I0824398

The TRIBE and I HAVE SPOKEN

The TRIBE and I HAVE SPOKEN

The Definitive (Unofficial) Lore and Legacy from the Game's Smartest Surviving Loser

Rob Cesternino

Host of *Rob Has a Podcast*

with ALEX KAVUTSKIY

Illustrated by SAM BOND

ATRIA BOOKS

New York Amsterdam/Antwerp London
Toronto Sydney/Melbourne New Delhi

ATRIA
BOOKS
An Imprint of Simon & Schuster, LLC
1230 Avenue of the Americas
New York, NY 10020

First Atria Books hardcover edition May 2026

ATRIA BOOKS and colophon are registered trademarks of Simon & Schuster, LLC

Interior design by Jason Snyder

Manufactured in China

3 5 7 9 10 8 6 4 2

The Library of Congress Cataloging-in-Publication Data has been applied for.

ISBN 978-1-6680-8747-3
ISBN 978-1-6680-8748-0 (ebook)

To anyone who keeps the torch of Survivor *alive in your heart—You are my tribe.*

CONTENTS

FOREWORD

I first met Rob Cesternino like most people did—on my television set. I was in casting for *Survivor: Tocantins*, and the casting associate told me I was like a cross between Rob Cesternino and Yul Kwon, two references that were at the time meaningless to me, since I was a shameful recruit. For research, I watched *Survivor: The Amazon*. I was dazzled. Rob not only brought a next-level strategic genius, roping in the outsiders to mastermind a cross-tribal alliance, but he also recognized that he was on a TV show. *The Amazon* is bursting with Rob's quips. He brought a Magic 8 ball as his luxury item and consulted it mostly about who would hook up. "He was the first player ever to go out of his way just to entertain the audience," Mario Lanza writes on his website, The Funny 115.

I couldn't believe it when I met Rob in real life at a party in 2009. This was not yet the Rob of *Rob Has a Podcast* (*RHAP*), although he had recently started messing around with the format, chatting with friends about the New York Mets and *Star Wars*. Rob wasn't involved then in the *Survivor* post-show community. I never saw him at alumni events or finale parties. Getting a Rob Cesternino sighting in the wild felt like stumbling on a rare mythical creature, an Italian unicorn in a pinstriped button-down. I nervously had a mutual friend introduce us and said something stupid, and we posed for an awkward pic.

It's not an exaggeration to say that meeting changed my life. Soon thereafter, Rob started podcasting about *Survivor*. He wasn't the first person to do that, but he was the first to bring in a rotating cast of old alumni to give insight into the show. Suddenly you could hear *Survivor* legends like Ethan Zohn and Jenna Morasca commenting on the latest episode. Rob was certainly the first to treat the medium with such zeal. "A long-form interview with the energy of a morning radio show, a combination of complex conversations with high-energy humor," described Mike Bloom, one of many up-and-coming journalists to whom Rob gave a platform.

> "He laid the blueprint for how to not just be a podcast. The irony is that the show is called *Rob Has a Podcast*, but what Rob built over time was far more than that. It's a network, a live experience, a business, and a community."
>
> **—Scott Yager, host of the *Challenge Mania* podcast dedicated to MTV's *The Challenge***

What was instantly obvious, as a friend and a weekly listener, was how much passion, humor, and depth Rob brought to every episode. He explored facets of *Survivor* that nobody talked about, and gave a platform to people you would never have expected to hear from again. I remember the fandom exploding in delight over his recap podcast with Billy Garcia, the second boot off *Survivor: Cook Islands*. Listening to his episode with Danielle DiLorenzo, where she explained how she was the secret mastermind on *Heroes vs. Villains*, made me realize that every *Survivor* player is the hero of their own story.

From a weekly *Survivor* podcast with his wife, Nicole, soon Rob was talking about *Big Brother*, co-hosting the internationally renowned *Survivor Know-It-Alls*, and launching a Patreon page to build out his community. There were exit interviews, merch, and a live show, where hundreds of fans from around the world congregated to celebrate their love of *Survivor*.

I was absolutely dazzled at those first live *Know-It-Alls*. There we were on the marquee at Carolines in New York City, trading obscure quips about *Survivor* maneuvers. Getting to mingle with *RHAP* fans from around the world has been one of the singular gifts of my life, and basically I got to do it because I was Rob's friend. Rob in his typical kindness and humility treated me like an equal partner, even though he worked for weeks to book the venues, organize the tech, and record the whole thing, while I—like Missy and Baylor—would just show up.

You'd think arriving to theaters with hundreds of cheering fans might give you a swelled head. But Rob remains unfazed. Before the show he's fixated on the logistics. Afterward, he's off mingling with his patrons. His humility, his kindness, his pure excitement to innovate and find new ways to engage people around *Survivor* and reality television have extended to all the projects we've done. He'll come up with genius idea after genius idea—our podcast the *Know-It-Alls*; the *Survivor Think Tank*; the *49 Laws of Survivor* strategy audiobook—and act like it was always our thing that we were doing together, rather than the truth, which was that I was a passenger clinging to his rocket ship as he built the biggest and most passionate reality television community that's ever existed.

> “The thing that continues to blow me away is Rob's dedication and work ethic. The sheer number of *quality* episodes he's produced and hosted is astounding. And you can tell it's not just about the output—it's about the love he has for the community he's built and the shared passion that drives it all.”
>
> **—Drew "Scooter" Ackerman, host of the *Sleep with Me* podcast**

> “We were all in the closet as *Survivor* fans until we realized through *RHAP* there were more of us, and when we got together live it was like something clicked. Suddenly you could be out about your favorite show and you didn't have to answer anyone about 'Is that show still on?' or deal with admitting you *like reality TV*. And then you realize that everyone else who likes *Survivor* is kind of just like you—it's such a smart, inclusive, diverse community with thousands of folks who would be your best friends if only you knew each other in 'real life'—but after a while, it was real life. And somehow I swear over the years *RHAP* has made it cool to like *Survivor*, and we don't care who knows it (even though we'll never come out of the closet about *Big Brother*).”
>
> **—Stephanie Townrow, *RHAP* patron**

That's the real beating heart of *RHAP*, the community that Rob has fostered. I realized at one of our live shows that people were excited to see our podcast, sure. But they were even more excited to see one another. There are events, hangouts, shared Airbnbs, dinners, and parties around every *RHAP* gathering. The podcast has spawned decade-long friendships, marriages, even babies. Yes, *RHAP* has spawned spawn. *RHAP* listeners have told me that through *RHAP*, they found their “people.” It's a wildly diverse group that shares a passion for reality television and strategic insight, but it's gone deeper than that, cutting into the quick of life. Rob gave the *Survivor* community a place to find one another. By loving something so deeply, and covering it so exuberantly, he opened the door for tens of thousands—honestly, millions—of other people who felt the same way.

Rob Cesternino hasn't just changed the community around *Survivor* and the other reality shows. He's fundamentally changed the way these games are played.

Players now go into *Survivor* having listened to hundreds of hours of strategic analysis—how to use an idol, navigate alliances, manage your threat level, curate your own personal winner's edit. They've heard firsthand from the titans of the show. That inherently pushes the gameplay further, because if everybody has access to the old ideas, it forces the best players to innovate new ideas.

Rachel LaMont, the winner of *Survivor 47*, was a patron of *Rob Has a Podcast*, as were Nick Wilson, the winner of *Survivor 37*, and *42*'s mastermind, Omar Zaheer. That doesn't even scratch the surface of all the listeners, like *42*'s winner, Maryanne Oketch, and Christian Hubicki. "*RHAP* was a godsend in understanding the history and the nuances of the game," Maryanne told me. On *Ghost Island*, Kellyn Bechtold reported singing the *Know-It-Alls* theme song with other contestants as a way to bond on the long frigid nights.

All that is to say, you hold in your hands the perfect *Survivor* tome for both the casual and the convert. Nobody in the world is a better guide to *Survivor*, and nobody loves the medium more.

> "Listening to Rob and being part of the *RHAP* community felt like doing the ACT prep. It gave me the confidence that I could enter the game ready. Even though most pregame strategies fly out the window the moment you hit the beach, the internal confidence I carried in with me was immeasurable. I'll always be grateful for that because it made the whole experience feel even more special, like I was part of something bigger than just the game itself."
>
> **—Rachel LaMont, winner of *Survivor 47***

Rob has endlessly talked strategy and shaped the game itself. He's equally accessible to fans tuning in for the first time and the ones who listen to hours of *RHAP* content each day. He can engage the newbie while slipping in deep-cut references that only the true devoted will catch.

If you're a longtime *RHAP* listener, you already know you're in store for something special.

If you're new to the *RHAP* community, welcome to the family. We're so glad you're here.

Stephen Fishbach

The TRIBE and I HAVE SPOKEN

INTRODUCTION
Rob Has a . . . Book?

Coming to you live from my apartment, it's *Rob Has a . . . Book*? Well, I guess technically a book is a little more "proofread and edited" than it is "live." And I live in a house now, but I've grown a bit attached to saying "coming to you live from my apartment," as it's how I've started over five thousand episodes of my podcast, narcissistically yet appropriately named *Rob Has a Podcast*. If you've never listened to *RHAP* (as we call it for short), it's expanded to covering all sorts of reality and scripted television, but the origin of the podcast, and still the main focus, is the CBS television series *Survivor*.

Now why would someone dedicate so much of their life to talking about and now writing an entire book about a twenty-five-year-old TV show? That's a great question that often rears its head late at night when I'm trying to fall asleep. The truth is I love *Survivor*. I just do. It's been my favorite show since it came out and I don't see that changing, no matter how many different ways they retool it. I assume that, if you're holding this book, you feel a similar way. That *Survivor* is not just another competitive reality show, but a special program that has transcended its genre.

Or maybe you've never seen *Survivor* but picked this up anyway because you're an incredibly curious, avid reader. In which case, yes, *Survivor* IS still on. In fact, it's going strong into its fiftieth season. Thank you for buying my book, but I would recommend setting it aside for a moment on your coffee table, getting yourself a seven-day free trial of Paramount Plus, and popping on season 1, episode 1 of *Survivor: Borneo*—or if you'd prefer dipping your toe into a more modern season, fire up season 28: *Cagayan*. But if you are still adamant about reading this book, I will do my best to guide you through. I'll put some spoiler warnings on the chapters, but tread lightly: This entire book is one giant spoiler.

I should probably introduce myself. My name is Rob Cesternino and, before I had a podcast, I actually got to play *Survivor* twice—on season 6: *The Amazon* and on season 8: *All-Stars*. That's right, I am an all-star. Or at least I was considered an all-star at one point in 2004. Am I still an all-star this many years later? That's not for me to decide. But there have been five Roberts to play the US version of *Survivor* (plus one Roberta and one Jean-Robert) and I'm confident that I'm at least the second-most memorable. If you were to ask a random fan about Rob from *Survivor*, they would tell you, "Yes, of course, Boston Rob is a legend of the show. He would easily make the Mount Rushmore of the most iconic castaways that have ever played, not to mention his dominance on *The Amazing Race, Deal or No Deal Island,* and *The Traitors*."* And you'd have to tell them, "No, I'm talking about the other Rob," and they'd get less excited and ask, "Oh, the Rob that sucks?" and then you'd have to say, "The one that wrote a book," and they'd get excited again and ask, "You mean *The Boston Rob Rulebook: Strategies for Life*?" and you'd have to say, "No, you're thinking of the wrong Rob again."

* And who knows what else by the time you're reading this!

While that Rob wrote a book of advice on how to win at *Survivor* and at life, my book's going to be a little different.* It's a collection of essays—thoughts I've had about the show over two decades of being invested in *Survivor* more than anyone should probably be invested in anything. Maybe you'll agree with some points, disagree with others, and that's what's so wonderful and enduring about the *Survivor* community. There is no one correct way to play the game, win the game, or even talk about the game. Underneath all the debates and hot takes, we share a deep connection as fans of this thing that is simultaneously just a game show on television and also the most important thing in the world.

So it doesn't matter if you've been a hardcore *Survivor* superfan from day one or just came across the show on Netflix during quarantine—this is for all of you.

Come on in, ~~guys~~.

* Although chapter six will outline exactly how to win so feel free to jump straight to that.

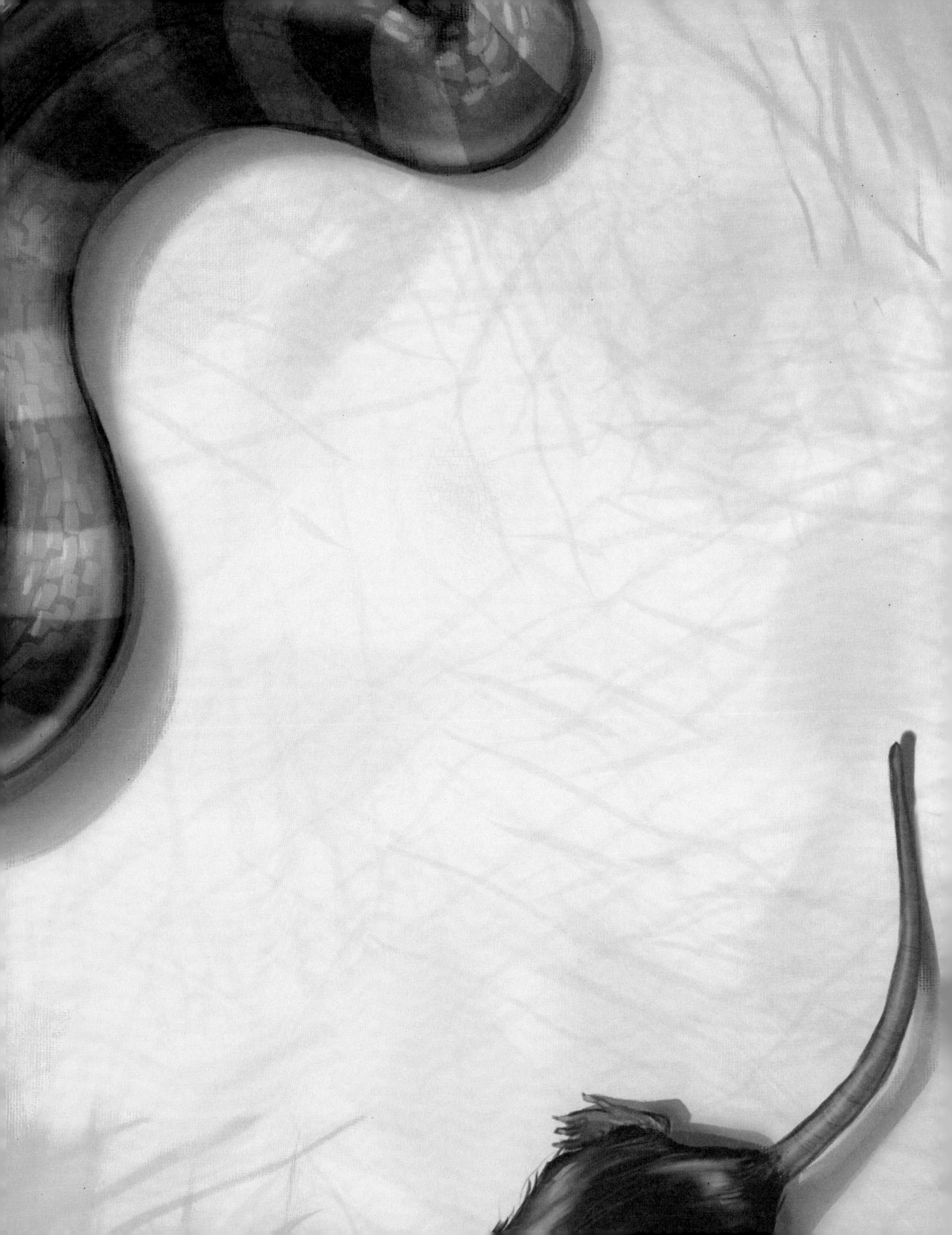

CHAPTER 1
Summer 2K

The Summer Television Finally Became Important

The year: 2000. The day: Wednesday, August 23. Al Gore and George W. Bush have just locked their respective party nominations as presidential candidates, Eminem has filed for divorce from Kim, and the number one movie in America is *The Cell* starring Jennifer Lopez. But nobody cares about any of that, because tonight, fifty-one million people are glued to their TV screens, dial set to CBS, as two contestants, who appear to be shipwrecked on an island and are covered in some sort of white, tribal war paint, are competing to see . . . who can stand on a log and keep their hand on a totem pole the longest.

These two competitors were Kelly Wiglesworth, a twenty-two-year-old river guide from Las Vegas, and Rudy Boesch, a seventy-two-year-old retired Navy SEAL from Virginia. Much like "Hands on a Hardbody," the infamous endurance competition where whoever kept their hand on a pickup truck the longest won the truck, this competition, known as "Hands on a Hard Idol," was just as much physical as it was mental. After a grueling four hours and eleven minutes, Rudy had a lapse in concentration, took his hand off the pole, and was eliminated. Kelly won the challenge and the producers thought maybe the show they were making was ruined. Yet the show wasn't ruined. It actually ended up an unexpected smash hit, bigger than anyone had ever imagined, changing the entire landscape of television. And, more importantly, the trajectory of my life.

That summer of 2000, I was what could safely be referred to as a "loser." I was twenty-one, completely broke, often seen digging around couch cushions for change so I could afford a pitcher of beer. As a senior studying broadcasting at State University of New York at Oswego, I wasn't able to graduate until completing a thesis paper on a subject I still hadn't picked or thought much about. Not to worry; I had a plan to turn things around. My three buddies and I were planning to stay in Oswego and . . . party harder than ever all summer. We designated this soon-to-be-unforgettable few months "Summer 2K."

Summer 2K got off to a rocky start. My share of the rent was $200, which my dad sent me every month, and I'd somehow already spent it all on school supplies (beer) before I could get it to my landlord. My landlord called my father, which is as humiliating as it sounds, and I was soon forced to return home to Long Island. There, I was sent to work with my mom at an insurance general agency, which served as the middleman between insurance companies and insurance agents and is exactly as fun as it sounds. Summer 2K was over before it started.

Instead of the summer of irresponsible binge drinking, it was a sleepy summer of responsible IT work and living in my parents' basement. There wasn't much going on until I began hearing a lot of chatter on the radio over some new, exciting TV show. Back when network TV was still king, this was a strange occurrence. We didn't get NEW shows in the summer. And we definitely didn't get any that involved . . . people shipwrecked on an island? Eating rats? Whatever it was, it sounded like a must-watch, and, back then, "must-watch" wasn't really something you said about TV. At the time, television wasn't important; movies were important. Nearly every week at the theaters there was an unmissable blockbuster like *The Matrix* or *The Sixth Sense* but every week on TV was like . . . *Becker* or *Dharma & Greg*. Now, no disrespect to sitcoms (*Seinfeld* was my favorite show at the time) but TV just didn't have any real stakes to it. You could miss an episode or three and jump right back in. But in 2000, something was in the water* and television was ready for its close-up. Dare I say, television was about to enter . . . a New Era.

Within just eighteen months, from 1999 to 2000, three shows came out nearly back-to-back-to-back that reinvented TV. The first, in January 1999, was *The Sopranos*, which was an award-winning critical success out of the gate and did pretty good ratings-wise, considering it was on a channel you had to pay extra for (believe it or not, most people found it outrageous at the time to have to pay extra for TV). *The Sopranos* was successful but a bit of a slow burn, seeping into culture over time and setting the standard for a prestige serial drama.

Then in August 1999 came the American version of *Who Wants to Be a Millionaire*, which may not get as many think pieces written about it as *The Sopranos*, but make no mistake: This game show was an instant and massive game changer.† Sure, we had other quiz shows, and sure, people won money on those, but those were more like . . . "Hi, welcome back to *Jeopardy!*, our three-day reigning champ has won thirty-five thousand dollars so far and blah blah blah blah blah." In this new show, Regis smacked you right in the face with WHO-WANTS-TO-BE-A-MILLIONAIRE?! Before you can even process the title, your subconscious is already screaming "ME!" It's not only a beautiful, round prize number, it's also such a visceral, life-changing amount of money. *Millionaire* was slick, sexy,‡ and you could play along at home. It became such a monster hit that if you were to look up the highest Nielsen-rated primetime

* And I'm not talking about Darnell taking an aqua dump too close to the shore.

† Almost as much as fan favorite game changer Sierra Dawn Thomas.

‡ In LJ McKanas speak, it was more "hot" than "cute."

shows of the 1999–2000 television season, the top three were *Who Wants to Be a Millionaire* (Tuesday), *Who Wants to Be a Millionaire* (Thursday), and *Who Wants to Be a Millionaire* (Sunday).*

Between *Sopranos*, where each episode cost nearly as much as an entire movie, and *Millionaire*, where you could knock out half a dozen episodes in one day on the same set, it's no surprise that it was the success of the latter that other networks were frothing at the mouth to replicate. Everyone was after their own game show, their own crack cocaine programming. British producer Mark Burnett found himself in the right place at the right time to create just that. He had recently bought a "format"—essentially IP for a reality show—from fellow British producer Charlie Parsons, for a Swedish show he produced called *Expedition Robinson*. Named after two marooning stories, *Robinson Crusoe* and *The Swiss Family Robinson*, it was a much more involved kind of game show—one where you'd drop real people off on an island, and only one would walk away with 500,000 Swedish kronor (equivalent to around $54,500). Burnett pitched this concept to then-president of CBS, Les Moonves, and he said . . . no.

Not only was it unheard of to fund a new series for the summer, but Burnett refused to do just a test pilot for the network; he demanded they pay for the whole season. Which does make some sense—it would be pretty silly to cast sixteen people, fly everyone out to Malaysia, have them vote off one contestant, and then send everyone back home. Burnett believed in this concept too much to take no for an answer. So he went directly to the advertisers. His pitch to them basically boiled down to this: We all know how much a Bud Light costs in the real world, but how valuable would a Bud Light be to a desperate, starving person on an island?† How badly would they want to eat Applebee's? How much would they love a chance to get a sneak peek of the new hit Adam Sandler film *Jack and Jill*? Advertisers ate it up and immediately jumped on board. CBS had no choice but to give in.

* Edging out *ER*, *Friends*, *Frasier*, and Monday Night Football.

† Famously, however, the Borneo cast revolted and refused to compete in a challenge when the reward was only a single Bud Light. The producers had to build a whole bar for the reward that Kelly wins in episode 12.

Thus, thanks to Mark Burnett, Charlie Parsons, Les Moonves, and Reebok, *Survivor* was born. The first episode aired on Wednesday May, 31, 2000, with a grand prize, of course, of one million dollars, which everyone agreed was slightly more enticing than $54,500. *Survivor* wasn't the first reality show—it wasn't even the first game show to offer a million dollars as a reward—but it was the first major show to have one sole winner. More thrilling than the prize was that the players would be eliminated one by one—a structure that, by design or by sheer luck, tapped into the two biggest draws of the two other biggest new shows of the new millennium. *Survivor* combined the money at stake from the game show *Millionaire* with the dark, visceral core of *The Sopranos*. The serialization of a show like *The Sopranos* connects with us on a primordial level. Each week we tune in because we're dying to know who will, literally or figuratively, die. On *Survivor*, somebody would be voted out, aka *whacked*, every episode. Unlike soothing sitcoms and formulaic procedurals, where we'd see the same characters for a decade or more, any one of your favorite characters on *Survivor* or *Sopranos* could go at any moment and you'd never see them again.* Other shows might've had cliff-hangers at the end of seasons, but every episode of *Survivor* had the stakes of a finale.

The specific magic of *Survivor* came from placing that addictive suspense of a serialized structure within a competitive format. It wasn't some writers' room deciding who would stay and who would go . . . it was the players themselves! Like *Lord of the Flies*, they would make their own society and decide amongst themselves who would be banished from it. Therefore anyone could win, anything was possible, and it was more exciting, unpredictable, and engaging than everything that had ever come before. Some could say that, as a society, we were not even ready for something that addictive . . . or maybe it was exactly what our primitive monkey brains had been waiting for all along. British anthropologist Robin Dunbar developed a theory known as the "social brain hypothesis," which basically states that, counter to the theory that human intelligence developed due to food-related reasons (such as sophistication needed for hunting and gathering), human intelligence actually grew as a means to survive

* Unless, of course, there was an *Edge of Extinction* or they appeared in a dream sequence as a fish later on.

in large and complex social groups. The bigger the group hominids started living in, the bigger our brains needed to become to navigate the subtle intricacies of social interaction—of understanding the hierarchy and of building coalitions. As opposed to other animals where two alpha goats would ram into each other over and over again to decide who gets to mate with the female, we apes evolved to understand that, outside of physical combat, you could take down the "alpha" of your "tribe" simply by outnumbering them. Sound familiar? *Survivor* was the first show that managed to tap into the deepest, oldest, and most instinctual part of our psyches. As a result, television finally had real stakes. Television was finally important.

> "The things we were doing, it just wasn't happening on TV. Like, you know . . . we're eating rat. Who's not going to watch this show? And we're eating rat. Now, granted, I thought the biggest thing would be I would get recognized at a restaurant and get a free meal. So me and Joel [Klug] had gone to New York for a charity event for the New York Giants and the Jets . . . and got recognized because some of the players had watched the show. So that was that moment where we were like, 'Wait a minute, we're with professional athletes. They just recognized us from a show that was on the other night.'"
>
> **—Gervase Peterson, October 12, 2020**

Tragically, I can't claim to be a day-one fan of the show. The first time I tuned in was the fourth episode, so technically I'm a day-four fan.* Like millions of others, *Survivor* had me instantly hooked. Episode 4 was the one where Ramona Gray, the twenty-nine-year-old biochemist from New Jersey, got voted out over Gervase Peterson, the thirty-year-old YMCA basketball coach from Philadelphia. Now, in the grand scheme of *Survivor* history, this was a fairly boring, straightforward vote, but, at the time, the layers

* Or a day-twenty-two fan if you're counting the exact days from the show's premier. Or a day-ten fan if you're counting the days played in Borneo.

and intricacy that went into such a simple vote melted my brain. On one hand, we had Ramona, who was seen as not contributing enough to camp life. On the other hand, we had Gervase, who was flopping in the challenges his tribe desperately needed to win. It boiled down to Gervase's charm winning people over, since Ramona had been sick and therefore hadn't bonded enough with the tribe. There wasn't one obvious person that had to go; there was good reason to keep or get rid of anyone. I became instantly obsessed with the social politicking and maneuvering needed to avoid getting voted out, to the point that one episode a week wasn't enough for me. How could I get more of this?!

The options for becoming completely lost in a fandom in the year 2000 were limited. This was well before the era of recaps and discussion shows, so, like a junkie looking for a fix, I would go on the CBS website, reading and rereading bios of the cast, hoping to glean any new information about literally anything between episodes. I ripped the soundtrack off Napster and would blast it regularly. It's crazy to say, but *Survivor* quickly became the most important thing in my life.* What's even crazier is that it may have remained the most important thing in my life ever since. It became my identity. While I can't say I was there from day one, I can confidently say that there are few people who are as much of an expert on the show as I am. Not only have I been on the show, but—and sorry to brag here—outside of the people actually producing the show, there is no chance anyone else has talked about *Survivor* as much as I have.† Over the course of fifty seasons, Jeff Probst himself might've put in his hours, days, months, and years talking *Survivor* in production meetings and editing bays, but put me up minute-to-minute against Probst on who's talked more *Survivor* into a microphone and it's not even close. When I die, the first line of my obituary will unironically be about *Survivor*. It won't be about how we miss Robert Kristopher Cesternino, the computers project coordinator at some insurance company. It'll be about how Robert Kristopher Cesternino was a two-time *Survivor* contestant‡ who

* Yes, even more important than Mug Night at Woodshed Tavern, where you'd pay for a mug once and then only pay 50 cents per refill of beer.

† And if you think you have, please go outside.

‡ Maybe a three-time contestant by the time I die.

went on to dedicate the rest of his life to championing and podcasting about *Survivor*. Leaving behind my wife and two children* would only be briefly mentioned at the end.

It's hard to overstate how big the show was when it first came out. Nowadays, there are so many streaming platforms and subcultures that it's easy to be in your own bubble, fully unaware of something incredibly popular. Back then, monoculture meant that we worked ourselves into a complete frenzy over each shiny new thing. We didn't have shows trending on Twitter but we had fifty million people, nearly *one-fifth of the entire country*, watching *the same thing together*. *Survivor* was everywhere. Everyone was talking about it, every commercial was doing some parody of "the tribe has spoken." Even cable news like MSNBC would report what happened on the show like it was breaking news. Can you imagine popping on *Morning Joe* now and seeing Willie Geist breaking down how Kaleb's Shot in the Dark hit? A current season of *Survivor* is like the latest iPhone model—yeah, it'll have some new emojis or fire tokens, but you basically know what you're in for. But the first season of *Survivor* was the first iPhone; it was historic. I wouldn't dare say it was man-walking-on-the-moon historic, but in its own way, the original cast were like astronauts to many of us, pioneers forging into the great unknown.†

While it may have been morbid curiosity that led us to tune into a game show where contestants had to eat bugs, what kept me and the rest of the world hooked were the complex *people* that were eating those bugs. Audiences weren't growing week after week to see who would or wouldn't help collect firewood; they wanted to see all the drama ensuing out of who would or wouldn't help collect that firewood. Take Richard Hatch, the thirty-nine-year-old corporate communications consultant from Rhode Island, placed in the same tribe as Sue Hawk, the thirty-eight-year-old truck driver from Wisconsin. Sue wanted everyone to get to work, while Rich wanted everyone to discuss the process by which they would discuss what work would be done. This right here is why *Survivor* became a phenomenon. Here was a blue-collar woman from

* Maybe three by the time I die.

† Yes, I am aware Borneo is the third largest island on the planet, divided by three different countries, with a population of over twenty million people.

rural America who wanted to work and a white-collar man from corporate America who wanted to talk about talking! While it was undeniably a blast to watch contestants compete at gross-food-eating challenges, what made the show a sensation was the culture clash that resulted from the completely different people who, if it wasn't for the massive casting call *Survivor* had put out, would have never otherwise met. The most captivating aspect of this whole experiment was the unpredictability yet relatability of human relationships.

It wasn't just the clash of culture; unexpected friendships also developed. The aforementioned septuagenarian Rudy was partly put on the show because he was a cranky old man who had a problem with gay people and they could stick him on the same tribe as an openly gay man, Rich. The producers thought they'd found a surefire (albeit a little cheap) way to create some television drama. But, as *Survivor* constantly proves, humans are often less predictable than we think. The friendship that developed between Rich and Rudy was one of the major highlights of the season. "He's fat," as Rudy eloquently put it, "but he's good." Turns out, Rich was a much more complicated person than his sexuality, and wasn't the gay stereotype that Rudy had in his head. In 2000, this was a major step forward in media representation, considering that at the time many onscreen nonheterosexual characters were defined and pigeonholed by their sexuality.

Survivor ended up recruiting the kind of people you wouldn't normally see on TV. The unscripted conversations they had didn't feel like those you'd see in other shows or movies. And due to the conditions, the deprivation, and the newness of reality TV, the cast was shown more bare (literally and figuratively) than maybe anyone on primetime had been before. The cast reminded you of people you knew, people you liked, people who annoyed you, people you might even see yourself in. Greg Buis, the twenty-four-year-old recent Ivy League graduate from Colorado, who jokingly chatted away on his fake coconut phone, was someone you could see yourself being best friends with. Colleen Haskell, the twenty-three-year-old advertising student from Miami, didn't necessarily look like the models they would put on covers of *Maxim* magazine; she looked like the girl you might've had a crush on in your office.* The appeal of the sixteen castaways was that they were just regular people you might run into on the street.

Ironically, what made the first season's castaways seem ordinary is what made them famous overnight. Every contestant, after getting voted out, would get a whole media tour—they'd start on *The Early Show* with Bryant Gumbel, call into all the major radio stations, do the whole talk show circuit. Even if you got voted out third, you'd still get a big Reebok spot. Colleen became America's sweetheart and starred opposite Rob Schneider in *The Animal* (although she seemed about as interested in being there as she did on *Survivor*). There was a week where *Survivor* contestants would co-host *Live!* with Regis Philbin. Sue Hawk even got to interview George W. Bush.† If only she had warned him that it would prove harder to track down WMDs in Iraq than to find a reliable source of tapioca on the island of Borneo.

* Though some contestants would later find themselves in *Maxim, Playboy,* and others.

† Richard Hatch also appeared naked in a sketch with Donald Trump, but this was long before he was a presidential candidate.

Crucially, because these were real people, we all thought we were experts in what was happening. Just as we'd play along on *Who Wants to Be a Millionaire*, we all felt qualified to discuss the merits of who should stay, who should go, and how the game should be played. But unlike trivia, where the correct answer is always moments away from being revealed, there *never was* one right answer. Everything in *Survivor* is so context-dependent and case-by-case that what works in one scenario might not in another—and something crazy that shouldn't work in a million years could come to fruition with all the stars aligned.* This made the conversation about the show endless, and soon after its premiere, it naturally became the ultimate water cooler show.

At the insurance office's water cooler, I found myself dissecting the show with the only other human I knew who was watching, a lovely older woman named Fran. Years before Stephen Fishbach came into my life, the *Survivor Know-It-Alls* were Rob and Fran, Thursdays at lunch, breaking down last night's episode: who we liked, who we didn't, who we thought was getting voted out next. *Borneo* started with two tribes competing

* See *Micronesia* or *Cagayan*.

against each other—the younger, fun-loving Pagong and the older, harder-working Tagi. Like the rest of America, Fran and I were rooting more for the Pagongs. Believe it or not, the guy living in his parents' basement preferred the tribe that just wanted to have a good time. What Fran and I didn't know at the time was that the two tribes were about to become one. Until I heard Mark Burnett explain the merge on the local New York radio show *Opie and Anthony*, I had assumed that they would just keep eliminating players until one tribe was fully gone.* But no, instead, the tribes merged into one—which increased the social politicking by ten. Thought you were getting used to living with a handful of strangers whose quirks were getting on your nerves? Well, here's a handful more with new neuroses, stirring up new conflicts and paranoias. On top of that, the players getting voted out would form "the jury" who decided the winner of the whole show. Yeah, the people you screwed over voting out are the people whose votes you desperately needed in the end if you wanted that million bucks.

Fran and I were convinced early on that Gretchen Cordy, the thirty-eight-year-old preschool teacher from Tennessee, was a lock for that million. When you broke down the cast, some seemed too crazy or got too much on people's nerves, but Gretchen felt like Goldilocks, just right. She was well liked, respected, and could hold her own in the survivalist elements. She was the levelheaded center of the carefree Pagongs. So it was an incredible gut punch to us all when Gretchen was the first one voted out after the merge.† This blindside was as big as when on *The Sopranos* they killed off—well, I wouldn't wanna spoil it for anyone so I'll just say . . . "Long Term Parking." Turned out, four members of the Tagi tribe had formed a voting alliance and strategically targeted Gretchen directly, *specifically because* she was the Goldilocks contestant. Yet another layer of the show was uncovered—you had to not only be good at *Survivor*, but also hide that you're good at *Survivor*. The world was shook, the Pagongs were shook, I was shook. But no one was more shook than Gretchen herself. "Oh my God," she said to herself as Jeff read out the votes, "it's me."

* Turns out I was nine seasons ahead of the curve.

† Or "merger" as we incorrectly called it back then.

That's when the fuzzy pre-merge of Borneo, where our favorite characters would explore the island and take dips in mud volcanoes, turned to the brutal post-merge. The next major blindside to the audience was Gervase. Before edgic* even existed, internet sleuths found something curious on the CBS site: Whenever a castaway was voted out, they'd replace their photo with the same headshot but marked with a red *X*. Clicking around the page source and URLs, it was discovered that every castaway had this red *X* headshot ready to go . . . except for Gervase. We still don't know if this was an oversight or a purposefully planted red herring (considering the show also slipped in a fake final-four shot of Gervase, Colleen, Sean, and Rudy just to mess with people). So everything we predicted would happen was wrong, none of the clues we had led to anything, and we would just helplessly watch our beloved Pagongs be eliminated one by one by the Tagi 4,† led by the original *Survivor* villain: Richard Hatch.

And what would reality TV be without villains and controversy? Richard was (and, safe to say, continues to be) controversial. He proudly walked around naked so much that the number one thing people were talking about was "can you believe that gay, naked guy on *Survivor*?" He was openly obnoxious and smug, and not even a writers' room could top his job title of "corporate communications consultant" to sound more off-putting to Middle America. But worst of all . . . he had formed an alliance. People strongly felt this shouldn't be allowed, that it went against the spirit of the show. Even Rich himself said he was going to do something underhanded. Choosing to vote someone out—whether because you felt they weren't helping the tribe in the challenges or because they were a pain in the ass around camp—was supposed to be an individual decision. Conspiring with others to vote for someone simply because it would help you get into a better position to win the money was viewed as some evil plan. When Jeff Probst overheard the Tagi 4 forming an alliance while standing off to the side of a challenge, he truly believed they were cheating.

* "Edgic," combining "editing" and "logic," is the online *Survivor* community dedicated to predicting who wins each season purely based on how all the characters are being edited.

† Ever since, watching a tribe getting voted out one by one has been referred to as a "Pagonging."

“It seemed so real sitting there around the fire and, you know, and just the whole ominousness of it. . . . And then the night that I got voted off, I couldn't sleep. And I just got up and I thought, I'll just walk up and down the beach. . . . I saw this Styrofoam, and I'm like, what is that? And it turns out it was the back side of tribal council. And then I remember thinking to myself, like, oh, it's a game. It's a game. It's all make-believe, you know, and it was a really odd coming-to-Jesus kind of moment where you're like, oh, my God, I took it so serious.”

—Gretchen Cordy, July 2, 2019

It's possible that Richard figured out the show before anyone making the show did: that, on top of the physical and the social aspects, *Survivor* was also a numbers game. The show itself originally seemed more interested in the social experiment of mixing people of various walks of life than in the strategy. The editors leaned heavily into the adventure aspect of survival, with the gameplay element being an afterthought. The producers wanted to compete with TV's biggest game show and arguably ended up inventing the greatest game show television had ever seen, but the irony was that they were expecting their game show contestants to neither acknowledge nor treat the game show they were on . . . as a game show. For the contestants and the viewers, this was happening in real time. Later in the season, when the contestants are about to compete in a trivia challenge, Colleen gets excited because it'll be just like a game show, only to suddenly realize: "Wait a minute . . . we're *on* a game show." Naturally, if you set up a game for a million dollars, you can't expect the players to not attempt to optimize their chances of winning. Greg sardonically compared voting someone out with playing the board game *Sorry*—it's part of the rules, something that has to be done, so you might as well do it in a way that benefits you. Fran and I also debated if the dirty a-word, *alliance*, should be allowed. While we hadn't yet grasped the strategic component of the show, it was surely inevitable.

Eventually, during the season, I was able to make it back to Oswego. Summer 2K was back on! Only I hadn't returned a simple college student, I was now a *Survivor* evangelist—trying to get anyone I knew to watch. My roommate Floyd and I would throw weekly parties where we'd get drunk, watch the show, and tape it so we could rewatch it the following day more carefully (and soberly). These tapes proved to be rather important in the future whenever we didn't pay our cable bill and our only choices of entertainment were a *Survivor* tape and our copy of *The Phantom Menace*.

Survivor had become our life. When we came home from bars, we'd get pieces of paper and vote out our own friends. I sometimes found myself crashing in a hotel room with four or five other guys after a night of drinking and I'd sleep on the floor jokingly telling everyone that was my way of preparing for *Survivor.*[*] We threw a big party for

* Though subconsciously, maybe not so jokingly.

the finale with what constitutes an "island theme" for college students in upstate New York: a pot of rice. I even made a coconut bikini for a girl to wear—but although someone was willing, bless her heart, it proved to be rather uncomfortable so we nixed it.

> "I couldn't go out there and act like a complete fool or a villain. And because, A, it's not me. I'd be faking it, but B, is that, you know, I have a career that I can't look that way on a grand public scale. I mean, it's just—it's not professional, and it's not who I am, but it's also not professional. Imagine if your doctor was out there and doing what Richard did. . . . Everyone would be like, 'That's your doctor? I don't want to go to him,' you know? . . . But like I said, I was really trying to win. I'm confident in my reasons for voting in alphabetical order, why I did it, and it was very strategic. I'm sorry. No one else recognized the strategy. I kept it secret from the producers because I didn't want the producers spilling the beans."
>
> **—Dr. Sean Kenniff, August 5, 2018**

All of the infamous Tagi 4—Rich, Rudy, Sue, and Kelly—barreled their way to the final four. Sue got cut at four, then Rudy at three, leaving just Rich and Kelly as the final two. But losing Rudy, who was far and away the fan favorite at this point, didn't ruin the show. It set the stage for something even better than a feel-good ending. The contrast between Kelly and Richard at final tribal couldn't have been starker. Rich was the mastermind of the cutthroat alliance, while Kelly was the one who'd made friends with most of the cast.* Now they had to face the jury, who arrived emotionally raw, with tough questions ready to go. And the final two weren't allowed lifelines; they could not phone-a-friend, and any wrong answer could cost them a million dollars. Kelly came in stressed, like she was about to face a firing squad, while Rich seemed relaxed, thinking the jury would be fun. Kelly's opening speech to the jury was a plea that they would vote for the

* Despite this, Kelly Wiglesworth was the first person on reality TV to say the iconic line, "I didn't come here to make friends."

"better person," while Rich's suggested they vote based on the "better gameplay." Therein lies the core of why *Survivor* is endlessly fascinating to this day, over twenty-five years and fifty seasons later; why fans are still watching, why we're still podcasting and writing books about it. How much is *Survivor* a game and how much is it a reflection of real life? Is it possible to separate how you play from who you are? Will the jury vote for who they liked better or who they feel played the game better? Every single jury member on every single jury has different criteria on what "played better" means and how they want to choose who wins the game. Much like they created their own society, the voted-out castaways get to create their own criteria for how their season's champion will be crowned.

The tie-breaking vote that season came from Sue Hawk, who stood in front of the jury like a hunter, both guns loaded, and fired them at full blast. In a piece of pure poetry, she pontificated that the island was pretty much full of two things: snakes and rats. She compared Rich to a snake: Yes, he's an openly arrogant, pompous loser in life, but he's frank, and he accomplished exactly what he set out to do. Kelly, she compared to a rat, running around two-faced; despite her claims of playing a more honest way, she was actually duplicitous and didn't own up to doing exactly what Rich was doing. Not one to mince her words, Sue let Kelly know that if she were to ever pass her in life and she was dying of thirst, Sue wouldn't give her a sip of water and would let the vultures take her and do whatever they want with her. Sue ends her fiery speech by declaring that they owe it to the spirit of the island that they have come to know to let it be, in the end, the way Mother Nature intended it to be—for the snake to eat the rat. Even though rankings are arbitrary and reductive, to this day, Sue's speech remains the most iconic moment in the show's history and it was the most insane thing I had ever seen on television—we sat there with our jaws dropped as someone was completely eviscerated on television. And in that moment, the question of how much of *Survivor* is a game and how much is real life was answered. It's both. *Survivor* may be strategic like a chess game, but every pawn, rook, and knight* is an actual person, and when you're playing with people, things are going to get very messy, very fast.

The snake did, in fact, eat that rat. In a 4-3 vote that Jeff counted then and there,† Richard Hatch cemented himself in history as the first ever winner of *Survivor*. The season 1 finale was watched more than any other episode of the show. So then why did the producers think the show was ruined while they were filming it? Well, because they (correctly) predicted the straight-shooting veteran Rudy would be who the audience rooted for to pull out the win. They were partially right; the seemingly nefarious Rich winning was a complete shock to the audience. In a poll taken going into the finale, 45 percent wanted Rudy to win, 42 percent wanted Kelly, and only 11 percent wanted Richard (with the sad remaining 2 percent for the robbed Sue Hawk). In a poll taken after the finale, only 31 percent felt the right person won, with 69 percent feeling the wrong person did.

Ultimately, Richard winning was the best thing to happen to the show. He was the perfect winner and mascot to capture both what the show wanted to be and what the show needed to become. While on the island, the producers thought the audience would have been too disappointed to see the beloved veteran lose to the villain, at home, more and more people began embracing Rich as the deserving winner. The show realized that leaning into the strategy would create an even better format for their social experiment to flourish. When Jeff Probst introduced the preview for season 2, *The Australian Outback*, he highlighted the extreme heat and harsh environments they had to fare against, but asked the bigger question of how contestants would fare with each other. "Because, as we have seen, surviving each other—surviving the social politics—is what this game is all about." This was just the beginning. As the players evolved

* Even Zane Knight.

† The winner for seasons 2 through 40 would be revealed at a live show instead. The live show was killed in season 41, bringing the winner reveal back to the island. Will season 50 have the return to the live finale?!

to meet the game, the game evolved to meet the players. Things got more cutthroat, more complicated, and dare I say, even more captivating. But the question that still lingers to this day is how much of *Survivor*'s success can be attributed to Richard's win.

> "On one of the neighboring islands, our last day, 39, there was like a floating university thing, and there was like a piracy attack, and some people were beheaded. . . . That stuff doesn't always make the news in the US, but, you know, production, they were like, well, we want to make sure that our people's family don't think it was them. So they let us make a phone call home and . . . I remember calling my mom, like, 'Hey, I don't know if you heard about this whole beheading thing, but that wasn't us. Like, we're safe. I'll be home in a few days.' . . . And she said, 'Are you okay?' And I didn't say anything. And she goes, 'You're not okay. Are you?' And I didn't say anything. And my mom goes—I've never heard her say a swear word in my life—and she goes, 'Oh, my God, you won the whole damn thing.' And then I just started blubbering. . . . I didn't say yes or no. I just started crying because I'm like, oh, great. Like, rub it in, Mom."
>
> **—Kelly Wiglesworth, January 24, 2021**

And the bigger, maybe more hyperbolic question, is how much *Survivor* is to blame for the complete decline of culture. When the show premiered, the media covered it like it was the downfall of civilized society. They said getting naked and eating rats for money appealed to the lowest common denominator of people. It was dystopian, like the real-life *Hunger Games.** What has television become? It is undeniable that *Survivor* was the spectacle that led to the boom of reality television, and that reality television permanently changed culture. Before, you got on TV because you were famous, because you excelled at acting or singing or sports. Suddenly, everything flipped. You

* Although the show predates *The Hunger Games*, which was probably inspired by *Survivor*.

didn't go on TV because you were famous, you got famous *because* you were on TV. *Survivor* paved the way for people to, with all due respect, become famous without merit.* The more people that succeeded at becoming famous just for being famous, the more others pursued a similar path. And the higher ratings reality television got, the more this led to the media covering everything like it was reality TV. We eventually even got a president who came from a reality TV show, also created by Mark Burnett.

While there is some truth that *Survivor* satisfies a dark part of human nature—every episode is, indisputably, akin to a ritualistic murder—there is also something beautiful about *Survivor* that resonated with counting-couch-cushion-change-to-buy-beer college student Rob then and resonates with a lot of people from all walks of life now. Two other tribes were formed that first season of *Survivor*: those who found it to be a trash show, damaging the social fabric of society, and those who found it to be a smart show that revealed often unexpected aspects of human nature. A separation between people who got it and people who didn't. The people who got it have been my tribe ever since. To me, Rich wasn't the reason *Survivor* became the monster hit that it did. And *Survivor* wasn't the reason reality TV took over the world. These events were inevitable and already in motion—Rich and *Survivor* just happened to be in the right place at the right time. If Kelly had won the jury vote, it was still a matter of time until a Brian Heidik or a Boston Rob or a Cirie Fields or even a different punk named Rob would come on the show and advance the game. Even if Mark Burnett and Les Moonves hadn't taken a risk on adapting Charlie Parsons's Swedish show *Expedition Robinson*, someone else would've had their finger on the pulse of what was happening. A year before *Survivor* hit the airwaves, *The Blair Witch Project*, the found-footage horror film, was a huge phenomenon (so popular, it inspired a challenge in the first season of *Survivor*). The era of real people filming themselves for our entertainment had already begun. The reality TV wave was about to hit the shore—if *Survivor* hadn't capitalized on that precise moment in culture, a different show surely would've.

* I say this fully aware it includes me.

What's ironic is that, over time, this show that many thought was garbage TV would be recognized as a class above the other reality and game shows that would follow. Just like we've had plenty of *Sopranos* knockoffs that thought the key to success was throwing in some nudity, some violence, and a whole bunch of swear words, we've had plenty of reality TV where the goal is just to cram in as many salacious moments as possible.* What made *Survivor* endure for nearly three decades, much like *The Sopranos* (both of which had major renaissances in streaming during the pandemic), is the intricate level of care put into the characters and an unmatched level of sophistication put into the storytelling.

Rewatching *Borneo* now is like opening up a time capsule—like jumping right back into Summer 2K. I had no idea where my life or *Survivor* were going to go. Turns out, my fate and the story of *Survivor* ended up being deeply intertwined. We were both finding ourselves at the same time, we got together when we needed each other, and we eventually concurrently reinvented ourselves. Malcolm Gladwell could probably write an entire book on how I was born at the exact right time to be the exact right age to be old enough to appreciate *Survivor* when it came out and young enough to be able to play it when I did. That podcasting technology came out when I was old enough to take advantage of it and that YouTube thankfully wasn't available when I was younger, more irresponsible, and would've really, really regretted having permanently recorded that version of myself. Honestly, everything good in my life has come from *Survivor*. Even the existence of my children could be traced to someone seeing my *Big Brother* audition tape† and throwing me in the mix for *Survivor* casting. My wife, Nicole, was my younger sister's best friend and had come by the house dozens of times, paying me absolutely no mind until my parents threw a watch party and she saw me on *Survivor: The Amazon* (she hates when I bring this up, but it's true). I went on *Survivor* to meet women and I ended up meeting just one because of it. For all the

* And no shame to fans of those kinds of shows; I'm one of them.

† I apologize for the major plot twist of casually revealing at the start of my love-letter-to-*Survivor* book that I actually applied for *Big Brother* first.

flak I got for constantly jumping alliances on the show, I will point out that I've been going strong with my most important alliance for twenty-three years.

Popping *Borneo* back on now is almost like watching home movies. The gameplay may not hold up but the characters certainly do. Everything is so vividly burned into my brain, from Gervase hitting himself in the head repeatedly to pump himself up to eat the bug larvae, to that strange little wiggle dance Richard did after he won individual immunity in the fire-making challenge. Every moment of *Borneo*, big or small, immediately brings me back to Oswego, on the edge of my seat, with an unworn coconut bikini at my feet. And when the season was over, I knew that everything had changed. Summer turned to fall, *Bring It On* took over *The Cell* at the top of the box office, and I ended up writing my thesis paper on the impact of reality television—finally graduating from SUNY Oswego, a feat not even Jerry Seinfeld managed. I may have started that summer a loser, but I ended it so much more than that . . . I was a loser who loved a TV show.

KS

CHAPTER 2

The Great and Powerful Jeff

Wanna Know *Who* You're Playing For?

"Do you like me at all?" Jeff Probst asks me without warning on February 10, 2020, at the premiere of the fortieth season of *Survivor: Winners at War*. Some moments take years to become iconic, others become iconic the moment they happen. This might be one of them. I was conducting red carpet interviews, having just finished up with *South Pacific* winner Sophie Clarke, and it was time to talk to the big man himself. Jeff was warm and friendly as we chitchatted a few moments before the camera was on, but as soon as we were rolling, he dropped that bomb on me, harder than Ben dropped all those Ben Bombs on Chrissy. To be fair, I did come into the conversation rather hot, asking him the burning question of, "How are you?" Say what you will about Jeff, but the man knows how to make a TV moment.

The rest of the interview went more smoothly. We got into it and Jeff wasn't actually upset with me, he was more frustrated with who I represented—everyone and their mothers who spew their own hot takes on what Jeff and *Survivor* does right or wrong. And while I feel like I've always been a generally positive commentator around the show, with the occasional (very fair) critiques, Jeff might've taken that moment to respond to the haters. Through my many years of podcasting, I seem to have become the unofficial *Survivor* customer service line. Fans have a problem with the show, they don't have Jeff's number, so they hit me up instead. It's understandable that Jeff takes a lot of the negative feedback personally. He has not only been the face of the show since day one, but gained more and more creative control until suddenly, he was running the whole operation. He may have entered Mark Burnett's *Survivor* chocolate factory as Charlie, but he's sure as hell Willy Wonka now. So he gets to enjoy the acclaim of producing the most delicious chocolate around, but that also comes with facing the critics who may not love that he's turning children into giant blueberries or taking their votes away.

The day *Survivor* was born, so was Host Jeff, and they basically grew up together. Jeff and *Survivor* are so intertwined that the journey of Jeff has been the journey of the show. You can't even say *Survivor* without instantly conjuring up the image of Jeff, in his patented blue shirts of various shades and khaki bottoms of various lengths, always donning a little necklace that could only beat the effing stick as far as fake immunity idols go. And while it may be impossible to recap every season and episode and moment of *Survivor* in a book (although, believe me, I've tried in podcast form for God knows how many hours), it could be possible to track the story of the show through the story of Jeff. So what is the story of Jeff?*

Embryo Jeff

In the late '90s, Jeff was broke and considering leaving the entertainment industry entirely. He had worked as a TV presenter for nearly a decade, hosting shows like FX's *Backchat* and VH1's *Rock & Roll Jeopardy!* and was a correspondent for *Access Hollywood*. He was booking commercials and corporate videos but he wasn't happy, turning down hosting gigs left and right. They felt hollow. He wondered what else could be out there. It wasn't until he heard Mark Burnett describing *Survivor* on the radio that he realized what his calling was. This wasn't a guy who wanted to read from a teleprompter (which is a hard skill in itself and something he's very good at); this was a guy who had already written and directed a movie, was in therapy, and loved Joseph Campbell. This was a guy who took a serious interest in the psychology of humans. So when he heard about the premise behind *Survivor*, he had the same reaction many of us had—that it sounded like the greatest thing ever.

Mark Burnett wasn't sold on Jeff at first. Maybe it was because he's a handsome guy (after all, he would be ranked *People* magazine's 32nd most beautiful person in 2001, a few spots above Heidi Klum) but Mark felt that Jeff wouldn't be able to cut it

* Or "Jeffrey," as Courtney Yates would say.

when it came to the adventure, wouldn't be able to handle the rats and bugs crawling all over him. But Jeff was persistent, even printing out mock newspaper articles about how the show became a hit all thanks to its unknown yet likable host.* Eventually it came down to Jeff and Phil Keoghan (who went on to host *The Amazing Race*) but Jeff got the edge—which Mark said is due to an *Access Hollywood* interview he had seen where Jeff interviewed Sandra Bullock. Jeff teased Sandra about showing off a lot of cleavage, but she teased back about him being the one looking, so he teased further that she's the one showing it, and she teased again asking him to show his, to which he, without hesitation, unbuttoned his shirt (again, something he can pull off, being *People* magazine's 32nd most beautiful person). Mark felt that a host who had the boldness for this sort of interaction could be the man for the adventure he was setting sail for. He made the right call. From sitting in the pouring rain at tribal councils to being wiped out by a wave during *Millennials vs. Gen X*, Jeff has never flinched from being down and dirty, in there with the players and the elements. The question still remains on how the interview would've gone if Sandra Bullock had tried to throw Jeff off his game by asking him if he liked her at all.

> "I don't kiss ass. It's not what I do. But Jeff is legitimately the best host in all of TV. The guy is amazing. I mean, he's really good. He can get something out of nothing. . . . Jeff's a good guy. . . . I think one day, me and Jeff are gonna have a beer together."
>
> **—Russell Hantz, January 28, 2012**

* Jeff had no idea that Mark had *also* drawn up mock newspaper stories about *Survivor* being a hit when pitching the show to CBS.

Baby Jeff

It's without question that Jeff Probst is the best host on television. I respect that RuPaul "slays" and Alan Cumming "understood the assignment" but it's still not even close. When they introduced the Outstanding Host for a Reality or Reality Competition Program award at the Emmys, Jeff won the first four in a row, after which I can only assume the Academy of Television Arts & Sciences was forced to hold an emergency meeting about needing to spread the love.

Probst's magic wasn't just sitting there on the beaches of Pulau Tiga when they first arrived; he wasn't born fully formed. Much like the players were trying to find their place in their tribe, Jeff was trying to figure out exactly how he fit into *Survivor*. A lot of what we now associate with Jeff wasn't present in the earliest seasons. He didn't narrate the challenges, he didn't host the reunion show, and he wasn't quite the imposing authority figure that he is now. He was on the same level as the castaways, often joining

them at the beach or on the rewards they won. "Hey guys," Jeff would say to the final five of Thailand, rolling up on them in a brand-new Chevy Trailblazer. "What do you think of the ride? Big Ted, take the front." Then he personally chauffeured them off to the challenge. Back then, Jeff seemed to want to be everyone's friend. At the first tribal council ever, Jeff commended them for their courage in making it that far and seemed truly saddened to be tasked with the unfortunate responsibility of having to snuff someone's torch. And did the castaways appreciate his kindness and friendship? No, they took it for granted and spat in his face. At the second tribal council, Pagong even wrote his name down to be voted out. Even though tribal council was designed to be a group therapy of sorts for the tribe, to his dismay, Jeff quickly learned that players would strategically treat it as a form of theater, lying to *him* at tribal. Lying to the other players in a deceptive game? Of course. But lying to the host himself?! Jeff was quickly hardened by the streets, or the jungle trails, of Borneo. He was going to have to earn the respect that he deserved.

One-of-the-guys Baby Jeff didn't last long. Having already been the host of a hit TV show, he was treated with a bit more reverence by the cast of *The Australian Outback*—rather than as a substitute teacher. Jeff started coming into his own, started to form a little bromance with Colby, and started commentating on the challenges (they had found in editing *Borneo* that the challenges felt a little empty hearing just the contestants and the music). Shooting season 4, in the islands of Marquesas, Jeff found his place in the show, revealing in a later interview that that's where he met "Survivor Guy." From my understanding, Survivor Guy was a hallucination Jeff had of himself but with longer hair, tattooed, and dressed in animal skins with a feather necklace.* This Survivor Guy showed Jeff the way to take things to the next level. While it was Mark Burnett who almost thoughtlessly came up with "the tribe has spoken," Jeff credits Survivor Guy with coming up with the iconic catchphrases of "got nothin' for you" and "worth playing for?" as well as the later slightly-less-iconic catchphrases of "spin and grin" and "sorry for you." With Survivor Guy by his side

* Many speculate Jeff had seen a vision of Coach from the future.

(and allegedly summoned every time Jeff looks at his feet before a challenge), Jeff boldly took his first steps, said his first words, and got ready to dig deep and become the host with all the fixin's.

Teenage Jeff

Maybe it was because he was getting more comfortable in his role or maybe it was because, like a few of us, he didn't seem to care much for many contestants of *Survivor: Thailand*, but season 5 ended up being a major turning point for Jeff. He had lost all his baby teeth and now had some real bite to him. In the third episode, the players competed for reward in a competition known as Pilfering Pirates, where they would have to race across bamboo pathways over water and steal items out from the opposing tribe's boats. But this challenge came with a twist: There were designated "attack zones" in the course where you could grapple with the opposite tribe and attempt to push them into the water. This was the first ever *Survivor* challenge that involved physical contact with your opponents, and Jeff was forced to step it up and flex his authority. "Whoa, whoa, whoa, you were not in the attack zone when you first made contact," Jeff warned them. "Don't get too cute in the attack zone, guys." But the members of the Sook Jai tribe just wouldn't listen and *did* get too cute in the attack zone. "No, no, no, Robb!" Jeff yelled at Robb with two Bs. "You were not in the attack zone when you grabbed Clay around the throat." The problem clearly wasn't the choking of Clay Jordan, may he rest in peace, but the blatant disregard of the attack zone rules. "Stephanie, what are you doing?!" Jeff yelled, completely flabbergasted. "You were in the water. Nowhere *close* to the attack zone!"

Up until this, CBS had wanted Jeff to remain neutral in his commentary, but they loved this Spicy Jeff and thankfully kept these interactions in the edit. Jeff's color commentary during the challenges became one of the biggest staples of the show. It's hard enough competing in these physical competitions while sleep-deprived and starving, with a million dollars on the line, but now, you had to worry about Jeff, in real-time,

"Probst would say, 'Once you get to tribal council, here's where the honesty begins. Here's where you really find out.' And my feeling was, yeah, once my vote is read. . . . We don't sign an agreement that says we have to be honest at tribal council. So why would you give away information? You can give a lying answer and I like Probst to be more open—I don't like steering, you know? It's fun as a viewer. I just don't like it as a contestant, personally. But as far as good television, yeah. I mean, like, you know, go destroy everybody's game, I don't care. As long as it's good TV, it's fine. But if I'm a contestant, just like, well, this sucks. Like, shut up."

—Jonny Fairplay, March 4, 2016

announcing in great detail exactly how hard you're flopping. So if you get frustrated with a difficult puzzle and kick it, you'll instantly hear a sarcastic, "Michaela, kicking the puzzle, which always helps." He's tough but he's fair. It didn't help Michaela and it surely didn't help Jake, who still holds the record of breaking the most challenges in frustration (1).* Spicy Jeff wasn't just restricted to the challenges where he had to disqualify multiple players. He started popping his head out at tribal council, most notably when Clay wrote "bye bye Denver Diva" on his voting parchment when casting a vote for Ghandia. "I have no idea what this means," Jeff scolded Clay. "In the future, write a name down. No more nicknames." The floodgates were open. No longer was Jeff expected to be a totally objective emotionless news anchor, a traditional game show host; he was now able to authentically respond to what was happening in front of him.

Season 5 was the first time Jeff himself hosted the live reunion show and he came in hot. First he poked fun at Brian for losing a challenge because he misspelled "road trip" and then questioning him on his strategy—how could he have been only one vote away from losing to the not-well-liked Clay? Jeff kept the show moving and grilled the cast, never letting them off the hook with vague answers. CBS was surely embarrassed that they ever thought they needed Bryant Gumbel or Rosie O'Donnell when they had Jeff Probst right there—a determined teenager confidently growing into the man he was always meant to be.

Dad Jeff

By the time I was with Jeff in the Amazon on season 6, he was fully formed, commanding all of his power on set. Don't get me wrong—Probst was a lot of fun, too, but he'd only joke around with you on his terms, without ever letting you forget who was really in charge. He wasn't trying to buddy-buddy with us like he may have been in season 1. He was like our dad whom we never wanted to disappoint. During the

* Kyle may have broken a challenge in season 48, but it was more of an accident.

merge vote, I did a (pretty solid) impression of DJ Casey Kasem dedicating a song from myself to the late Roger Sexton: the classic '60s chant from the Steam hit "Na Na Hey Hey Kiss Him Goodbye." I was walking back from the podium, pretty proud of this confessional, when Jeff proceeded to angrily tell me, "Just so you know, that will never ever make it on the air."* At the final four tribal, I remember smiling over at Deena on the jury and Jeff warned me not to pander to her. Can you blame me, Jeff? I was only trying to win a million dollars. But the challenge earlier involved us running around blindfolded in a maze and I got an eyelash or something caught in my eye. So at tribal, I was maybe blinking a little more than usual, which really pissed off Dad—I mean Jeff. "That's it! I saw you winking at Deena!" It was like he was threatening to turn the car around. Jeff, please, I wasn't winking! I had a medical condition! Don't turn the car around, I'll be good. I still wanna go to Disneyland, not Ponderosa.

Because Jeff was our dad, there was always jockeying amongst the survivors to be Dad's favorite. For a brief moment, I felt like I was Jeff's favorite and, boy, did that feel great. At the challenge and at tribal, he'd ask questions to everyone, but if you were giving answers he liked, he'd call on you more and more. Modern *Survivor* players are more aware of stuff like this and targets form on "Jeff favorites." But at the time, there was no downside to being the brownnoser and I loved being Jeff's go-to guy. Before the *Amazon* reunion, Jeff called me (as he called everyone) and ran through some of the questions he was planning to ask me. He really enjoyed the way I strategically played and wanted me to discuss how poorly he thought Jan and Helen played the Thailand endgame. It was half a year later and he still wasn't done kicking *Thailand*! Not only was he already working as a producer of the live show, Dad Jeff was clearly already thinking as a producer of the main show, by encouraging the sort of captivating gameplay he wanted to cultivate more of. And I tried my best, preparing my answers, hopefully making Dad proud at the reunion.

* Joke was on him, it did. And then the joke was on me when it was removed from streaming due to copyright infringement. My deepest apologies to Paul Leka, Gary DeCarlo, and Dale Frashuer. I learned my lesson writing this book and not being allowed to print the exact lyrics I had once said on CBS primetime.

Two seasons later, on *All-Stars*, I stopped being Jeff's favorite.* It's a painful process to see your father start to prefer a different sibling, and it's definitely salt in the wound if that other sibling shares your first name. But that's what happens when you go from being the smartest player to never win the game (Jeff's words, not mine!) to being the first one booted from your tribe by the more beloved Robert. You can't be a go-to guy anymore when you're voted out early. Then you're fly fishing with Rudy and Tina, while Jeff is calling shotgun to ride up front with golden child Robert in the Chevy Malibu he has just won, with Amber, Rob's number one ally, public showmance, and future mother of his four daughters, forced to ride in the back. Before the *All-Stars* reunion, I didn't get a phone call to prep for the questions I would get asked. Because there's no need to prepare for questions that aren't coming. However, a week later, at "America's Tribal Council" (a special where the cast of *All-Stars* got together just for fun to award Rupert a million dollars for no reason), Jeff did throw me a dig, disguised as a question, about how thanks to *Survivor* I was able to land a girlfriend way out of my league.

> "If I ask you a question at tribal council and the best you can come up with is 'I don't know,' I will pummel you. . . . But if you're smart and I ask you a question, you've already been thinking about it while you laid in the sand all day, and you've got an answer that gets it off of you and onto somebody else . . . If you really show up and you haven't thought one f—ing moment about tribal council, you're an idiot."
>
> **—Jeff Probst, November 19, 2012**

Jeff seemed to be in the same boat as me about not enjoying the *All-Stars* experience. He publicly stated that he felt a season of returning players was antithetical to the premise of the show, which is strangers living together. A returnee season

* I stopped being *anybody's* favorite.

felt like cheap stunt casting, akin to *Two and a Half Men* casting a naked Jeff Probst himself to show off his bacon bits. Jeff has since come to terms with bringing favorite players back again and again (and, in some cases, again and again and again), saying he understands the show and television much better now. But I think the real reason he didn't enjoy it the first time was because he had finally found his footing as the authority of the show, when suddenly here comes the likes of Jenna Lewis from season 1, clowning him. He didn't quite command the same fear and respect from the earlier cast members and part of him regressed from being the dad of the show to being the adult son coming home for Thanksgiving, only to find his parents still treating him like a little kid. Jeff wasn't planning on going backward. He was eyeing more creative involvement and was moving full tilt boogie ahead.

Middle-Aged Jeff

As the series went into its double digits and entered its middle ages, which many consider the prime of the show, Jeff was also at the top of his game. He was sharp, present, and vocal. When he was pissed, he'd let you know. When he was amused, he'd let you know. And when you were barely digging in a challenge like a small rabbit, he'd definitely let you know, Cassandra. But while we remember and quote the snarky Jeff moments the most, Jeff's genuine empathy and compassion for the players shines through, as well. "Candice? From Raro Tribe?" Jeff asked Billy Garcia, with absolute curious delight, who on the second episode of *Cook Islands* had proclaimed that he and a castaway on another tribe had experienced love at first sight. While it may arguably be one of the most unexpected, insane things that has ever happened on the show, one of the main reasons it's such a beloved moment is because Jeff had the composure to handle Billy's feelings with great precision—delicately but directly. Not to mention how incredible his facial expressions were during this exchange.

A critique Jeff often catches is being too involved in the game and asking the tribes potentially leading questions. But I think his emotional investment in the game is the best part of Jeff. His greatest strength as a host is how much he cares. He operates with the authority of the host but views the game through the lens of a fan, asking players the questions he'd be screaming at the TV if he were watching from home. This is why Jeff was turning down other quiz show opportunities in the '90s; he's not read-from-the-teleprompter guy, he's gonna-get-in-there-and-prod-around-without-letting-anything-slide guy! Yeah, why don't the people on the bottom just form their own alliance and flip the power structure? Yeah, Candice, a kiss from Adam is nice, but if it were love, he would've given you that immunity necklace.* Should've given Billy a chance!

Jeff also catches a lot of flak for playing favorites. His bromance with Boston Rob was so apparent that after the latter got voted out of *Heroes vs. Villains*, Jeff snapped at Courtney over it . . . who didn't even vote for Boston Rob to go! Maybe because Jeff developed personal friendships with players like Colby Donaldson and Andrew Savage, the assumption is that he prefers the alpha males of the game. But this theory doesn't really hold water if you look up his interviews and see which players he speaks about with the most excitement. His favorite winner is Cochran, not quite the poster child of an alpha. His favorite players definitely include some stronger men like Tony or Tyson, but also plenty that don't fit that mold like Sandra, Parvati, Cirie, Spencer, and Wentworth. When you lay them all out, a common thread appears. Outside of being great at playing *Survivor*, the one obvious thing they all have in common is that . . . they get a lot of screen time! Some of you are probably screaming at this book right now, "See! Jeff gives his favorites the most airtime!" The truth is that it's probably the other way around. They don't get the most screen time because they're his favorites; they're his favorites because they get the most screen time. His favorites are the ones who make the best TV. With some rare exceptions—like Jeff treating Chris Daugherty rather unfairly at the *Vanuatu* reunion show because Chris backstabbed Julie Berry (who Jeff was a huge fan of in and out of the game)†—Jeff's producer brain prefers

* Although John Cody, who I have no doubt IS in love with Candice, did NOT trade places with her to be on Redemption Island either.

† Chris has said that Jeff did the classy thing and called him up to apologize about it.

those who will help him make the most exciting television product. "It was worth a shot," Adam Klein tells Probst right after unsuccessfully playing the podium "idol." "Always," Jeff responds, beaming with pride. He'll always love the players willing to risk it all to give us the best show.

Gone are the days when Jeff was shocked that players lied to him at tribal. The savvier players became aware that he is a tool to be used in the game, just like anything else. The relationships formed between Jeff and the castaways can sometimes become the highlight of the show, with nothing ever topping the banter Jonathan Penner shared with Jeff over multiple seasons. "Oh please, Jeff!" Penner would snap at Jeff's challenge commentary. "Jonathan, getting frustrated . . . by me," an amused Jeff fired back, a real pro turning Penner's commentary about his commentary into commentary. "I mean MY ASS," Penner shouted out when the tiles he was trying to smash in a challenge seemed to not be smashing. "You gotta stop bitching and start throwing," Jeff threw back. There was such joy seeing Penner and Probst reunited again nearly ten seasons later. Within moments of the season starting, Penner was already challenging Jeff. He had just told the whole cast they had ten seconds to get off the boat. "Before what happens?" Penner demanded to know. And without missing a beat, Jeff shot back, "Before you gotta get off the boat, brother! You've played this game before." Jeff calling you *brother* is the Schrödinger's cat of *Survivor*—it could be a warm sign of respect or it could mean you really pissed him off. "I got the message, brother," Jeff coldly told Colby, who was a little too eager to get to a challenge he was sitting out of. "We'll go when I'm ready."

Although Jeff was possibly at his most-beloved here by the fans and his metaphorical *Survivor* family, as it tends to go with life, Host Jeff was starting to go through a bit of a midlife crisis.

Midlife-Crisis Jeff

It's no secret that Jeff has considered leaving the show multiple times. It may have been due to wanting to try new things, or maybe he was having a bad time with seasons he considered less successful, such as *Fiji*, *Gabon*, and later, *San Juan del Sur*. While those seasons have definitely found their cult followings, maybe living through a trainwreck season is more exhausting than consuming it on a binge watch. Fortunately, the seasons Jeff liked less seemed to always be followed up with absolute bangers. Every time he thought he was out, someone like Coach, using all that life experience in a kayak, would pull him back in. When Mark Burnett fully stepped away from the show after season 20, it wasn't a surprise—he had said from the beginning he would have other shows to focus on and would eventually fully hand over *Survivor*. But to Jeff's surprise, Mark personally chose him to take over the show creatively—perhaps as a way to keep the wandering-eyed husband at home where he belongs. Much like a chief in a small village dubbed Coach a warrior, Jeff was officially dubbed the showrunner.

Heroes vs. Villains would've been a tough act for any producer to follow, so I don't blame Jeff for starting his showrunning career with a bit of a rough patch. The early 20s of *Survivor* seasons have notoriously been known as the dark ages of the show and that's partly due to new production twists that Jeff oversaw. The first questionable choice was the Medallion of Power, which allowed the tribe holding it to get an advantage in the challenge they were competing in and led to pretty predictable challenge results. Jeff has gone on record that he never liked the Medallion of Power, but maybe not wanting to rule the show with an iron fist right off the bat, he didn't speak out loudly enough against it.

Conversely, the next season's twist, Redemption Island, Jeff proudly takes credit for. Ever since he was a kid playing Little League, he loved the idea of a losers' bracket, that someone eliminated would still get a chance to win. This, however, was also not a hit with many fans who passionately felt that getting voted out should mean just that . . . you're out.* But even though it may have struck out with the fans, much like a little kid who couldn't hit a baseball to save his life, Redemption Island still got four more chances to return in various forms.

Like some fans, Jeff started having less fun during these times. Spicy Jeff's fun challenge commentary seemed a bit meaner—which, to be fair, is pretty great to watch. It may be less fun if you're the Pathetic Alicia throwing worse than Jeff's nephew or Tarzan experiencing general failure or the Completely Ineffective Katie, really slowing her tribe down on the easy portion of the challenge. His best line of the era has to be "Benry makes the best move of the challenge for the yellow team with the ceremonial loser dismount." I'm on Jeff's side here. Who the hell performs a full *backflip* after *losing* a challenge? And while we're at it, what the hell kind of name is Benry anyway?! Are you a Ben or are you a Henry?! Oh, his full name is Benjamin Henry? Sorry, I think Spicy Jeff is rubbing off on me.

It's not just that Jeff was frustrated with the casts he was being fed; it seemed like his attention was shifting elsewhere. Jeff has always had other ambitions, and he wanted to start other families outside of *Survivor*. He directed his second film right after booking *Survivor* originally, and in this era of the show he was working on his third. He had also recently sold another show to CBS called *Live Like You're Dying*, where he would take a terminally ill person on the adventure of their life. Most importantly, in 2012, Jeff got his very own talk show. He was originally up to co-host *Live!* with Kelly Ripa but she went with Michael Strahan instead. Much like a different Kelley blindsided Savage out of *Survivor: Cambodia*, this Kelly blindsided Jeff into getting his own show instead, appropriately named *The Jeff Probst Show*. It was a syndicated daily talk show and didn't exactly catch on as quickly as *Survivor* had. I had only been doing *RHAP* a couple years at that time and I was openly supporting *The Jeff Probst Show*, in a thinly veiled attempt to try to get the big guy to come on my podcast. Maybe it was a bit transparent, but, who cares, it worked! Jeff, I thought, gave a terrific interview, but when we got to the end of the

* Although I would welcome in any season a Redemption Island or Edge of Extinction or whatever battleback challenge they throw at us, as long as it ends at the merge.

show and I gave him a chance to plug the talk show, he already seemed defeated about it. Usually when people promote something, they tell you where and when to check it out. Jeff's answer was more like, hey, people will watch it or they won't, it's fine. It seemed he saw the writing on the wall and accepted his fate. People just weren't tuning in—even when it was co-hosted by co-star of *Survivor: Philippines* Lisa Whelchel.

The Jeff Probst Show was sadly canceled after only one season, his third movie *Kiss Me* never got a proper release, and *Live Like You're Dying* (I apologize in advance for this pun) turned out to be short-lived. But Jeff's struggles outside of *Survivor* coincided with a curious turnaround inside of *Survivor*. Seasons 25 and 26 ended up being . . . really good.* Maybe it was a little case of the grass being greener and Jeff noticed the grass was pretty damn green in the Philippines. By the time season 27 came around, we were already fully out of the dark ages, and Jeff's head was out of the clouds. There was no more one-foot-in, one-foot-out; Jeff had ended his extramarital affairs with other shows and was 150 to 200 percent committed to *Survivor.*

Golden Age Jeff

It appeared that Jeff went from an identity crisis to fully accepting who he was and settling into the prime of his life. If Jeff Probst ever had reservations about his name being synonymous with *Survivor*, that was a thing of the past like the dodo bird or the rites of passage segment in the finale (which Jeff was finally able to kill off in *Caramoan*). Jeff returned to *Survivor* on season 27 all-in, kicking this era off with the inspired themes of *Blood vs. Water*, where players play with their loved ones, and *Brawn vs. Brains vs. Beauty*, which, like many of the great *Survivor* concepts, is fairly self-explanatory. These themes were so popular, they repeated them both immediately. The casting seemed to get more dynamic but, more importantly, so

* Yes, I'm well aware how some of you feel about *Caramoan* but I'm higher on it than most. It gets a bad rep for its pre-merge, but it's very fun overall.

did the gameplay, due largely in part to how hard Jeff Probst was championing the big moves. "She voted out her mom!" Jeff would constantly shout about Ciera. Sir, this is a Wendy's (and maybe the bigger move would've been voting *with* her mom to overthrow the power structure of Tyson, Gervase, and Monica). It seemed that the harder and more creatively players played the game, the more invested Jeff got—unless, of course, they got creative in how they approached the auction or the coconut chop challenge.

Jeff retained his edge, especially if you were the "completely ineffective Wardog" who has "never thrown a baseball before" or Monica slowly unspooling rope like it was "a Sunday picnic for the church," but he was clearly starting to show a gentler side. Getting softer is just something that comes with age,* and although he was already metaphorically our father, he literally became one in 2011 when he married Lisa Ann Russell and became a stepfather to her two children. *Survivor* was always a show people watched together, but it started to become more outwardly presenting as family friendly and a show about looooooove (and I don't just mean Jeff being an ordained minister, offering to marry Taylor and Figgy right then and there). Jeff wanted more families to watch and wanted young children to start planning to apply when they were older. The family visit took on more importance (contrasted with the time Jeff threatened that the losing loved ones would be taken and executed in *Nicaragua*), building to the biggest family visit ever on *Winners at War* with forty-two loved ones visiting!† That's a family so big, not even Boston Rob could carry it on his back!

The run of seasons from the late 20s through the early 30s is probably one of the best the show has ever seen. So much so that it started to get difficult for Jeff and the show to top themselves—they definitely had their work cut out for them after capturing lightning Tony in the *Cagayan* bottle. It didn't help that, due to financial restraints, safety concerns, or just convenience, the show decided to permanently

* Just ask my critics!

† And it could've been a few more if Sandra hadn't raised the sail on the Edge.

settle in Fiji. Unable to rely on new locales, Jeff and the team became a bit stretched for fresh theme ideas to separate the seasons. *Second Chance* was an exciting theme with built-in narratives, but *Heroes vs. Healers vs. Hustlers* didn't quite hit as hard (personally, I'm a hustler sun with a healer rising). Jeff also brought back his pet Redemption Island in the more punishing form of *Edge of Extinction*, letting contestants stick around forever. For *Winners at War*, Jeff went from not wanting the all-stars to return at all, to ensuring that they were in every single episode. But as scrutinized as Jeff gets for pushing certain themes, you can't say he doesn't go all-in. Who can deny that the original dream of the show was fully realized when people from completely different walks of life came together in the poignant discussion led by Jeff on if Millennials and Gen Xers spell *you* "y-o-u" or "u" while texting?

Jeff had found his place as the showrunner. He was always willing to try new things—even if the audience yelled at our televisions that what he got ain't broken!

> "When I see Jeff talk about a new season, he's so invested in these concepts like *David vs. Goliath*. You ask him about the show, you ask him about the theme, and he doesn't skip a beat. It's like, well, David is this and Goliath is that. I mean, certainly not every person who was a David or Goliath, I would argue, was a perfect embodiment of David or Goliath. But the point was still there. He had this kind of story he was looking to tell or some kind of question. . . . That's one of the things that made me realize that this show was kind of an ambitious kind of show."
>
> **—Christian Hubicki, May 9, 2019**

Grandpa Jeff

During the 2020 pandemic, Jeff and *Survivor*, and the rest of us, were forced to take a little break and reflect on things. While some of us stayed home, rewatching *Survivor* and podcasting about it, Jeff locked himself in a garage with a whiteboard and went down a deep rabbit hole to figure out the next era of the show. He envisioned a fire token economy and Rick Devens running a shop on the island. This was famously put to a halt in one phone call with Mike White, who asked Jeff if that sounded fun.* And Jeff instantly erased his whiteboard. Although I don't disagree with Mike White, the influence celebrities have on the state of *Survivor* is always a frustrating point for the fans. We love the show, but we know our wants and desires are a tier below those of Mike White, Tyler Perry, and, most influential in recent times, Exploding Kittens creator Elan Lee, who all have a direct line to Jeff. It'll take Jeff seven seasons of the fans kicking and screaming that we don't want the Sweat or Savvy challenge for him to address it, but if Jon Hamm rang him up and suggested a hidden immunity pickle, you best believe the next season will be *Island of the I-Dills* with Rick Devens running the beachfront delicatessen.

Season 41—drop the four, keep the one—Jeff broke the fourth wall into our living rooms with his new, long pandemic hair, welcoming us into the New Era. We've gotten rid of the themes and the two-tribe format but we have all sorts of new twists and turns and now a season is only twenty-six days.† Did all this pass the Mike White "is it fun?" test? Hey, they're still figuring it out. A huge change overall was the focus on the player's journey. Going on *Survivor* became sort of like going to Oz. You go to this faraway, colorful, magical place; you form an alliance of four; you search for the wizard because you want something (a million dollars); but once you get there, you realize the real prize was inside you all along. You go so far on this big adventure,

* At press time, it is unclear if this will be a bone of contention on *Survivor 50*.

† Originally due to Covid-related quarantining but stuck around due to budgetary considerations.

backstabbing the Tin Man along the way, just to learn there's no place like home. And sometimes, you may even see monkeys.

Also hailing from Kansas, Jeff became like the Wizard of Oz. His focus shifted from the exciting moves players could make to their personal growth. After forty-eight seasons, we finally saw Jeff moved to tears when Joe comforted Eva after she won a challenge. If Cirie crossing the balance beam soft-launched the New Era, then the straw that broke the camel's back was that twentieth fire log Ethan defiantly brought back down from the top of the Edge. When I interviewed Jeff for the podcast's 5,000th episode, he told me he was no longer interested in casting villains on the show. Despite some criticism, Jeff has denied that what they're looking for are "sob stories" and has spoken out harshly against Adam Klein's business as a casting coach helping young hopefuls get on the show by helping bring out their inner stories (sob or otherwise). I guess when Jeff told Adam that it was "always" worth a shot, that didn't apply to somewhat-successfully gaming his casting process.

> "I'm maturing along the way, so things that I might have said back in 2004, I might not feel today, you know? And I probably didn't understand the show as well and I didn't understand television. . . . I love this show. I love finding people that want to play. I love spending most of my year trying to figure out, what's something we could do that would twist the game so that when they get there they go 'oh s–t, now what am I gonna do?'"
>
> **—Jeff Probst, February 10, 2020**

But the fans started to miss the tougher Probst. The one who really gave quitters a hard time, who laid down Purple Kelly's and NaOnka's torches, who told Colton he never should've gotten up off that couch—although maybe in retrospect he was a little too hard on the staph-infection-ridden Osten and definitely too hard on my friend Jenna Morasca, who, needing to be with her sick mother, probably had the best reason out of anyone to take herself out of the game (even Boston Rob had to tell his boy Jeff that it wasn't right to question her motives). It's not exactly the same Jeff when he says the reason he's been hosting *Survivor* all these years is because of how moved he was that Heather struggled with navigating the trip wires to catch a ball. Season 1's cast took Jeff's kindness for granted and so did the New Era casts, leading to the nearly back-to-back quits of Hannah and Sean in 45, who Jeff was way nicer to than, say, Julie McGee from *San Juan del Sur*—where after she left, Jeff hosted a little roundtable with the rest of the tribe to trash-talk her. But Hannah and Sean may have finally been the bridge too far, because Jeff admitted to Kelly Ripa on *Live!* (whose host is now Mark Consuelos, and still not Jeff) that he's been going too easy on the contestants and will no longer snuff* the torches of the quitters. We all excitedly

* Or "smuff," as NaOnka would say.

welcomed back our beloved Spicy Jeff as he stabbed a bag of rice, demanding players sit out the immunity challenge or starve.

The New Era brought us Grandpa Jeff, where you're never really sure which Jeff you'll get. You might get the cranky old man who tells you tales of how back in the day, they had to walk ten miles uphill both ways to the water well, or you might get the sweet grandpa who you beg not to spoil your kids but who can't help trading them eighteen eggs for the chickens they don't want.

The Wizard of Fiji

Over the years, we've seen the whole span of Jeff. From the harsher host who told Russell Hantz that one of those dumbass girls beat his ass to the gentler one who massaged Brandon Hantz's shoulders until he calmed down. We've constantly seen Jeff try new things and keep growing. Just compare how he handled the Ghandia situation his first time hosting a reunion show, or the infamous China reunion where he demanded to know if Courtney had an eating disorder and if Erik is still a virgin, with how he handled the Zeke tribal in *Game Changers*. That man is out here and he is trying.

Do we need one more Jeff Probst metaphor? He's like Tom Cruise.* Slightly short-in-stature but absolutely larger-than-life. He's charismatic, he's bombastic, and he's addicted to trying to top himself. And you know what? When Tom Cruise did his stunt taking the Olympic flag from France on a motorcycle to a plane, skydiving it to the Hollywood sign, that was nothing compared to all the motorcycling, skydiving, Jet-Skiing, and taxi-calling Jeff himself has done getting that voting urn back to the States for the live reading of the votes (which we all miss). Trying to understand Jeff Probst is like trying to understand Tom Cruise. They're both almost . . . not human. You look into their eyes and you truly cannot tell what's in there. When I watch a

* Tom Cruise also happened to be *People*'s 4th most beautiful person of 2001. And they've both been spotted with Boston Rob.

Mission: Impossible film, I don't doubt for a second that Ethan Hunt would go to the ends of the Earth to save his girlfriend. But when Tom Cruise is on screen with Rebecca Ferguson or *White Lotus** star Michelle Monaghan, I'm not fully convinced that he experiences the human emotion of love as I myself know it. And I don't doubt that Jeff is a wonderful husband and deeply loving father to his children. But when he's narrating that family visit, explaining that the interesting thing between a brother and sister is that they're both family but neither of them is the parent, he doesn't seem too unlike an alien who has just crash-landed on Earth, trying to understand what it means to be a human. I'd say the big difference between Jeff Probst and Tom Cruise is that Jeff is at his best when he's off-the-cuff and at his worst when he's got a little something prepared to say. On the other hand, when Tom has something prepared, he breaks records at the box office, and when he's going off-the-cuff, he's breaking viral video records by jumping on Oprah's couch. Both Jeff and Tom, if they tell you to "dig, woman" . . . believe me, you're digging, woman.

If you still have a problem with Jeff, guess what—he already knows. Jeff has always had a complicated relationship with the fans. He loves them, he openly does the show purely for them, and yet he constantly has to weather their complaints. He tries to have it both ways, seeking out their input by creating the interactive living room (live-tweeting a show before live-tweeting was a thing) and telling the audience to tweet all their thoughts at him . . . but then also saying he probably won't read them anyway. He began the New Era with a monologue about how he missed the fans and ended it with an incredulous, "What do you want from me?!" already annoyed at the backlash that hadn't come yet. He even started a podcast, taking a page out of my book,† so he can explain his creative decisions directly to the audience. During his podcast's first season, he had a segment on the show called "Why Jeff Sucks" where he responded to emails about what he does wrong—although some, not me, might say

* The incredible and even underappreciated *White Lotus* (in case you're reading, Mike White).

† His however is the OFFICIAL *Survivor* podcast, which sadly makes mine the lowly UNOFFICIAL one.

that those emails were cherry-picked a little bit to leave out the fairest criticisms of the show. Season 50, *In the Hands of the Fans*, does attempt to give the fans some say as to how the season goes. Jeff opened elements such as tribe swaps, the live reunion, and idols up to a public vote. We'll see how it plays out, but the wording on the ballot makes it quite clear where Jeff stands on every issue. Would you rather have a super-thrilling awesome forced fire-making challenge at final four or an incredibly boring, dull, normal final four vote where everybody's favorite unceremoniously goes home?

To come back to the original question from Jeff—if I like him at all—of course I like Jeff. I love Jeff. When you pull back the curtain, he's like my dad. I look up to him, I'm intimidated by him, and sometimes I'm frustrated by him. He really is a dad to us all. And sometimes we don't see eye-to-eye and sometimes we're mad at each other and sometimes we get embarrassed because Dad read something online and now thinks he'll get canceled if he says "guys," but, at the end of the day, he's still our dad and we love him. Say what you will about Jeff, but you can't say he's been an absent father. He hasn't missed a single birthday, piano recital, or tribal council in over twenty-five years.* And that's how you do it on *Survivor.*

* Missed a few challenges but that's all right.

CHAPTER 3

The Heroes and Villains Hall of Fame

The Good, the Bad, and the Sprint Fan Favorite

In the *Epic of Gilgamesh*, the oldest known written story, the brave king Gilgamesh (spoiler) is able to defeat the anthropomorphic demon Humbaba. In 2019's *Avengers: Endgame*, the second-highest grossing film of all time, Tony Stark (spoiler) is able to vanquish the alien warlord Thanos. From the first bedtime story a caveman told their cavechild about whichever cavegods they believed in, there has been a common thread in the narratives which dominate our cultures. Luke Skywalker vs. Darth Vader, Harry Potter vs. Voldemort, Sugar Kiper vs. Randy Bailey. Whether you look to fiction, politics, religion, or history, the most universal story is the battle of good versus evil. The battle of heroes versus villains. It's no different on *Survivor*.

If you pull up any list ranking the *Survivor* seasons, be it by fans, critics, or yours truly, the top spot is almost always the landmark 20th season *Heroes vs. Villains.* Sure, it's a rather lukewarm take, but a take doesn't have to be hot to be correct. The main reason *HvV* is so beloved is obviously the cast—the best the show has ever assembled (and quite possibly will ever assemble).* Everyone is firing on all cylinders, making big plays and even bigger blunders, all while delivering incredibly funny character moments. But what really elevates the season is the theme itself. This anniversary season's conceit allowed the players to lean into their designation of "good guy" or "bad guy," or to subvert the expectations put on them. Season 20 asked us, without mincing words, who we were rooting for.

Even back when the show was just a twinkle in Mark Burnett's eye, he knew that heroes and villains would be a major part of the show's success. Stripping everything away from the players would bring out their inner selves and force them to make tough choices. And the ways they chose to navigate the game would define them. But what makes someone a "hero" or a "villain"? In the real world, what we generally consider heroic could be a firefighter rushing into a burning building or a single mother working multiple jobs to provide for her kids, or the aforementioned Iron Man, sacrificing his own life with the Infinity Stones. What we generally consider villainous could be a mobster breaking some guy's legs or a politician acting on behalf of his wealthy donors or the aforementioned Darth Vader building a literal *Death* Star to destroy entire planets. Simply put, heroes care for others, while villains look out only for themselves.

I was a blatantly self-interested player, back in the era where you were supposed to hide that. I took great joy in only looking out for myself, the mark of a true villain. "When TV provokes a philosophical argument about evil, the subject matter isn't usually more profound than Rob's treachery on *Survivor*," *Time* magazine wrote about me in their review of CBS's mini-series *Hitler: The Rise of Evil*. I don't particularly love being lumped in with Adolf Hitler in any category, but I'm glad critic James Poniewozik

* I'd almost call them the Avengers of *Survivor*, but I wouldn't dare mix metaphors since the Avengers are all heroes.

at least acknowledged that Hitler breaking the Munich Agreement was slightly worse than me breaking my word to Christy Smith.*

But *Survivor's* a game, right? If you're a real-life slumlord, raising the rent on an old lady who has lived in her neighborhood for decades, of course you're a villain. But if you're playing Monopoly and bankrupting your own grandmother because she landed on your luxurious Marvin Gardens hotel . . . tough luck, Nana, charge it to the game. *However*, if your aging nana is blind in one eye and you take that opportunity to sneak money from the bank . . . yup, villain move. Going outside the set rules of a game is cheating and cheating is . . . well, bad. But what if you're playing with some friends and fake a phone call that your grandmother has died in order to garner sympathy and get some favorable railroad trades going? I've checked the Parker Brothers Monopoly manual closely and they don't have a rule against that. You may lose some friends in the process and conjure up some bad karma, but it's allowed. And that's *Survivor*. There are mechanical rules in play—you can't knock over someone else's puzzle pieces or steal someone's idol†—but when it comes to things that are generally not okay in the real world, like lying or looking through people's bags, it's up to the other players, the fans, and even the editors to decide which lines should or shouldn't be crossed.

So let's take a look at the most important heroes and villains that have graced our *Survivor* screens. At the great heroes braving the way, who literally macheted their way through the jungles, and the evil villains lurking in the shadows, who metaphorically macheted their way through other people. These iconic giants have shaped not only the landscape of the show but also our perception of morality on a game show. Who we call heroic and what we consider villainous doesn't just reveal how the show has morphed over the years. It's a rather telling reflection of ourselves as a fan base and a culture.

* Although I still do feel a little bad about it.

† Unless you're playing in the fifth season, *Survivor South Africa*, the only season I know of across the worldwide franchise that allowed this wild rule change.

RUDY BOESCH

Borneo, All-Stars

Rudy Boesch was the first hero of *Survivor* and basically hit the trifecta of virtues that, early on, the show pushed as heroic. 1) As a former Navy SEAL, his military background presented him as a hero outside of the show; 2) he was a hard worker around camp, which meant he literally helped his tribe survive; and 3) he played a loyal and honest game, never betraying his allies and never compromising his own values. All this combined with his frank, curmudgeonly attitude and inherent underdog quality of being the oldest player out there, and it's no mystery why he was such an adored fan favorite. And no surprise as to why he was brought back on *All-Stars*—where he was sadly booted second. As someone whose time in *All-Stars* was also cut short, I cherish the time I got to spend with Rudy on our pre-jury trip and can attest he was as great of a guy in person as he seems on TV. Even if he maybe-not-so-heroically threatened Jerri and Jenna on his way out of the game.

RICHARD HATCH

Borneo, All-Stars

The show's first villain was the first hero's closest ally. Richard Hatch made it clear he was willing to step on anyone he needed to in order to win the money, which maybe now is considered smart, but back then, was viewed as selfish. As a smug corporate suit, Richard's focus in the game was on forming and maintaining a (not-so) secret alliance with the set goal of getting himself to the end. Even when Richard caught fish for the tribe, it wasn't because he couldn't bear to see Dirk go hungry; it was a manipulative tactic to make himself indispensable to his tribe. A squid pro quo, if you will.

"Truth is, it's more about real life than most of what's on TV. People make fun of reality television, but you really get to see how people, even though they're— It's a game, and I don't think it's about ethics and all the rest of that any more than it's football. You know, football players aren't out tackling people on the street. They're doing what they're supposed to do within the game's rules to win. And that's what's happening on *Survivor*. But in *Survivor*, you get a better peek into how humans interact and into what's going on in our minds, into how we deal with each other socially and what's important and what limits we have. I mean, I find it fascinating, and I love watching people be exposed in the way they are on *Survivor*. No pun intended."

—Richard Hatch, April 23, 2010

Whether this was intentional or not, the game of *Survivor* by design favors heroes in the first half and villains in the back half. When everyone is broken up into tribes, the players that are most beneficial to keep are the ones who do well in the challenges and do the most around camp. But after the merge, it's an individual game and the ones who thrive are those most able to navigate interpersonal social politics—a task difficult enough in itself that proves even harder if you aren't willing to lie. Over the years, we've seen many heroes competing their hearts out to win immunity, but Richard's greatest play was purposefully losing the final three challenge. It was him versus Rudy versus Kelly, and he calculated that whichever of the other two won would be forced to bring him to the end—Rudy out of loyalty and Kelly out of having a better shot against the jury.

And conversely, he realized if he himself won, he was screwed because he'd either have to take Rudy to the end just to lose to him or betray Rudy by voting him out, hence losing his jury vote to Kelly. The only way to win was to lose. So while heroes never quit, never surrender, villains are willing to throw challenges . . . should it benefit them.

Looking back now, the way Richard played is the bare minimum of how players should approach the game. We want to see players try to win. But Rich was viewed as incredibly underhanded and was never able to shake his reputation. Not on *All-Stars*, not on *House of Villains*, and certainly not with the IRS. Could've been interesting to see how his gameplay held up in *Heroes vs. Villains*, but being on house arrest in Rhode Island does tend to get in the way of popping over to Samoa.

COLBY DONALDSON

The Australian Outback, All-Stars, Heroes vs. Villains, In the Hands of the Fans

In Colby, *Survivor* gets its first leading man. I mean, what can be more American than our leading man being a Texas cowboy? Calm, cool, strong in challenges (still tied for the record of individual wins), his popularity caused the baby name "Colby" to jump all the way up to the top 100 in 2001. Not only was he the star of the show, but he was also the first marketable star that was maybe going to win it all. "All I know is I was damn close to that million dollars," Colby would later say to a different type of survivor in a cameo playing himself on *Curb Your Enthusiasm*. He was in fact damn close—after winning the final immunity challenge, he had a choice between keeping Keith Famie and winning or keeping Tina Wesson and losing. Colby may have genuinely thought he had a chance to beat Tina. And to Tina's credit, she probably got into his head a little bit, making it emotionally difficult for him to cut her. Most interestingly, Colby was probably hyperaware of his image on the show as "the hero." While everyone understood how Richard had won the previous season, the players weren't yet ready to admit they were there to vote out the people who are getting in the way of the prize money. Instead, there were a lot of discussions about who were the "right" people who "deserved" to go further. So when Colby was faced with the choice between the chef Keith that got on everyone's nerves and the well-liked Tina who had bravely saved the tribe's rice from the flood, he went with who "deserved" to be in that final two. Because heroes do what's "right," not what stuffs their pockets. If you're the hero of the biggest show on television, maybe that helps your chances of breaking into Hollywood after . . . but of course, that's not what heroes think about in the moment; they just act with no concern for themselves.

> **"I met a lot of people that named their dog Colby. But, you know, that's the funniest thing. Like, 'I named my dog after you,' and I kind of think that's a compliment? I don't know whether that's a compliment or not."**
>
> **—Colby Donaldson, December 6, 2017**

Colby's return on *All-Stars* showed a different shade of him. His confidence came off more like arrogance. As one of the bigger names coming into the season, he didn't seem to want to work with the lesser pissants. And as returnee seasons often go, it's the quote unquote pissants who end up getting the last laugh over the superstars. His third appearance on *Heroes vs. Villains* came with more nuance. A bit older and a bit out-of-touch, he struggled greatly with the social politics, the strategic gameplay, and the physical challenges.* Everyone on the season was disappointed with the decline of Colby. His fellow hero James, who used to idolize him, even referred to him as

* Though one challenge flop was clearly his brother's fault. C'mon, Reed!

"Superman in a fat suit." Despite being humbled, he outlasted his tribemates and ended up being the last hero standing. "I don't know how to quit," he states in his final, incredibly dramatic confessional, while outnumbered by villains four to one. "It's just not in me." There's only one way for him to play *Survivor* . . . and that's full tilt. So what version of Colby will we see on *50*? The washed-up hero or one ready to prove himself again?

JERRI MANTHEY

The Australian Outback, All-Stars, Heroes vs. Villains

Does a great hero need a great villain? Can the Batman exist without the Joker? What about Catwoman? The polarity between an iconic hero and an iconic villain on the same season only amplifies the iconic nature of both. Thus, we got the first great *Survivor* rival pairing in Colby Donaldson and Jerri Manthey. While Colby was the rugged cowboy, Jerri was the she-devil in a blue bikini, the Wicked Witch of the West, Man-Eater Manthey. While Colby was strong and stoic, Jerri came across lazy and annoying. She was the first reality TV villain who transcended the show into the news and tabloids. She openly had a crush on Colby, which may've been a reciprocal flirtation but was presented as one-sided. While Jerri graphically described her fantasy of covering Colby's body in chocolate while having sex with him, Colby made it clear he ain't no Hershey Bar* and blindsided her out of the game—a move that should've been considered villainous in this era but was hailed as Jerri getting her just desserts (which sadly was not chocolate). Colby and Jerri ended up appearing together on the same season not once, not twice, but, to the chagrin of both, all three times they played.† On their final season together, *Heroes vs. Villains*, they fully leaned into their categorized alignments with Colby and Jerri landing on the beach

* As iconic of a quote as this is, it never really made total sense, since you don't cover a Hershey Bar in additional chocolate.

† Feels a bit wrong that we'll be seeing Colby on a season without Jerri.

in contrasting white and black cowboy hats. When the heroes and villains finally merged and had to pick a communal tribe name, Jerri suggested the "All Villains," a name which really disgusted the overly sincere, incredulous heroes Colby and Rupert.

But was Jerri really a villain? Looking back, especially compared to villains to come, what's the worst thing that she did? Get on the nerves of some people who were all paranoid and sleep deprived? Maybe someone who yawned a little too expressively on television didn't deserve to be the most hated person in America? At the live *All-Stars* reunion, Jerri got booed off the stage for making the point that all the contestants appear on the show as entertainment. They're edited as characters and don't deserve the hate they get as people outside of the show. At the time, being in that room, it did feel like Jerri was being a bit melodramatic—I mean, no one held a gun to her head and forced her to return to the show. But as the years went by and social media developed as it did . . . maybe the "she-devil" had a bit of a point.

> "Any of us who have kind of been like the female villain of our season, like, we kind of have like a back-channel connection to each other. I haven't reached out to Tori [of 42] yet. I should just to kind of be that support for her. But I remember during my season, like, Kass reached out and Chrissy reached out and like, so there's this little, you know, secret society of villain women. . . . I haven't talked to Jerri. I have to talk to the original, you know, the OG."
>
> **—Angelina Keeley, April 22, 2022**

Jerri's three-season arc was kind of the reverse of Colby's. She went from the black widow who got her revenge on those who had wronged her—Colby in *All-Stars* for *Australia* and Boston Rob in *Heroes vs. Villains* for *All-Stars**—to . . . well, I wouldn't go as far as saying she became a hero, but even in the words of her longtime rival Colby, she really chilled out and got a more levelheaded vibe. A villain turned fallen angel, who was mere seconds away in an immunity challenge from winning the whole thing. Now, the same vocal fan base that booed her off the stage is now booing that the show left her off of the cast of season 50.

> "And on Day 3, I went out in the woods just to have my prayer moment . . . And so the Lord, He said, 'I want you to play your game, but I also want you to play based on the rules. The rules say to outwit, outplay, and outlast, and you're not doing that yet. You're trying to be this Christian, this high and mighty Christian. No. Play their game, lie, backstab, do all that stuff. And then they're gonna turn around and they're gonna be shocked because they're expecting you to be this Christian, good Christian girl, but do what you need to do.' And at that point, that's when I started to play."
>
> **—Vecepia Towery, November 24, 2020**

* Although, from where I sit, it seems like Lex did her much dirtier in *All-Stars* than Rob did.

HUNTER ELLIS

Marquesas

Hunter Ellis is possibly the least memorable name on this entire list, probably due to the fact that he was the third person voted out of his season. But every superfan knows that you can't tell the history of *Survivor* without mentioning his appearance on the show—more specifically his infamous elimination. On paper, Hunter couldn't be more of a prototypical hero. Leader of the tribe, check. Military background, check. Good-looking guy, check. Everything we knew about *Survivor* told us he should've made it deep into the game, but if *Survivor* were predictable, it wouldn't have lasted five seasons, let alone fifty. When this Navy fighter pilot got shot down early, his parting words to camera were that he was camping with a bunch of knuckleheads and couldn't understand the logic behind voting him out. Survivalist Hunter saw *Survivor* as a camping trip when it was seen as a strategic game by the emerging villain on his tribe who orchestrated his blindside . . . Boston Rob Mariano.

BOSTON ROB MARIANO

Marquesas, All-Stars, Heroes vs. Villains, Redemption Island, Island of the Idols, Winners at War

Before the merge, *Survivor* was generally viewed as a team sport—it's your tribe against the other tribe(s). But not for one young construction worker from Boston. Rob Mariano landed on the beach of Marquesas ready to look out only for himself. So what if his tribe desperately needed Hunter's strength in the challenges? Rob didn't care if his alliance was strong physically or mentally; what was important to him was that they would obey. Each of the six times he's played, Rob's priority has been seizing and maintaining control. He literally plays like a mob boss, even quoting *The Godfather* about using fear to keep his alliance players loyal. Hunter couldn't be controlled, so Hunter had to go.

Sure, Rob was cunning and manipulative, but what really made him stand out as a villain was how incredibly charming he was. I still give him credit for being the best ever at fostering a relationship with the audience. When he talked to the camera about what he was plotting, he wasn't just letting us know what he was thinking—he was bringing us in, making us co-conspirators in his evil plans. Rob was the show's first villain that we would root for. Though he didn't make it past the first vote of the merge in his first season, his innovative strategic thinking permanently changed how future players approached the game. When I first went on the show, the two game styles I most wanted to replicate were Dr. Will Kirby's from *Big Brother 2* and my namesake Boston Rob's.

It's possible that Rob, like Hunter, could've ended up just a notable footnote in *Survivor* history, but as fate would have it, he was brought back on *All-Stars*. And it really was fate, because out of the nine men in the cast, he was, at the time, the ninth most popular amongst the fans. Yup, as hard as it is to believe now, *I* was the more famous Rob in the cast. If Brian Heidik wasn't such a villain outside of the show, he probably would've taken Boston Rob's spot (and thus probably married Amber). Rob did not squander his opportunity his second time out and played a much more successful mob boss game. As the first returnee season, *All-Stars* was the first season where it wasn't a bunch of strangers playing together. These were people who knew each other outside of Panama—and in the case of Rob and Lex van den Berghe, they were very good friends. But Rob was able to separate his close personal friendship with Lex from the game he was playing and betrayed him.

From its inception, one of the central questions of the show has been how much of this is a game and how much is real life. Is who you are when you play *Survivor* who you are when you're back home? In the case of Rob and Lex, there was no more dodging the question. Did Rob make the right strategic game move or did he sell out his character, values, and friends for a stack of greenbacks? If you ask Lex (or Grant Mattos from *Redemption Island*, who got similarly snaked), he might lean on the side that Rob's choice was a moral failing—I don't believe he and Rob ever fully mended that friendship. But history is written by the victors.

"I'm a villain?" Rob half-jokingly asks Jeff in the opening mat chat of *Heroes vs. Villains*. While undoubtedly one of the most iconic villains of the show, Rob is such a fan favorite in large part because of the heroic side of him: He's a good-looking, charming guy; a strong tribe leader who gives everything he's got every single challenge; and, of course, he's the romantic lead of not just the best love story *Survivor* has ever seen, but the best love story *reality television* has ever seen—just watch the live proposal to Amber and look at how strong their marriage is to this day . . . I mean, any idiot can see that. Rob came into *Heroes vs. Villains* wanting to play like a diplomat, rather than a dictator. While it got the best of him and he quickly reverted back to his mob boss ways, he came out of the season as the most heroic villain—his image definitely helped by the fact that he was next to Russell Hantz.

> “[Boston Rob] created this game called 'Who's Got the Stick?' . . . Everyone would shut their eyes, and Rob would hand a stick to somebody with their eyes closed. And then when everyone opens their eyes, everyone has to try to figure out who has the stick . . . of course, he's just watching. He knows exactly who has the stick, and he's watching that person and figuring out what it looks like when they lie.”
>
> **—Adam Klein, May 26, 2020**

On Rob's fourth go on *Redemption Island*, he employed his tyrannical game style flawlessly. He played like a mob boss, a general, a cult leader—whatever metaphor you want to use. He ran his tribe with an iron fist, using his patented buddy system to control what they ate, when they ate, who they talked to, and, of course, who they voted out. Only this time, the show edited him like someone we were supposed to be rooting for. Yes, he was still the Robfather, placing his hand on the shoulder of the person he wanted his loyal soldiers to put a hit out on, but he was doing it for his family—literally carrying them on his back as he beasted out challenge after challenge. Rob won in such a dominant fashion that his reputation preceded him into both *Winners at War* and *The Traitors*, so he wasn't able to make another deep run. But while he was around, everyone understood who was boss.

So is Rob truly a hero or a villain? The question is actually most amusingly asked on his appearance on *Deal or No Deal Island*. Rob was closely aligned with a young, dorky kid named Aron and they developed a sweet bond—in a similar way to how Hollywood loves to keep making movies where a big action star is softened when they're forced to babysit a precocious child. Aron has heard Rob was on *Heroes vs. Villains* and asked Rob if he was the hero. "No, I was a villain," Rob confesses with a don't-be-mad-at-me smile, completely shattering Aron's world. This guy who took me under his wing, who seems to totally have my back . . . is a villain? Thankfully, we never had to see Rob betray Aron. Hero to some, villain to others, Rob Mariano is definitely both the villain and the hero that the show needed to become what it became.

RUPERT BONEHAM

Pearl Islands, All-Stars,
Heroes vs. Villains, Blood vs. Water

With his bushy beard, gravelly voice, and tie-dye shirt, Rupert Boneham arrived on the seventh season of *Survivor* a fully formed fan-favorite hero. He was so popular that they instantly brought him back the following season for *All-Stars*. And since he didn't win *All-Stars*, they let America vote on which additional player deserved to also get a million dollars . . . to no one's surprise, it was Rupert. It's not hard to see why Rupert was so instantly beloved. He's a big, strong, gregarious guy; a provider for the tribe who happens to also be overly sincere and sensitive. He was bullied and now works with troubled teens. Rupert is so earnest that, in his four times out on *Survivor*, his most underhanded moment was probably walking around with a rock in his pocket so that Russell would notice and think he'd found an idol.* Even when he does a villainous act, like stealing the shoes from the opposing tribe in the opening *Pearl Islands* challenge, he's treated like the hero—after all, he's a pirate, pirates steal, and he's stealing *for* his tribe. When he's screaming at Jonny Fairplay for writing his name down, ready to rip his head off, it's not seen as someone much bigger picking on someone much smaller. No, it's the hero of the story standing up to the dastardly villain. The show treats Rupert with such reverence that the episode where Fairplay finally gets the upper hand and blindsides him is edited like a Greek tragedy. A dark, brooding tale. "So much for my dreams," Rupert says on his way out, with a heavy heart. While every player tends to view themselves as the hero of the story, Rupert *really* saw himself as the protagonist of the epic saga that is *Survivor* . . . and the fans and the show agreed. The *Pearl Islands* DVD was the only one they put out without placing the winner front and center on the cover—that slot was for Rupert, our hero.

Incredibly self-serious, without an ounce of disingenuousness, Rupert committed so hard to the theme of whatever season they put him on, be it pirates, all-stars, heroes, or loved ones—sacrificing his place in the game for his wife minutes into the start of *Blood vs. Water*. He was a pop culture phenomenon. Unless you were forced to live in his flooded below-ground shelter,† who isn't a Rupert fan?

* Possibly the most successful fake idol ploy in *Survivor* history.

† Or were an Indiana voter in 2012.

"And it was hysterical on *All-Stars* when [Rupert] got these profound moments . . . I'd be sitting there, like, having some cool conversation with Colby or somebody, and all of a sudden, the cameras are going, 'Oh, my God. Rupert's having a profound moment. Okay, we're gonna break away from you guys, and we're gonna follow Rupert!' Rupert was, like, such a camera king, and it drove us crazy because he really didn't do that much."

—Kathy Vavrick-O'Brien, May 15, 2010

Well, I guess one person who is definitely not a Rupert fan is his rival. The Lex Luther to his Superman. *Survivor*'s greatest hero needed its most diabolical villain . . . Jonny Fairplay.

JONNY FAIRPLAY

Pearl Islands, Micronesia

Jon Dalton, more commonly known by his moniker Jonny Fairplay, went into *Survivor* with a mission: He was going on with the express purpose to be hated. Fairplay came from the world of professional wrestling, where he loved playing the heel—his nickname came from the fact that he, in fact, did *not* play fair. And he brought that same energy into *Survivor*. He'd get drunk, flip people off, take glee in kicking someone out of his tribe, and flash his signature peace sign fingers. While he wouldn't shy away from getting into confrontations with others (Jeff included), his real villainy was his shady backroom dealings. Compared to the big, heroic Rupert catching fish for the tribe, Fairplay was like a little weasel sneaking around, cooking up devious plans.

Heroes act, villains scheme. Of course, Fairplay is most infamously known for his dead grandma lie. During the loved ones visit, he prearranged for his buddy Thunder D to come bearing the devastating news that his grandmother died, dude. So while his very-much-alive grandma was back home, watching *Jerry Springer*, Fairplay was cashing in on all the fake bereavement sympathy.

Fairplay thrived off being hated. An entertainer at heart, he understood the value in getting an extreme reaction from the audience. The worst thing you can be on television is forgotten. But what made Fairplay such a lethal villain was how naturally good at the game he was. Unlike other flash-in-the-pan wannabe baddies who play the role of bad guy by talking smack in the confessionals, Fairplay knew when to be a showman and when to dial it back. He lied constantly, but the lies he would tell were so believable and mixed in with truth that he kept slipping deeper and deeper into the game. Heck, he probably would've won the whole thing if he wasn't taken down by a courageous troop leader who happened to take some aerobics classes.

> **“I still say if it would have been [Fairplay] and the devil sitting at final tribal council, I would have given the devil my vote.”**
>
> **—Rupert Boneham, January 20, 2014**

Fairplay's return to the show on *Fans vs. Favorites* was obviously a disappointment. Despite coming into the season with such a wicked reputation, his social play instantly landed him in the prime swing vote power position. Unfortunately, he claimed to be missing his pregnant girlfriend and asked to be voted out. The show's editing portrayed this as a quit, a former supervillain losing his edge, but it's now pretty well known that it was actually a legitimate medical situation. Prior to coming out to Micronesia, Fairplay was power bombed by Danny Bonaduce during Fox's 2007 Reality TV *Really Awards* and broke his jaw. He seemed to have been coming along in recovery until fan favorite hero Yau-Man smashed Fairplay's head against a boat during the season's first challenge. Since he wasn't allowed his pain medication on the island, Fairplay peace-signed his way out of there.

Fairplay's legacy looms heavily over *Survivor* and reality television in general, especially in the realm of contestants realizing they are often cast on a show to play a part. Whether hero, villain, or comic relief, playing into a character makes the producers happy, engages the audience, and gets you more screen time. Win, win, win. However, this only works if you seem authentic in the role you're playing, and Fairplay definitely nailed the authenticity of being a villain. It breaks a hero's heart to have to hurt someone, but it brings a smile to Fairplay's face to send someone packing. Over the years, Jon's started a family, found Christianity, and maybe mellowed out a bit, but it's still perfectly fitting that he was the first villain to enter the first season of *House of Villains*.

SANDRA DIAZ-TWINE

Pearl Islands, Heroes vs. Villains, Game Changers, Island of the Idols, Winners at War, Australian Survivor: Blood vs. Water

In a season dominated by the big personalities of Rupert and Fairplay, there is still room for Sandra Diaz-Twine to shine. Sandra not only went on to win the game but came back to become the first two-time winner of the show. She's certainly the Queen of *Survivor*, but is she a villain? We have to categorize her as such since the show placed her on the Villains tribe of *Heroes vs. Villains*. Not to mention, she was the villain who won out.

But on paper, isn't Sandra clearly a hero? She's a mother, a military spouse, aligned with the biggest hero of the season Rupert, and opposed to the biggest villain of the season Fairplay (and the biggest villain of her following season, Russell). But the obvious trait that paints her as a villain is that she is a grade-A, unmatched trash talker. Sassy Sandra can get loud, too, what the f–k?! To the camera or to someone's face, Sandra drops more iconic lines per episode than most players get per season. "Last time, I was mean," Sandra says in her opening *Heroes vs. Villains* confessional. "And this time, I'm meaner." Her call-it-like-it-is attitude pairs well with her deeply unbothered nature. While everyone was offering Jonny Fairplay condolences for his recently deceased grandmother, Sandra either saw through his BS or just couldn't have cared less. "It's not about you all the time," she tells Fairplay when picking his buddy to send down the plank during the loved ones challenge. When her tribe caught a goat in *Game Changers* but decided they needed to let her go, Sandra was the one dissenting voice. She was ready to kill that mama goat, kill that baby goat, and, hell, kill Bambi if he was out there, too. Good ol' country boy J.T. had a conscience; Sandra had an appetite.

But deeper than her attitude, the core of Sandra's alleged villainy is her patented "anybody but me" strategy. Heroes are loyal to their allies, but villains cut those in their way. I'm not saying Sandra isn't a loyal player—no one can say she isn't loyal to her allies. But when your mindset is that anyone can go home that isn't you, that means sometimes you do have to say adios to your friends. Sandra never betrayed her bestie Christa, but when Christa took the blame for the fish that Sandra dumped out in anger . . . well, Sandra wasn't about to set the record straight. Sandra never betrayed her bestie Courtney, but when the vote was between the two of them, Courtney voted for Jerri and Sandra wrote down Courtney. Was it smart gameplay? Absolutely. But would Harry Potter throw Ron Weasley in front of a curse Voldemort was shooting his way? Probably not. Maybe in the newer books, now that J. K. Rowling has entered her villain era.

Outside the show, Sandra is an extreme couponer, which to me is a perfect metaphor for how she plays. She knows that a little here and a little there will make a whole lot of difference eventually. Sandra won't just tell a lie; she'll tell a good lie. Does she actually mean "anybody but me"? Yes and no. Yes, she's willing to let anybody else go, but no, she's a bit more cunning and sophisticated than that. She knows she can use the "anybody but me" cover to subtly push her own way and keep herself under the radar. Let the big egos battle it out, while she slips on by to the end and collects another million dollars. This strategy worked amazingly on *The Traitors*, almost bringing her home yet another win.

You can slip under the radar once and win. And apparently you can pull that off a second time. But a third time is trickier. Sandra's target couldn't have been bigger going into *Game Changers, Winners at War,* or her foray into *Australian Survivor.* Forced to play above the radar, Sandra's sneaky tactics had to be turned into active, overt strategy. She may have dumped out Rupert's fish by accident, but she definitely ate J.T.'s sugar on purpose. Interestingly, there are portions of the fan base that give Sandra more credit for her losing games than her two winning ones. Odds are we won't get to see a three-peat *Survivor* win from her, but . . . I don't know about that.

TOM WESTMAN

Palau, Heroes vs. Villains

Tom Westman was a natural tribe leader who, despite his tribe getting a bit of a rocky start after losing their supplies in a canoe flip, successfully brought Koror to an unmatched winning streak. His physical prowess continued into the merge where he went on to tie the record of five individual challenges won, culminating in the longest endurance challenge *Survivor* had ever and will ever see—hanging on to a buoy against his number one ally Ian Rosenberger for twelve whole hours!* On top of all this, Tom wasn't just a firefighter . . . he was a *New York* firefighter in post-9/11 America. He was a hero the audience rooted for all the way to his dominant win.

There isn't much to criticize about Tom's game, but what lingers is the question of how heroic or villainous he actually was. He definitely kept a tight alliance from the

* Making Christian Hubicki's five-and-a-half-hour endurance performance seem more like my four-minute result in the *Amazon* finale.

start, which, in reality, probably wasn't too dissimilar to the mob-like way Boston Rob ran things. Through the modern lens, Tom being able to win out both physically and socially would be seen rather positively—after all, the best *Survivor* players, like the best poker players, play the hand they're dealt. And if that hand contained a young, impressionable Ian, then manipulating his emotions was probably the best play. But at the time, the producers probably felt that the audience wasn't ready to cheer on a brave firefighter gaslighting a naive dolphin trainer half his age.

Tom's return in *Heroes vs. Villains* cemented him even more as an icon. After getting to see him play a game from a position of power, we got to see Tom's chops when he had his back against the wall. Although he didn't make the merge, he certainly left an impression on the season. "Tomorrow, we make our apologies. Tonight, we make our move," Tom coldly says while plotting his idol play that blindsides the powerhouse Cirie out of the game—maybe one of the most badass lines in the history of the show. Now I ask you, if we lifted this quote and threw it into an action movie . . . would it be said by the hero or the villain?

STEPHENIE LAGROSSA

Palau, Guatemala, Heroes vs. Villains, In the Hands of the Fans

Season 10 wasn't a story of a hero versus a villain; it was a story of two heroes. Dual protagonists on opposite tribes. On the unstoppable Koror was Tom, and on the very-stoppable Ulong was Stephenie LaGrossa. With the exception of Rupert, Stephenie was the biggest superstar the show had ever produced, definitely helped by the fact that she was the first woman to be a true hero. Prior to Stephenie, the women were positively presented as "sweet" or "cunning" or "motherly," but she was the first presented with attributes that were typically reserved exclusively for the male heroes. You don't have to watch more than a few minutes of *Heroes vs. Villains* to witness her dislocate her shoulder and pop it back in like it was no big deal. Her valiant efforts in the challenges were never fruitful, since Ulong lost every single challenge, but this only multiplied her standing as a scrappy underdog, culminating in her being the last person on her tribe—the only time this would happen in *Survivor* history. It was the lone Stephenie against all of Koror.

Like Rupert, she was brought back immediately the following season. Stephenie from *Palau* to *Guatemala* is one of the show's most interesting case studies. Here was the same person, playing the same game back-to-back, but she went from being portrayed as a hero to a villain. The main difference had to be that she was no longer the underdog in *Guatemala*. The confidence the fans loved in her was now seen as arrogance as her dominant alliance picked off the minority one by one. Maybe due to buying into her own hype, she came off as less of a badass and more of a brat (the fans even nicknamed her StepheMe). She successfully made it to the end, but her cast disliked her game so much that she lost the jury vote in a landslide to underdog Danni Boatwright. Tom being edited as a hero and Stephenie as a villain in their respective games where they led powerhouse alliances probably boils down to the fact that Tom won and Stephenie lost, and the show generally likes to tell a story that explains why the winner won and why the loser lost.* If Tom had lost *Palau* to Katie, he'd probably be edited like a jerk, closer to how Coby viewed him in the game. If Stephenie had beat Danni, she'd probably have an unmatched hero winner edit.

Stephenie and Tom were reunited on *Heroes vs. Villains*, where they were both placed on the Heroes tribe. And they were instantly both scrappy underdogs who

* The editors of *41* did not seem to get this memo.

forgot to pre-game. To all the little girls she inspired, it was sad to see her go out of the game second, but, I'll tell you this, it's nothing that a filet mignon pizza can't cure at her (now-closed) restaurant Gigi Restaurant and Lounge.

> "*Survivor* comes down to a lot of luck in the end. And if you piss off too many people, you're not going to win. . . . But if you ever ask anybody, 'Do you remember *Survivor: Guatemala* and who won?' I'm not even kidding you. Most people do not remember who won. They're like, 'I remember you went to the end, didn't you? But who won?'"
>
> **—Stephenie LaGrossa, June 20, 2019**

TERRY DEITZ

Panama, Cambodia

Terry Deitz is an interesting turning point when it comes to the heroes of *Survivor*. In a similar mold to Tom, he was a fighter pilot who was a great tribe provider and leader, and, after the merge, he went on to tie Tom and Colby's individual immunity record. Yet despite his physicality, Terry was actually the underdog of the season. He was the last of his tribe against the unbreakable Casaya and was forced to win challenges and find an idol to survive. He eventually lost his balance in the final challenge and was eliminated (a spot where many great heroes fail due to their balance). Though he was sometimes portrayed as a bit of a prick, he improved his social game on his second outing—only to have no choice but to leave Cambodia after receiving news that his son needed a heart transplant. Everything about Terry screams textbook

Survivor hero: Captain of Sports Danielle DiLorenzo was placed on the Villains tribe purely because she dared vote him out. But what's most notable about Terry as a hero is that, when it came to the audience voting for the *Panama* fan favorite award, they didn't pick the expected underdog challenge beast. The tides were turning and the fans went for a new breed of hero . . . Cirie Fields.

CIRIE FIELDS

Panama, Micronesia, Heroes vs. Villains, Game Changers, Australia vs. the World, In the Hands of the Fans

Cirie Fields not only won the fan favorite award, but she's probably the most universally liked contestant ever. While all the major stars like Boston Rob, Parvati, or Cochran have their dedicated group of haters online, it's tough to find trolls even in the dregs of the internet badmouthing Cirie. Cirie is the woman who got up off the couch, representing the every-person who loves to watch *Survivor* but doesn't have any survival skills. As an ex–couch potato, she entered Panama the ultimate underdog, scared of leaves, and left it a strategic force of nature to be reckoned with. Beloved castaway? Undeniably so. But a hero? For the purposes of this chapter, I'll label her as a hero for the same reason I've labeled Sandra as a villain—that's how the show itself categorized them. Cirie could be painted as a hero because she's a mother and a nurse who bravely left her comfort zone to go on *Survivor*. But out on the island, she definitely played like a villain. Heroes like Terry win challenges, while villains try to steal advantages that don't belong to them and manipulate others behind the scenes. "My mama always told me, you might not be able to beat them with these," Cirie said, pointing to her bicep, "but you can always beat them with this," pointing to her head, before letting out a laugh. This, of course, was right after she led the Black Widow Brigade in tricking the poor Erik Reichenbach into giving up his immunity necklace and getting blindsided in possibly the most humiliating way. So how could someone who takes such delight in deceiving others get classified as a hero?

> **"I found out it was *Heroes vs. Villains,* I really felt this. I felt like I could go either way. I didn't feel particularly heroic, and I didn't feel particularly villainous. I felt like I fell somewhere in the middle. But after getting out there and playing with the people I played with, I think I would have fared much better if I was a villain."**
>
> **—Cirie Fields, September 17, 2010**

In the same vein as Boston Rob, a lot of Cirie's popularity comes from the effortless ease with which she connects with the audience during her talking head interviews. Similarly to Rob's *Godfather* references, Cirie refers to herself as a gangster. But she's not like a mean gangster; she's a nice gangster with a smile. A gangster in an Oprah suit. Cirie has an incredible smile and infectious laugh that comes out both when she's plotting Ozzy's brutal blindside and when she's examining Shane's chafed penis. She's having such a delightful time out there that it's impossible to see her as the bad guy. Cirie prompted a real *Survivor* vibe shift for the fan base, moving them from rooting for the traditional alpha male to the strategic mastermind.

Although heavily lauded by the show itself, I do think Cirie is still underrated in how they present her. The "she got up off the couch" branding is an inspirational message they use as a rallying cry to encourage fans to apply. However, this "if she can do it, so can you" implication does a disservice to Cirie's superpowers. Anyone can get up off the couch and have *some* sort of experience playing *Survivor,* but not just anyone can get up off their couch and permanently change the way it's played. Her most notable influence is probably voting out the not-so-well-liked Courtney Marit who everyone wanted to sit with when facing the jury. It's not just the threats you gotta watch out for; the goats* could also be taking up your spot at the end! After Cirie was unable to cross a balance beam during a reward challenge in *Game Changers*, everyone stayed behind and rooted her on to keep going and finish it anyway. While I'm sure that was a meaningful moment for Cirie personally, I'm not sold that this was as incredible as the show tried to sell it. All right, so she's not great on the balance beam; is it so important that we see her overcome that? She's so gifted in other areas. Why don't we wait after a challenge for Rupert to figure out how to do a 3-2-1 vote split? We'd be waiting there all day!

Despite her villainous plays, Cirie's legacy will always be that of a hero, because now she is a permanent tragic figure of the show. After losing in fire, a surprise final two, and getting idoled out during a split, Cirie has never gone home due to a typical majority vote. Not to mention Advantagegeddon, where Cirie leaves the game at the *Game Changers* final six while having *zero* votes cast against her, just because, due to a mix of bad luck and poor production planning, the other five players all had various forms of immunity. On *Australia vs. the World*, superfan Lisa Holmes from New Zealand ended up being the audience surrogate, rooting for Cirie more than herself even—and exited a conversation about Advantagegeddon being too triggered to hear the tale recounted again.

Cirie is probably the best player to never win the game,† but the fans got the satisfaction of seeing her use her superpower to dominantly win the first US season of *The Traitors* . . . as a villainous traitor, of course.

* On *Survivor*, a "goat" does not generally refer to the "greatest of all time" but rather a dud you can drag to the end and slaughter.

† Did she end up pulling it off in Australia? Can she pull it off for *50*? You probably know better than me by the time you're reading this.

OZZY LUSTH

Cook Islands, Micronesia, South Pacific, Game Changers, In the Hands of the Fans

Oscar Lusth, more commonly known as Ozzy, is almost a mythical figure. The second he landed in the Cook Islands, it already seemed like he was back home. Half-man, half-animal, Ozzy would effortlessly catch fish or climb trees for coconuts, just like Mowgli in *The Jungle Book*. Not since Colby had there been someone as dominant in the challenges—especially in the water, where he could rip through the waves faster than a dolphin. It's no surprise he became an instant fan favorite, especially with the younger fans of the show. On top of that, Ozzy was the last remaining member of the original tribe and one of the post-swap, post-mutiny outnumbered Aitu Four. He was the underdog of the underdogs!

The four times we have seen Ozzy play so far, he's mostly had the same three-part strategy: 1) provide for the tribe; 2) win challenges; 3) that's it. He seemingly has no use for any aspects of the game that aren't physical. This is interestingly contrasted on *Cook Islands* against his ally and rival Yul. Though clearly no slouch physically, Yul is a game-theory driven, rational, strategic player. The surprise final three of the season led to not only one of the most competitive end results, but the one with the starkest differences in play style. Godfather Yul versus Warrior Ozzy. And though Yul eked out the win by just one vote, to Ozzy's strategic credit, if the season was a typical final two, Ozzy was only one challenge away from cutting Yul and beating Becky for the million.

After *Cook Islands,* Ozzy returned as a fan favorite and he knew it. On each of his returns, Ozzy came back a bit more cocky and entitled, even throwing temper tantrums when he didn't get his way. Which maybe isn't "heroic," per se, but is very fun to watch. Who doesn't love seeing someone take glee in planting a fake immunity idol stick and then being blindsided himself with the real deal? But despite him acting as a "stupid bitch" at times (Cochran's words, not mine!), his challenge dominance remained unparalleled. In *South Pacific*, he really made Redemption Island his home, even volunteering to get voted out pre-merge so he could beast his way back into the game—making him the only player to ever be voted out three times in the same season. It's quite possible that Sophie's winning move was finally beating Ozzy in the final four challenge.*

> "A greatest player doesn't always mean, like, winning. It's the way they played the game. Ozzy always had fun. Ozzy makes it look fun. Like freaking Tarzan . . . Who doesn't want to go camping with their friends, play a bunch of games in the forest? Like, everybody wants to do that. He made it look fun."
>
> **—NaOnka Mixon, December 10, 2020**

You're probably not going to get a much different Ozzy every time he plays. His biggest character growth is going from voting out Billy after he professed his love for Candice to professing his own love for Amanda Kimmel. But he still brings an interesting flavor to any season he's on and remains one of the most popular contestants to ever play. So popular that he now has a website only for his fans. I haven't personally visited it but I hope his acting on there is a little stronger than his Redemption Island tirade for revenge . . . basically.

* Though she might've pulled it off in the final five challenge had Albert just dropped his stack and helped!

PARVATI SHALLOW

Cook Islands, Micronesia, Heroes vs. Villains, Winners at War, Australia vs. the World

"What did we do that was so bad?" Parvati asks Jeff at the start of *Heroes vs. Villains*, as to why she's on the Villains tribe. Well, most notoriously, she ran the all-women Black Widow Brigade alliance in Micronesia where, in her words, they would spin the guys around as much as they could until they didn't know which way was up and devour them one at a time. But even as Jeff recaps the diabolical exploits of the BWB, the camera cuts to Cirie and Amanda—two of the other members of the brigade, both on the Heroes tribe. The simple explanation is that a lot of the casting decisions in themed seasons are arbitrary. It's rumored that Parvati was originally on the Heroes tribe but once they saw they also had Cirie, Amanda, and James there, they realized they couldn't fill half the tribe from season 16 and decided to toss Parvati over to the Villains. Then to balance things out, they had to toss a female villain over to the Heroes tribe, and thus we inexplicably get the mutineer Candice Woodcock Cody as a hero.

But the more intriguing explanation for why the show declares Parvati more of a villain than her cohorts is that she very openly uses the strategy of flirting to get her way. Should that brand someone a villain? A bigger issue for a different book on gender bias. When we look at mainstream storytelling, the femme fatale *is* often portrayed as the villain. Not that every *Survivor* player needs to be slotted into a trope out of a film noir, but Parvati definitely slides much more into the femme fatale role than the damsel in distress. She's so successful at playing that role, and the alliance she led was so dominant and powerful, that to this day, a woman can't smile at a man or talk to another woman without somebody going into a panic and declaring that they are

Parvati 2.0, 3.0, 4.0, etc.* Her threat level was so high going into *Heroes vs. Villains*, she couldn't just keep claiming she was an innocent little girl. She had to work with anyone willing to work with her . . . which, in this case, meant Russell, the biggest villain of them all. But I don't mean to imply she was somehow a victim of being saddled with the villain label. She loved it and loved leaning into it. She giggles in her confessionals about how she's going to eat J.T.'s heart after Russell is done stabbing it. She's such an iconic villain that she couldn't even shake her infamous reputation at a Scottish castle on *The Traitors* or on the Banker's private island on *Deal or No Deal Island*.

Her villainy, charisma, challenge prowess, and multiple high placements (not to mention her iconic double idol play) secure her place comfortably on the Mount Rushmore of *Survivor*. Yet she still has aspects of her game that are simultaneously overrated and underrated. Now, before you get your pitchforks because I used the words "Parvati" and "overrated" near each other, what I specifically mean is the level of threat she is perceived to have, as if she can walk into any room and trick any man into doing anything she wants. Yes, at the root of it, *Survivor* is a social game, and yes, Parvati knows how to turn on the charm and make anyone feel special when her attention locks in on them. But she's no magician. She can't pull a rabbit out of a hat unless the rabbit kinda wants to be pulled, and probably won't succeed if the rabbit has already seen her screw over a bunch of other rabbits on TV. Her flirtation might work on Ozzy in the hot tub, but it doesn't work on Yul. If she truly had this mythical siren ability, she would've used it on Boston Rob and Tyson and gotten into the majority early, rather than slumming it with Russell.

But where Parvati is still underrated is her social game with other women. The key to her successful gameplay is coming across as a cool girl that other girls want to work with. This is not a trait that fits the caricature of a femme fatale. Getting Erik to give up his immunity necklace (which was probably more Cirie's handiwork) might have been the flashiest moment of season 16, but her winning move was pulling in Natalie Bolton and Alexis Jones, who seemed to happily play for fourth and fifth place and let

* By this logic, *Vanuatu*'s Julie Berry should be Parvati 0.0.

Parvati win. It was the same in *Heroes vs. Villains,* where Danielle appeared perfectly content to lose to Parvati at the end—and if it wasn't for Russell's (basically correct) paranoia, Parvati would've been our first two-time winner with Sandra on the jury, asking Parvati how her gameplay resonates in the bedroom.

I won't spoil *Australia vs. the World* here, but it was a delight to see her return in full force, reunite with fellow Black Widow Cirie Fields, and play all her greatest hits.

J.T. THOMAS

Tocantins, Heroes vs. Villains, Game Changers

J.T. Thomas came out of *Tocantins* as golden as a golden boy could be. Hardworking, good-looking, and so fierce in challenges, he'd spit out a tooth that got knocked loose and keep going. The only people who loved J.T. more than the audience who voted him the fan favorite were his alleged opponents who mostly seemed to be going out of their way to make sure he won. J.T. was like *Africa*'s beloved Ethan Zohn with a Southern accent, which, until Russell hit the scene the following season, made people assume you were an honest gentleman. J.T.'s good ol' boy nature was amplified by being in the underdog Jalapao alliance against the baddies on Timbira, and contrasted with his number one ally and best friend Stephen Fishbach. J.T. and Stephen are still the most beloved duo in *Survivor* history—the straight-shooting country boy and the neurotic city slicker. While Stephen got more of the strategic credit, J.T. got to be more overtly out in front. Kind of like in an action movie where the rugged star is doing the big stunts while the nerdier sidekick is on a computer somewhere, hacking the mainframe.

J.T.'s perfect reputation does get a bit tarnished every time he comes back on the show with diminishing results. On *Heroes vs. Villains*, due to a bad mix of wanting to prove himself as a strategic force and being overly afraid of Parvati's seductress powers, he passed villain Russell the idol he found—an idol that he himself got taken out with. If being taken out with your own idol wasn't bad enough, he managed to get voted out pre-merge in *Game Changers*, with his idol still back at camp. It's easy to poke fun at J.T.'s subsequent performances—especially since his idol pass came with an overly sincere and slightly condescending letter to Russell—but if his incorrect read happened to be correct and Parvati *was* running another woman's alliance on the villains' beach . . . well, his mistake could've actually gone down as one of the greatest plays of all time. You gotta respect J.T. for always taking the big swing. Baseball fans who cheer the grand slam might boo the same player who strikes out. But Babe Ruth only held the home run record because he also held the strikeout record. And Babe Ruth also got pissed at Lou Gehrig for finishing up the sugar in the Yankees clubhouse.

TYSON APOSTOL

Tocantins, Heroes vs. Villains, Blood vs. Water, Winners at War

One of the baddies J.T. was originally up against was the iconic Tyson Apostol. Now Tyson is known as a villain less so for his actions (he often plays a loyal game) and more so for his snark. Not your typical Mormon, he's a little mean, a bit of a jerk, and loves to see people cry when he crushes their dreams, but his bluntness and confidence (some might even say cockiness) cause others to gravitate to him. Some do feel that his behavior toward Sierra in *Tocantins* borders on bullying, but if you ask him, he'll tell you Sierra sucked, everyone hated living with her, and he was a hero for taking her down a notch.

Even though Tyson is a natural entertainer, he's also incredibly cutthroat and cunning. Not to mention a force of nature in the challenges. There are heroes who the audience roots for to win challenges and there are villains who are the obstacles in the challenges to take down. If he was in an action movie, he would be the final boss the hero has to defeat (or the really funny henchman of the final boss). Tyson is so dominant in challenges that one of his best strategic moves was playing up his shoulder injury on *Blood vs. Water* to lower his threat level and win it all.

Tyson's legacy on the show is demonstrating how much fun villains can have. He's mischievous, rustling feathers, always doing something "sneaky and hilarious"—whether that's stealing coconuts with Gervase or hiding peanut butter on the Edge. He's incredibly self-aware and doesn't take things too seriously, and was able to laugh at himself when he was blindsided the same night he was describing how awesome it'd be to blindside Sierra. He admitted he was the victim of his own stupidity when he swapped his vote from Russell to Parvati and basically got himself voted out of the game—the first victim of Parvati the reputation rather than Parvati the player. But truly one of the great joys of seeing Tyson play over four seasons is to watch him grow. He's always the same Tyson, but his winning game came from him being able to kick it into a different gear when he was playing for his then-girlfriend, now-wife Rachel. He's always stayed mouthy, but as we hear him describe spending time with his kids on *Winners at War*, we see that, as much as he'd deny it, he's a villain with a ticking heart. To be determined how much heart he actually plays with on the third season of *House of Villains*.

COACH

Tocantins, Heroes vs. Villains, South Pacific, In the Hands of the Fans

"We're throwing underhand, breaking tiles. None of us have ever done this in our lives," Brendan Synnott says in the middle of a reward challenge. Coach's hand goes up: "I have." His birth certificate may read Benjamin Wade, but everyone has to refer to him as Coach, just as the women's soccer team he used to coach at Southwest Baptist University in Missouri did. One of the most polarizing characters in the show's history,

Coach arrived in Brazil a fully formed character, telling tales of how he's been through a hurricane, attacked by a shark, had a run-in with a crocodile, and got captured by a native tribe. So cartoonish, so over-the-top, it's hard to even fathom that this person really exists. Where did they find this guy? Who is this jackass?! The show portrays Coach as a villain, not because he's doing bad stuff, but because he's such a ridiculous figure who appears to lack self-awareness—the editors love throwing in that eagle screech sound effect every time he's on screen. Love him or hate him, it's fun to root against him. Unlike Boston Rob (who Coach worshiped on *Heroes vs. Villains*), Coach doesn't bring the audience behind the curtain in his confessionals. He doesn't wink at us and let us know he's putting on an act. Is it even an act? We don't know, and he passed Jeff's lie detector test about his life at the reunion!

The truly unique thing about Coach, in contrast to, say, a Jonny Fairplay who came onto the show to play the villain, is that he views himself as a hero. There's nobody there that's honorable, he tells us, except for himself. He plays with honor, integrity, and loyalty, taking the monastic approach at Exile Island. Coach is a samurai warrior who believes in taking the strongest to the end. Unless, of course, that strong player is Brendan, who Coach blindsides at the merge. Even when Jeff calls out this hypocrisy, Coach doesn't see any contradiction there. In fact, he calls Brendan a dragon and dubs himself the Dragon Slayer—the hero of his own fairy tale.

It was a no-brainer choice to bring Coach back on *Heroes vs. Villains*. But while his fellow tribemates like Rob and Parvati leaned into their villain labels, Coach seemed genuinely hurt that he's viewed that way. Coach and Jerri instantly share a bond over being misunderstood by the world. After Sandra challenged his work ethic at tribal council, Coach had a mini-breakdown and needed to be comforted by his assistant coach, Tyson, leading to one of the show's most endearing moments. Tyson gave him some tough truths—if he doesn't want to be mocked, he shouldn't wear feathers in his hair, tell his wild stories, and do his tai chi in the open. Coach's internal struggle comes out of how desperately he wants to be the hero.* "You're a little man," Rob tells him on his way out of the game. Not just because Coach betrayed him, but because he betrayed him in a cowardly way by throwing his vote away and not admitting that he played "dishonorably."

Coach's inability to reconcile "being honorable" with playing manipulatively cost him the game in *South Pacific*. He controlled his entire tribe all season with Halloween jokes, Chuckie the Cheese jokes, and using religion (which was slightly gross) to keep his crew together. All he had to do was tell the jury that he played *Survivor* and he would've won . . . but he couldn't do it. He was able to pretend to enjoy the film *Jack and Jill* but he couldn't bring himself to admit he lied on a lying show. Maybe this is because he was playing for something more than the million dollars. As they say . . . with friend and foe, we march to the battle plain. Some to seek success, others to seek fame. We play with honor for the love of this game. And with armor or without we will toil in vain. So that someday, someone, somewhere will remember our name. And Coach is definitely a name that will be remembered.

RUSSELL HANTZ

Samoa, Heroes vs. Villains, Redemption Island, Australian Survivor: Champions vs. Contenders

I've always referred to Russell Hantz as *Survivor* Viagra. A decade in, the show was getting a little soft, and Russell was the exact kick in the pants it needed. It wasn't that they were hurting for big characters—especially not after Coach or all the kooks on *Gabon*—but we were a bit lacking in ways to play the game. So here comes the villain so bad that the entire promotional material for *Samoa* was centered around how this season had the devil incarnate, blasting "Bad to the Bone" in the commercials. After all this buildup, onto the island steps a stout man at 5′6″ who is missing a tooth, and,

* And sometimes he is, like when he frog-marches Colby in the season's first challenge.

with all due respect, looks like a bridge troll. And he wasted no time revealing his true colors. On the very first day, he was already pouring out other people's canteens, making up a sympathetic story about how his dog died in Hurricane Katrina, and burning his tribemate Jaison's socks just because he believed the more miserable people were, the easier it'd be to control their minds. He hit the beach running, forming final two alliances with every "dumbass girl" out there, without a care in the world if they compared notes. After all, if they dared to question him, he'd get their dumb ass voted out of there.

The show loves to highlight when someone has a great reason to play *Survivor*, like if they need the money for their family or want to prove something to themselves. But that's not Russell. He boasts that he's already a millionaire and has nothing to prove to nobody. He just wants to show how easy it would be for him to dominate. And . . . he did succeed. He not only started running circles around the rest of his cast but also outfoxed production itself. Prior to Russell, the only way players got idols was by getting a clue (or multiple clues) and following it to where the idol was hidden.* But Russell didn't wait around for a clue—he figured the idol must be hidden somewhere, so, as long as he was willing to look longer, he was bound to find it sooner or later. And find it sooner he did, inside the trunk of a tree. Other players got clues leading them to that tree, but it was too late. And after Russell played the idol at the merge, he went out and found *another* one without a clue under the bridge. Thanks to Russell, every modern *Survivor* player has to spend endless hours idol hunting.

Russell was also the first player to use the hidden immunity idol offensively. While Yau-Man in *Fiji* and Amanda in *Micronesia* played idols to save their own behinds, Russell used the idol as a weapon, understanding that the threat of an idol was often worse than the actual playing of it. Russell's intimidating use of the idol has paved

* Or in the case of landscaper Gary Hawkins, wait for Judd to find an idol clue, have him tell you, "It's definitely on the ground," watch him searching the trees for it, and find it yourself.

the way for players such as Tony, Domenick, and George from Australia, who found unorthodox ways to play the trinkets they find on the island. Much like Parvati turned every smiling woman into a threat, any player going off into the woods alone can get themselves instantly voted out thanks to Russell. Nobody is less trustworthy than someone looking to find an advantage. When players claim to want to play a Russell-type-game, they usually mean they want to be . . . mean. It wasn't until Gabe of season 47 was the first player who claimed to want to play a Russell-game in the sense that Russell does technically play a loyal game with his tight group of allies—it's just buried under all the smack-talking Russell does in confessionals.

> "I remember getting up to go to the bathroom, and [Russell]'s like, someone needs to follow her so she doesn't look for an idol. And I was like, dude, I'm taking the shovel for a reason. Nobody needs to follow me. And so what if I was looking for an idol? Who do you think you are? Like, that kind of stuff is just not, it's not cool on any level."
>
> **—Jerri Manthey, October 30, 2020**

How much you love or hate *Samoa* is directly proportional with how you feel about watching Russell, because never had a season been this lopsided in its edit. They did this not just because of how dynamic Russell was, but because, for the first time ever, the villain was the underdog. Russell's tribe Foa Foa came into the merge with four members, while the opposing Galu had eight. Now, it doesn't take a rocket scientist like John Fincher to calculate that's twice as many. But thanks to Russell's leadership, brazen tactics, and loyal soldiers (and some suboptimal choices made by Galu), the Foa Foa Four were able to run the merge and have three members filling out the final three chairs. The season doesn't have a hero because Russell was edited as the "hero." Not *heroically*, mind you, but as the true underdog protagonist succeeding against all odds.

One of the most fortuitous things to ever happen for the show is that they were subsequently filming *Heroes vs. Villains*. So instead of sending Russell home after *Samoa*, the producers just kept him in a hotel room for ten days and sent him right back into the game.* If *Heroes vs. Villains* was happening seasons later, sure, Russell would've certainly gotten a phone call—but then everyone on the cast would've seen him on TV already. Instead, Russell entered season 20 as a complete unknown, and was able to pull all the same stunts again. He immediately hid the tribe's machete and started forming more final two alliances with more "dumbass" girls. Despite being instantly in the minority of his tribe, Russell was able to, yet again, find the idol, play it perfectly, and barrel his way to the end of the game.

Now, Russell may have gotten to the end back-to-back, but he also lost the jury vote back-to-back. In *Samoa*, they gave the win to Natalie White because they despised him on a personal level. In *Heroes vs. Villains*, they gave the win to Sandra because they not only despised him on a personal level but also despised that Parvati worked with someone they despised so much. Both times, despite not winning over the jury, he won the audience fan favorite award. For *Samoa*, that was basically a given, but for *Heroes vs. Villains* he beat out the great, powerful Rupert! The good guy, the second coming of Christ, Rupert! Possibly the most telling fan favorite vote ever, it showed that the mainstream audience wasn't just watching the show for the honest knights in shining armor . . . they wanted players who were there to play the game as hard as possible. Even the good Christian boy Matt Elrod told Russell on *Redemption Island* that he's one of his favorites to watch, no lie. Is it a coincidence that around this time audiences were also rooting for a different fedora-wearing villain on *Breaking Bad*? Probably, but it still portends an interesting rise in popularity of anti-heroes.

Russell's third and final time on American *Survivor* was quite a disappointment. Russell's iconic rivalry with Boston Rob in the *Heroes vs. Villains* pre-merge† led to

* Rumors have it they had to kick either Shane Powers or Jonathan Penner off the cast to make room for him.

† He doesn't even *like* the Boston Red Sox; it's the Houston Astros, baby.

them facing off two seasons later on *Redemption Island*. This time, all of Russell's tribemates had already seen him on TV. When he tried to recruit his girls and find his idols, they were dead set on throwing a challenge just to get rid of the cancer of the tribe. He played once again on the Australian offshoot of *Survivor*, but despite magically finding an idol, he was unable to shake his treacherous reputation and was once again the first one kicked out of his tribe—being represented only by his infamous fedora on the reunion show.

Russell has often referred to himself as "the greatest of all time" and while the record shows he probably isn't, he's definitely the player who changed the game and television product more than anyone else. If you want to argue that player is Richard Hatch, you'd have to first make the argument that there was something before Richard for him to change.

Would Russell ever return to the show? Well, that's a question for CBS, who at one point was so into Russell, they even brought his nephew Brandon on twice. But the much more interesting question would be if Russell is capable of returning and playing a different sort of game. Clearly, the part of his personality that makes him such magnetic TV is the same part that makes it rather difficult to put on the charm (or fake charm, at least) and win people over on a personal level. Not to be an armchair psychologist, but there seems to be something in his ego that prevents him from faking that last bit of humility. Spoiler, but hubris was also the downfall of that other fedora-wearing fella, Walter White. As much as many fans would love it, it currently seems highly unlikely that we'll ever see Russell back on the show and implementing a strategy that doesn't instantly get him booted . . . but you never know. Keep hope alive.

PHILLIP SHEPPARD

Redemption Island, Caramoan

When Russell was in tears, eliminated at the Redemption Island arena because he loved the game so much, he looked up into the stands, and told a member of the opposing tribe that he is now playing on for Russell. That player was the Specialist himself, Phillip Sheppard. And he did, in fact, continue Russell's legacy by finishing in second place. However, he did not play a villainous game in the mold of Russell—his character lineage is more in line with Coach,* an over-the-top persona who never winks at the audience to let us know what's real and what's an act. He's an alleged former federal agent (which seemed to have been confirmed at the reunion show) who boasts about his ability to tell when anyone is lying but seems to lack other social awareness skills. He's someone that was fun for the audience to check in with for forty minutes a week but seems a bit insufferable to be trapped on a desert island with. From episode 1, Phillip already found himself antagonizing members of the tribe, such as Fransescwa, and as the episodes went on, things only got worse.

Similarly to Coach, Phillip gave himself a nickname—"the Specialist"—and went around giving others their not-so-secret spy nicknames and forming the Stealth R Us alliance that nobody took seriously. With his hot-pink briefs, his feather in his headband, and his communications in meditation with his great-great-grandfather Jessem Herring, nobody took much about Phillip seriously. Except for Boston Rob, the one player that tried to understand Phillip as a person, and more importantly, how useful Phillip could be to his game. Rob dragged Phillip to the end and easily beat

* In fact, the original conception of *South Pacific* prior to Ozzy being cast was supposed to be Coach vs. Phillip.

him for the million dollars. Phillip's version, however, grants himself more agency. He asserts that once he became aware of how much control Boston Rob had over his tribe, he deliberately played up an obnoxious persona so Rob would keep him around. If this was his intentional strategy, it's brilliant. True or not, Phillip was not able to successfully communicate this at final tribal, using most of his time to berate the jury instead.

When Phillip returned to the second *Fans vs. Favorites*, he brought along with him all his greatest hits. His pink underwear, Stealth R Us nicknames, and getting Fransescwa voted out first. But he also brought a new strategy. Much like many returning players attempt to replicate the winning games of their original seasons, Phillip wanted to play a domineering Boston Rob game. The domineering aspect he succeeded at, but that Boston Rob magic of actually getting people to follow your lead proved much more difficult. He was taken out in the exciting Three Amigos tribal, where Phillip was targeted less because he was a strategic threat and more because he was a pain in the ass to live with.

> "You do not compare Bach to Tchaikovsky because Bach was the original. Tchaikovsky came two hundred years later. You don't say that Plato certainly emulates Michelangelo because Michelangelo came seven hundred years later. So you cannot compare Coach to Phillip. You must compare Phillip to Coach . . . I was the original. Now, that being said, Phillip is an original. A lot of people said that he ripped off my shtick. If he did, imitation is the finest form of flattery."
>
> **—Coach, February 16, 2013**

We never saw Phillip on the show again, but maybe the closest successor we got was Debbie Wanner—overbearing, bombastic, with dubious claims of many former professions. As the show went on, especially after parting ways with legendary casting director Lynne Spillman, *Survivor* casting moved away from these over-the-top characters. On one hand, it's admirable that the show wants to portray humans in a more nuanced light, but on the other hand . . . we're watching a game show on an island. It's fun to throw in unbelievable people who stir up conflict out of nowhere. We haven't really gotten a New Era Coach/Phillip/Debbie. I'd consider including Q in this list but I wouldn't want him to cancel Christmas.

MALCOLM FREBERG

Philippines, Caramoan, Game Changers

Malcolm is the first real hero we've gotten since *Heroes vs. Villains*. Like the next Ozzy, he checks all our heroic boxes. Good-looking charismatic guy. Strong in challenges. An unlikely duo with the older Denise Stapley.* Part of the ultimate underdog tribe, with Matsing losing every challenge until the tribe was completely dissipated. But Malcom arrived in a post-Russell world, so he was the first hero-hero who the show seemed fine with presenting as openly strategic and conniving. Malcolm's idol hunting is presented positively. He's not a sneaky little sneak, looking for idols—he's smart and savvy, just doing what needs to be done.

Malcolm's legacy as a hero is underscored by him being a tragic figure. Despite having an advantage, he lost the final challenge and was immediately voted out. When he returned the following season on *Caramoan*, he was once again the underdog and, despite a fun run with the Three Amigos, couldn't make it to the end. The fans were thrilled to see him return on *Game Changers* and were shocked by how early he was cut, when during a twist joint-tribal council, he fell victim to yet another big J.T. swing backfiring horrifically. His first season, Malcolm was the runner-up fan favorite to the beloved

* A much more successful version of what I tried to form with Deena.

Lisa Whelchel. His second season, he did win the fan favorite. His third season, he was gone way too early to win anything . . . but, for what it's worth, he was voted Mr. Survivor by the listeners of a certain *Survivor* podcast.

Survivor has attempted to replicate this long-haired archetype many times, most notably with Joe Anglim (aka Joey Amazing) and Jonathan Young. But while these two did have the hair and the physicality and popularity amongst kids, they lacked the layered dimensions that Malcolm brought. While Ozzy and Jonathan's return to Fiji for season 50 made sense, it may have been more interesting to see Malcom's strategy in the New Era. Plus, we missed out on a lot of meme potential not getting to see Joey Amazing interact with somebody named Q.

ABI-MARIA GOMES

Philippines, Cambodia

Abi-Maria Gomes, the Brazilian dragon, has probably been best described by Stephen Fishbach . . . as a grenade. If you have her on your side, you can use her loyal vote as a highly effective weapon. The risk you run is that, the longer you try to keep her in your pocket, the likelier it becomes that one wrong move will set her off. *Survivor: Philippines* started off pretty well for RC Saint-Amour—she was building a coalition and even found herself a clue to the idol, which she openly shared with her number one ally. Unfortunately, that ally was Abi. Abi got paranoid whenever RC had conversations with others and, once trouble-maker Pete Yurkowski planted that shared idol clue in RC's bag, all hell broke loose—and by "all hell," I mean Abi. As much as RC tried, there was no talking to Abi-Maria once she made up her mind. If you "f" with her, you're dead. This led to RC's early exit from the game and an incredibly bitter

Ponderosa video, where RC still couldn't let it go. In fact, she couldn't let it go years later when she refused to be on the *Second Chance* ballot because she couldn't bear to be on the same beach as Abi-Maria again.

> "It takes a connoisseur to understand Abi."
> —Abi-Maria Gomes, December 13, 2012

The fans did unsurprisingly vote this firecracker back and Abi returned with the hopes of playing a bit of a calmer game. That dream died rather quickly when she inexplicably found her bracelet in Peih-Gee Law's bag. No amount of "I must've picked up the wrong bag by accident" could get Abi to turn the other cheek. But we don't love watching Abi because of her rationale; we love her raw, emotional reactiveness. She's not strategically plotting how to get to the end and win, she's a heat-seeking missile locked in on Woo. He wrote her name down twice so it's over for him. When it comes to players like Coach or Phillip, you can squint and see when they're playing up their personas here and there. With Abi, everything feels incredibly authentic. She might be a sweetheart in the real world, but when put into rigorous conditions, she seems to lack any bit of social grace. Jeff asked if some of this could be due to a cultural difference. But I don't know what sort of cultural differences lead to nicknaming someone Mr. Poopy-Pants when they're suffering from severe gastrointestinal distress.

TONY VLACHOS

Cagayan, Game Changers, Winners at War, Australia vs. the World

While Tony Vlachos is a one-of-a-kind *Survivor* unicorn (or, technically, *Survivor* llama), you can't start figuring out where to place his legacy without first comparing him to Russell Hantz. On paper, they have a lot of similarities—both highly aggressive players with polarizing personalities playing idol-heavy games. Both barreled their way to the end and faced harsh juries. But how does one reconcile Russell losing twice with Tony winning twice? The first thing to consider is that Tony's living in a post-Russell world; Russell took the bullets running in first and Tony came in after to collect the spoils of playing in a time where underhandedness is encouraged. At the end of *Samoa*, Erik Cardona gave a big jury speech about how Russell's tactics made him undeserving; nine seasons later, the young lad Spencer Bledsoe* made an almost identical speech about Tony's tactics . . . but making the case for why Tony *should* win.

Once you concede that Tony was playing in an era more welcoming to his style, you really have to credit him with his incredible social game. Undeniably, Russell played much more loyally than Tony did. Russell stuck with his people while Tony flipped back and forth, cutting allies left and right. But unlike Russell, there is a lightheartedness to Tony. He's playing hard and chaotic but without a menacing sheen to him. Maybe it was actually *because* of how much he would flip that people were less upset with him. Russell may've created an unbreakable "us vs. them" mentality, but Tony made it clear he was willing to work with anyone. Nothing felt personal because he was open for business.

Tony plays like a shark (even though he's terrified of them). He cannot stop moving forward or he will die. During the day, he's constantly running around, looking for idols, taking big swings, and making big mistakes. Then at night, he barely sleeps, looking for more idols and thinking up new angles to play. Even in his fourth time out on *Australia vs. the World*, he gets a new trick up his sleeve—or, more specifically, a new shoe to tie around his neck. With his spy shack, spy bunker, and spy nest, Tony sprints on ahead with the philosophy of begging for forgiveness rather than asking for permission. And that forgiveness usually comes courtesy of one of his most trusted

* Now going by his middle name, Reiman.

> "Every single night, I would just go to the beach, because during the day, you can't think of things outside of what you're talking with people with. You know, when I'm talking with people while I'm playing the game, I can't be thinking about what to do with A and what to do with B and what to do with C. You can't think strategy. So I used to go out at night all the time. Whether I was building things or making my bunkers or looking for idols, I would go out at night and I would just think. Because that's the only time you get to think about the game in advance."
>
> **—Tony Vlachos, June 18, 2020**

and levelheaded allies, Trish or Sarah, swooping in to clean up the mess he made. Things would play out like a parent bringing their spoiled child to your house. He makes a mess with his bag of tricks, his mother promises he's sorry and won't do it again, and before you know it, he's voting you out of your own house.

When his loyal partner-in-crime Woo brought Tony to the final two instead of Chaos Kass at the end of *Cagayan*, it was one of the most incredible moments in *Survivor* history. Did Tony fully get into Woo's head? Did Woo drastically miscalculate? We'll never truly know, but when we get a miracle like that from the *Survivor* gods, we don't question it. We surely don't expect it to ever happen again. Yet, it happened again. Tony's return performance in *Game Changers* was sadly foreseeable. Everyone had already seen all his tricks and antics on TV and he was voted out second. So when he returned again for *Winners at War*, we all figured Tony was playing on borrowed time. But out of his famous bag of tricks, Tony pulled out a brand-new gear, climbing that shaky ladder to victory. This is what truly separates Tony from Russell. Tony was able to take how people perceived him and adjust his gameplay. *Winners at War* Tony was still the same scheming goofball but he made sure to actively lower his threat level. He stayed under the radar just long enough to amass his army of lions and pounce to the end.

Casting has tried to replicate Tony many times with other bald hooligans like Joe Mena or Wardog, but these Temu Tonys just don't hit the spot like the name brand. Maybe Tony is so easy to root for because of how much heart he plays with. Forget Colby and Jerri, forget James and Amanda—it's the "Cops R Us" Tony and Sarah duo that have the best three-season arc. First in *Cagayan*, Tony blindsides her and wins the game. Then in *Game Changers*, Sarah emulates some of Tony's ruthless tactics to win. Finally, in *Winners at War,* Tony and Sarah really truly work together, making it all the way to the final four, where they are forced to go against each other in an incredibly emotional fire-making challenge—probably the most compelling one of the forced fire-making era. Tony wins in tears and goes on to get his second win, cementing himself as one of the top five, baby, players of all time.

MIKE HOLLOWAY

Worlds Apart

BEN DRIEBERGEN

Heroes vs. Healers vs. Hustlers, Winners at War

We're pairing Mike and Ben together as two winners in the classic hero mold of hardworking, salt-of-the-earth, blue-collar guys. One of them was literally on the Blue Collar tribe. Both were underdogs for the second half of their games; against the wall, they were forced to win immunities and play idols to stay in. Hard work on *Survivor* originally meant working hard around camp and providing, but as the game became more strategic, hard work started to correlate to winning challenges and out-searching other players for advantages. Due to the style of

their wins (especially since Ben was the first beneficiary of the unpopular fire-making twist), they are often ranked as lower-tier winners—even discussed by Andy and Rachel during season 47's final tribal council—but I think many fans forget that they were fun players with great stories. Ben's win probably deeply devalued Mike's. Mike was a good guy, stood up for Shirin against the bad guys, and went on an unprecedented run. But once we saw that run was replicable, it stopped being so desirable to see.

TAI TRANG

Kaôh Rōng, Game Changers

SCOT POLLARD

Kaôh Rōng

KYLE JASON

Kaôh Rōng

Tai, the refugee from Vietnam, is one of the most gentle souls ever to play the game and was placed on the Beauty tribe for his inner beauty. This gardener loves nature so much, he didn't want to hurt a single tree when digging around for idols. At the marooning, the tribe got a chicken, which he named Mark (after Mark Burnett*), and Tai took care of Mark the entire game—even bringing him to final tribal council, where he was finally set free. His care for animals inspired pop-superstar Sia to crash the live reunion show and give Tai $50,000 just for being a sweet, sensitive soul! The first of many "Sia Awards."† But Tai isn't just a big heart; he's also a crafty player. Incredibly patient, hardworking, and able to climb trees like a monkey, Tai's probably the best idol finder we've had since Russell. His small stature leads others to underestimate him, but when it comes to endurance challenges, he's an incredible competitor—lest we forget him dramatically beating challenge-beast Ozzy in the hanging-on-to-a-pole challenge.

* Apparently they named another chicken Jeff after Jeff Probst but that's the chicken the tribe DID eat. Although, Tai made sure no parts of Jeff went to waste.

† Yup, superstar Sia has given out over a million dollars in prizes to her personal favorites. She abruptly ended the award after season 46, but maybe if the live reunion returns, so shall she.

What really makes Tai a rootable force to watch is his struggle to separate his head from his heart. He tries to play the best he can strategically but he's always torn between who he feels he should work with and who he actually wants to work with. Tai is a fickle, grenade-type player like Abi was, but in a positive way. It's not that he might unexpectedly decide he hates you; it's that he might become a little more enamored with another friend. This poetically comes to a head in *Kaôh Rōng* when he finds himself allied with villains Scot Pollard and Kyle Jason, two of the last truly villainous players the show cast. Tai and Scot both found two halves of a Super Idol, which when combined can block any votes *after* Jeff reads them. This leads Scot and Jason to be extra cocky, believing themselves invincible. While they take Tai for granted and ignore his concerns, Aubry is able to win Tai over to her side. So after Scot receives the majority of the votes, Tai stands up for himself and refuses to share his half of the Super Idol, wiping the smug look off of Scot's face and sending him packing. No matter how many twists the show adds, the most satisfying turns come from the unpredictable nature of the human heart.

ANGELINA KEELEY

David vs. Goliath, In the Hands of the Fans

Through all the swirling rumors until the official cast release, Angelina Keeley was the most obvious lock for a season 50 return. From one perspective, Angelina might be the greatest hero the show has ever seen. Who else has sacrificed their chance at immunity to provide rice for the tribe? Who else risked their own life climbing a 100-foot ladder to get an idol and stop the evil Dr. Alison from finding it first? On the other hand, maybe her alleged self-sacrifice was a tad bit overblown and over-mentioned. Maybe that ladder wasn't quite that tall and maybe Dr. Alison was already going home so it was a little mean-girl to plant a fake idol for her.

Described by fellow tribemate Mike White as "Tracy Flick from *Election*," Angelina comes off as an overly transparent tryhard. But Angelina is easily one of the most iconic characters in the modern era, not in spite of her personality, but because of it. Demonstrating a deadly combo of out-of-touch and strong-headed,

"Just something that happened on my season was I also negotiated for rice with Jeff—that wasn't shown and, maybe, I didn't negotiate as articulately as she did it. You know, her delivery was definitely up there. But when I did it, you know, we negotiated. We had to give up our shelter . . . So did it turn into a whole debacle for Angelina because of what? The act of her actually doing it, or was it just the way she handled it and how she constantly brought it up and wanted to take credit for it?"

—Domenick Abbate, December 20, 2018

for better or worse, in every situation, she is the star of the show. She's considered a villain in the way Coach or Phillip are—because she seems oblivious to how negatively she comes across to others. There's few things audiences love to root against more than someone with a perceived lack of self-awareness. The *David vs. Goliath* jury happened to agree with the fans on this and awarded Angelina no jury votes, despite making it to the end . . . without a jacket.

SHAN SMITH

41

There was a time when *Survivor* was a battle of heroes versus villains. A little while later, it became a battle of heroes versus . . . healers and hustlers. By the New Era, *Survivor* has mostly become heroes versus heroes. Jesse Lopez backstabs someone nearly every episode yet he takes zero pleasure in it, doing it for his family. No one is truly a villain because everyone has a sympathetic backstory. Shan is the closest to a classic villain in the New Era. One of our main metrics of classifying someone as a hero or villain is how much glee they take in blindsiding others. What can be clearer proof that someone enjoys being bad than coming up with their very own anthem for their own villainy? Shan Smith, a pastor who is more than happy to break "Thou Shall Not Lie," hums her own little ditty (the Shanthem) whenever she is cooking up a scheme. These schemes usually involve building up a great amount of trust with someone right before slitting their throat. In the case of JD, he even trusted Shan to hold his extra vote, which she happily kept after writing his name down and sending him home. Shan was not only the biggest villain of *41*, but—similar to Rupert going home in *Pearl Islands*—her own blindside was almost treated as the climax of the season.

CAROLYN WIGER

44

With so many inspirational, good-hearted players in the New Era, it's tough to single out a singular hero. But here comes the eccentric and vulnerable Carolyn Wiger, one of the most unique players to ever play the show. Though her kooky personality might suggest she'd be sent home early, she ended up making it to the very end. The producers were clearly as enamored with Carolyn as the fans were, not only making her the star of the season but even, in an unprecedented move, starting the season cold with a Carolyn confessional blooper. Not a regular confessional, mind you, but a blooper where she's confused about how to go about introducing herself. A former drug addict turned drug counselor, Carolyn plays with her heart on her sleeve. She gets incredibly frustrated when other players don't take her seriously—like when Brandon and Danny fully ignore her on the journey—yet she's self-aware enough to use others' perception of her as a weapon. Not only was she underestimated, but her underdog alliance with Yam Yam and Carson was overlooked as they snuck through the game. But maybe *snuck* is underselling how loudly the Tika Three would bicker with each other.

Carolyn was the hero we were rooting for. Even though we could see her strategic acumen throughout the game, she wasn't able to get a single vote out of the jury. However, unlike older *Survivor* that tended to dunk on zero-vote finalists in the edit, Carolyn joins New Era players like Jake O'Kane, Owen Knight, and Xander Hastings who may not have earned any jury respect, but still heroically fought and persevered. Carolyn didn't win the million dollars, but she certainly won a million hearts (and a hundred grand of Sia's money . . . *on my podcast*), becoming the most shocking and notable New Era snub for season 50. She stole the show once again on *The Traitors*, where she was able to make another deep run after being similarly underestimated.

Over the years, *Survivor* has had many iconic heroes and villains battling it out. But as the show departed from its black-and-white portrayals, the lines blurred between what makes a hero and what makes a villain. While there's definitely an upside to editing players with more nuance, maybe part of us misses the epic fight . . . maybe the same part that drew the ancient Mesopotamians to the *Epic of Gilgamesh*. Yes, these are real people playing *Survivor*, but they're also characters on our television screens and we love our characters to be larger than life. We don't need to see a bunch of nice friends playing a board game on an island; we want to see competitors who are pushed to the edge. We want to celebrate great heroes prevailing and mourn when they fall just short. We want to see the biggest villains topple, but sometimes it's a thrill when they're able to pull their diabolic plans off. In classic Westerns, the good guys wore the white hat and the bad guys wore the black hat. The good guys didn't always win but you always knew who you were supposed to root for. But supposed to doesn't mean you have to. It's fun to root for the villain too.

“Number one, I put no stock in heroes and villains. You could tell me about how you're living your life at home, and I'll, you know, pass judgment on whether you're a hero or a villain. But in the game, I don't think there's such thing as a villain. I think that we've all signed on for this, and it is outwit and outplay and all that kind of stuff. So nobody there was a villain to me.”

—Tom Westman, June 6, 2020

SUPERFAN MODE
ON
DANGER: SUPERFAN

CHAPTER 4

Oops! All Cochran

How the Show Became about the Show

It was Day 13 and we had just received Tree Mail ordering us to send our youngest tribemate off to some mysterious reward. We sent Dave Johnson, who, at twenty-four years old, was just three months younger than me. Dave was a rocket scientist, but it didn't take a rocket scientist to suspect that a potential tribe swap was imminent. Or at least it seemed obvious to me, who had obsessively watched and rewatched the first four seasons of *Survivor* and whatever had already aired of the fifth by the time I was out in the Amazon, filming the sixth. It wasn't long before I noticed that my fellow castaways didn't have quite my level of *Survivor* fandom. Sure, they'd seen the show before—at least during the casting

process*—but they may not have been thinking about the game like I was. Actually, I don't know how many of them were thinking about the game at all. They were thinking about the adventure and being on television, and, in Dave's case, exactly as the producers had intended, he was definitely thinking about flirting with Jenna Morasca, the youngest member of the opposing tribe he was about to meet up with for a little picnic.

This picnic did, in fact, trigger a tribe swap. It was one of the many times when I could see what was coming before it happened. Jeff told me I was like Jamie Kennedy's character from *Scream* . . . the video-store employee horror fan living inside of a horror movie, enthusiastically pointing out the tropes to come. He was simultaneously amused and annoyed by me. Once during tribal council, Jeff got mad at me because I said being at tribal was much more nerve-wracking than watching it at home. "We're not here to talk about *watching* the show," Jeff scolded me. "We're only here to talk about *playing* the show." Back when the show was an hour long and seasons were thirty-nine days long, each episode cut down three full days of our lives into forty-two minutes. Think about how many conversations you've had in the past three days. Now imagine you didn't have to go to work or take care of your kids or focus on any responsibilities other than sitting outside with half a dozen strangers and chatting. What would you talk about? To me, being part of *Survivor* was truly the coolest, most exciting thing in the world—what else would I *want* to talk about? But producers would shut down any conversations around camp if I brought up previous seasons or players. They weren't trying to convince the audience that we were actually shipwrecked, but this mythical artifice still existed that we had to pretend we weren't actively and self-consciously participating in the most popular television show on the planet.

If you've only seen recent *Survivor*, this must sound crazy. Currently, nearly all of *Survivor* is about the show *Survivor*. Each new castaway talks about what the show means to them, how they watched with their families, and which former contestants

* Maybe not Matthew or Ryan.

they want to play like. Every other word out of their mouths is "*Survivor*." Every season, a contestant nervous about the first tribal council they're attending potentially being their last, says some form of, "Oh boy, it's a lot scarier being here at tribal than it is watching at home!" I'm not saying that I originally articulated some incredible insight . . . I just said the most obvious thing in the world. No matter how many tribal councils you watch, nothing can prepare you for that feeling in your stomach when you put your torch in the flame, sit up in front of Jeff, and wonder if everyone has been lying to you and you're about to be humiliated on national television. The big difference, though, between what I said in season 6 and what Omar Zaheer said in season 42 about how unbelievable it is as a superfan to actually attend tribal council, is that what Omar said not only made it to TV, but put a big smile on Jeff's face. And just an episode prior, at Zach Wurtenberger's first (and last) tribal council, he gets a laugh out of Jeff with the meta observation that, when you watch *Survivor*, building the shelter is just a minute-and-a-half montage, but once you're out there, you're the one who has to actually build it. This is moments after Jeff encourages Zach to recite his famous "in this game, fire represents your life. Once your fire is gone, so are you" speech. The show has evolved from desperately avoiding any acknowledgment of it being a television show to getting a "well done" from Jeff if you have all of his catchphrases memorized word-for-word.

Much like Jamie Kennedy didn't survive deep into *Scream 2*, my *Survivor* life was also cut short on my return to *All-Stars*. One of the many reasons I was disadvantaged heading into that season was the fact that I was genuinely starstruck. I couldn't believe it. I was actually on the same beach as Boston Rob and Sue Hawk and Big Tom . . . Colby, Lex, Kathy . . . there were so many icons surrounding me. Nobody was starstruck to see *me*. This could be chalked up to pretty standard stuff: *Survivor* alumni tend to be more reverent toward those that came before them than after them. You meet someone who played before you and it's like, "Wow, it's you!" You meet someone who played after you and it's like, "Wow, who cares?" I'm half-joking, of course. I genuinely love continuing to meet and develop relationships with newer members of the *Survivor* family, but I'm a forty-seven-year-old man now. I

have two kids. You can't expect me to be out in the streets, shipping and stanning. Yes, I enjoyed Drew Basile on both *Survivor* and *Jeopardy!*, and he's welcome back on the podcast any time, but I'm not starstruck by you, Drew. No disrespect, but waiting for you to join a Zoom link doesn't quite give me the same butterflies I had back in 2003 at the *Amazon* reunion show, getting to meet the legendary Peter Harkey and all of his holes. Back then, there was something so deeply uncool about being starstruck. I remember meeting Jenna Lewis and Amber at some charity event, and, desperately wanting to impress them, I told them I could name every survivor. They looked horrified and I was humiliated. Even on the show, my genuine enthusiasm was met with cold indifference—not just from the other too-cool-for-school castaways but from production itself. My fandom of the show and its stars was not what they wanted to present to the audience. Cut to thirty-some seasons later and they're building a giant Mount Rushmore-esque head of Boston Rob on Fiji! So, how did we get from me being doomed for being starstruck by Boston Rob to the entire franchise being starstruck by Boston Rob?

Survivor became increasingly more meta as they cast more and more superfans. The difference between a regular fan and a superfan is highly subjective. Personally, I'd say you might be a superfan if you think about *Survivor* during the parts of the week when you aren't sitting on your couch watching it.* It's my book so I can make the claim that I was the first true superfan cast on the show. When Mitchell Olson puts out *his* book, he can claim *he* was the first superfan cast, and I won't argue. Until then, I'm the OG. A crucial distinction to make is that I may have been a superfan who was cast on the show, but I was not cast on the show *as* a superfan.

The Amazon was the first season to pit men against women, and with the gender war theme came some obvious archetypes they wanted to see reflected in the cast. They definitely wanted some attractive women, as well as some good-looking fellas trying to get with said women. To round it out, how about a funny guy who lives in his parents' basement and can't seem to land a date? When they saw my *Big Brother* casting tape, they didn't think, "Great, the audience will relate to this guy who can name the *Marquesas* boot order forward and backward in his sleep." They thought, "Great, the audience will get a kick out of this guy's clumsy attempts to flirt with the babes."

> "We'd never had anyone like you. I mean, there really was before you. There was nobody that came on and said, I know the show inside and out. I know everything that's ever happened on every day. I can tell you who did it and why they did it and what happened after they did it. And so you were that, you know, that character. The thing I'm frustrated with is that we haven't figured out how to use you again because the story on you from a casting point of view was you were too clever for the game."
>
> **—Jeff Probst, November 19, 2012**

* If you're this deep into this book, congratulations are in order . . . you're a qualified superfan.

My fairly successful run on *The Amazon* could definitely be attributed to my fandom. By studying *Survivor*, as well as *Big Brother*, I understood the value of maintaining a great working relationship with everybody, not just my own alliance. I wasn't the first person to ever flip on an alliance—that would be Paschal and Neleh turning on John Carroll in *Marquesas*—but I'm pretty sure I was the first one to do it twice. While *Marquesas* had five players work together because they realized none of them were making it to the final four, I believe I was the first player to operate as a lone wolf, working to regroup with many different combinations in order to find a winning path. I didn't get caught up in the complicated moral quandaries Neleh had to wrestle with when she started playing the game on Day 24. I started playing Day 1. I can't take full credit for this, but I do believe my game had a significant impact on the evolution of *Survivor* strategy. Newer players were able to see the game a bit more fluidly than "stick with your original alliance and barrel your way to the end." The following season, Jonny Fairplay claimed to be motivated by watching me on *The Amazon*. He was a recruit who bought every season on VHS to prepare and was, allegedly, rather bored by the show until he watched me.

I didn't have any impact on casting more superfans because, like I said, the popular character of "Rob" on season 6 wasn't a superfan. And if they ever did happen to cast superfans like Skinny Ryan, Brian Corridan, Rafe Judkins, and Spencer Duhm, their fandom wasn't part of their on-screen character. Production didn't think anyone would care, and it didn't necessarily mean they'd have the edge in the game, either. Gary Stritesky, better known as Papa Smurf, was the only fan of the show on the cast of season 14 in Fiji. In fact, he was the only one who applied to be on the show (the rest were recruited). His fandom didn't end up helping him much, although who knows how far he could've gotten if he wasn't allergic to those dang bug bites. Todd Herzog was the first superfan to win, but like the superfans whose shoulders he stood on, his love of the show was not a part of his storyline. Todd was "gay Mormon flight attendant who is also smart"—no one cared what he liked to watch on television.

The first turning point in the meta was the casting of Cirie: the woman who dared to get up off her couch. Hey, I got up off the couch, too. I wasn't even allowed to mention it, but you couldn't shut Jeff up about Cirie's couch. The amount of times Jeff mentioned her couch, it surely must've been incredible—reclining seats, cup holders, not covered in beer stains like mine. All the more impressive that Cirie was willing to leave it to deal with Shane and Courtney's bickering on *Panama*. But the core mythos of Cirie's couch was the dichotomy between the safety of your living room versus the dangers of the jungle. The fact that she's one of the most dominant strategic forces to ever play is actually unrelated to her personal fandom of *Survivor*. It didn't necessarily matter if Cirie was on that couch watching *Survivor*, soap operas, or C-SPAN; "Cirie's Couch" is the story of someone who isn't necessarily outdoorsy or athletic thriving outside of her comfort zone. It was a stepping stone that *Survivor* proper was willing to acknowledge that the players watch the show that they're on.

Cirie returned on *Micronesia*, the sixteenth season, which was originally supposed to be *All-Stars 2* before they decided on a fresh, exciting theme of *Fans vs. Favorites*. Half of the cast would be beloved(ish) returnees, and the other half would be huge fans of the show. For some reason, they didn't end up filling the Fans tribe with real fans, but the theme itself was a definite vibe shift . . . *Survivor*, the television product that had many fans, was allowed to be mentioned on *Survivor* itself. During the loved one's visit, Erik Reichenbach (one of the actual fans of the Fans tribe) pointed out Jeff Probst to his brother Curt: "That's Jeff Probst! He's just standing there!" "Erik, you're a freak," Jeff says back to him with a huge grin. Sixteen seasons in, maybe it's not too self-indulgent to appreciate the joy that comes from fans experiencing being on their favorite show.

A seismic shift came in season 23. *South Pacific* was a captains' season—two returning icons, Coach and Ozzy, each helmed their own tribe. Ozzy's tribe had a wide assortment of folks: a country music singer, a retired NYPD officer, a spoken word artist, but most importantly, a twenty-four-year-old Harvard Law student named John. With his pink shirt, red sweater vest, and glasses, it's safe to say John was on the nerdier side of the cast (Sophie does refer to him as a dodgeball target). But we'd had nerds on the show before. Having the socially awkward John navigate his way around his physically stronger tribe is classic people-meeting-other-people-from-different-walks-of-life *Survivor*. What was incredibly unique about John, the television character, was that his defining trait was being a *Survivor* superfan. After Coach and Ozzy, he has the first confessional from the new players on the season, and he tells us he's, by far, the most *Survivor*-savvy player to ever play *Survivor*. That he's never missed a single episode and even wrote a prize-winning essay on *Survivor* in law school. I believe it was about how the *Survivor* jury system could be applicable to our legal jury system. I don't know what conclusions he came to, but I do know that if I'm ever on trial and I find myself facing the *Samoa* jury, let's just save everyone some time and give me the death sentence.*

Jeff is heavily involved in the casting process and by the time they hit the beach, he knows every contestant inside and out. Still, for the sake of the audience, he does a little song and dance at the opening mat chat, asking, "You in the back, what's your name?" John answers that his name is John, but he's hoping that Jeff would refer to him by his last name, Cochran. He breaks the fourth wall, pointing out that Jeff often calls his favorites by their last names and he feels that "Cochran" would fit nicely in the lineage of Donaldson, Penner, and Mariano. "All great players," Jeff admits. "Let's see if you live up . . . Cochran." And live up, he does. His *South Pacific* game is controversial, to say the least—how Cochran flips on his tribe at the merge is still debated on Reddit nearly every day.† But producers didn't care if Cochran was a great player or not. What mattered was that he made compelling television, which he undoubtedly did.

* I'd actually love to see a *12 Angry Men* type movie about Laura Morett wrangling the votes against Russell. We can call it *9 Angry Jurors* and I'll play Danger Dave Ball. Call me, Paramount Plus.

† Ironically, by people who look a lot like Cochran.

Funny and articulate, Cochran is often cut out to be one of the main narrators of the season. His insight into the game and charming self-deprecation had him dominating the season (in terms of airtime). Even though he placed eighth, he had the second most confessionals (61), only behind finalist and returnee Coach (78). That's more than fourth-place finisher and fan favorite Ozzy (48) and over twice as many as the winner of the season, Sophie Clarke (25). Cochran became an instant sensation with the audience and the long-held theory that the audience didn't want to hear players on the show talking about the show itself was proven patently false. When he was finally eliminated by Ozzy at a Redemption Island duel, Cochran summed up how much the experience meant to him, how he lives and breathes *Survivor*: "To hear you say, 'Come on in, guys,' before a challenge," a teary-eyed Cochran tells Jeff, "I think 'I'm one of the guys! He's talking about me!'"

> "I don't think I've ever told anyone this, but when *South Pacific* first came out and I saw Cochran on episode 1, I was like . . . holy crap, this kid, this guy is me. And I was like, this is what it would be like if I were on *Survivor*."
>
> **—Omar Zaheer, July 11, 2024**

Two things happened after Cochran's first appearance on the show. First was the following season, *One World*. This was peak recruiting era when it came to *Survivor* casting. The casts were filled with mactors (model-actors). A great way to get on the show was to be hot and hang out at Los Angeles bars, waiting to get noticed by a casting associate. *One World* was a season jam-packed with mactors, players who were the exact opposite of superfans. If some of the Manono tribe had watched the show previously, for example, maybe they would have known it isn't the smartest move to go to tribal council when you have already won immunity. The season obviously worked out for Kim Spradlin who trounced her competition in the most dominant fashion, but the audience and Jeff Probst himself were left less than satisfied. In an interview with Chuck Klosterman, Jeff very openly talked about how he felt the casting of certain low-IQ individuals made the game less fun for everyone and wanted "no more dumb people." The following season, we got Malcolm Freberg. Malcolm looked like a mactor, walked like a mactor, even acted like a mactor,* but he thought like a superfan. Suddenly, production could have it both ways. They could get a young heartthrob on screen, but one that wouldn't just sit there twiddling his thumbs, waiting to be voted out. Maybe casting players who watched and understood the show could make better television?

For season 26, *Caramoan*, the show's second *Fans vs. Favorites* match-up, Cochran and Malcolm were obvious choices to bring back. I remember saying how lucky the *Survivor* franchise was to have these two as the faces of the show—although, I did wish they'd put a little more care into the other "Favorites" . . . and nearly all of the "Fans." Cochran and Malcolm were the stars of the season, and with very different play styles, they were two sides of the same superfan coin. Cochran went on to win *Caramoan*, never having his name written down except when every single jury member voted for him to win. The way he dominated the season (and confessional count) locked him in as one of the show's most popular contestants. We already had iconic heroes and legendary villains, but the success of Cochran created a new category: the Superfan. The following season, Brad Culpepper even made it a point to look out for the "Cochrans" who end up doing well in the game. Maybe if this genre of player was officially recognized back in 2004, I could've won Best Superfan at America's Tribal Council instead of losing Best Villain to Jonny Fairplay.† The Superfan archetype became such a prominent staple of the show that, allegedly, when they were planning *Island of the Idols*, the initial conception was *three* idols: Rob, Sandra, and . . . Cochran. Three powerhouses of the show that all approach the game with different strategic mindsets. Unfortunately, that didn't pan out and none of the cast members of season 39 got to receive any game advice from Cochran—which was ultimately only reserved as a reward for Debbie during *Game Changers*.

* Malcolm appeared in three episodes of *The Bold and the Beautiful* in 2013 as the character Malcolm.

† And not even getting nominated for Sexiest *Survivor* Man!

When Hollywood makes a hit movie, they milk those sequels for all they're worth. *Survivor* casting is no different. In the same way *Survivor* tried to replicate the magic of someone like Russell Hantz, they were now after the next Cochran. The first sequel, Spencer Bledsoe on season 28, was also a box office smash hit. Writing that he'd play similarly to both Cochran and Stephen in his pre-game survey, the sharp twenty-one-year-old lad was placed on the Brains tribe of the first of two Brains vs. Beauty vs. Brawn themed brawls. As a chess expert, Spencer attempted to use his *Survivor* knowledge to move his fellow castaways around as pawns. Only nothing went his way all season, starting with a fellow castaway spilling rice all over his chessboard. His seemingly strong *Survivor* awareness, combined with his hapless misadventures, made him into a beloved underdog. As Cochran tweeted out, Spencer was the Charlie Brown of the season, always almost kicking that football but falling flat on his ass. The mere fact that Jeff would read out tweets during the live finale (whether from former players or random audience members) showed that the wall between the TV screen and the people watching it was crumbling.

Twitter launched in 2006 and was really hitting its stride by 2009. *Survivor* Twitter was in its infancy. Finally, there was a home for real online discourse for the show and, specifically, the game. Yes, prior to Twitter, message boards existed, but, while I'm sure there were some reasonable strategy talks on places like *SurvivorSucks*, they were mostly there to tear players down with vicious personal attacks . . . as the name of their message board would imply. And speaking of things that are named very literally, in 2010, a certain former player (me) started a podcast called *Rob Has a Podcast*. I wanted to talk about *Survivor* and I thought maybe people wanted to hear about *Survivor*. At first, the show had fewer than a hundred listeners. But when Ronald Reagan delivered his big "Mr. Gorbachev, tear down this wall!" speech in 1987, the media barely covered it at all, yet once that Berlin wall came tumbling down two years later, he got all the credit. Now, I'm not comparing myself to President Reagan,* but I do feel somewhat responsible for Mr. Jeff tearing down this fourth wall. As the *RHAP*

* Although I do have a similar trickle down economic patron system.

community grew, fans had more and more ways of talking about the show and the show was listening. The audience groaned when Cochran shouted out his Twitter handle during the *Caramoan* reunion show but now nearly every contestant is tweeting out their thoughts every season, getting into back-and-forths with fans and trolls alike.

In 2015, *Survivor* announced a fan vote. Much like how the fans were allowed to vote whether Jonny Fairplay or I were *Survivor*'s greatest villain,* now the fans were going to get to vote on which former cast members would be brought back for a second chance to play on season 31 in Cambodia. We've had many other returnee seasons, but this was a thrill for the fans themselves to choose who would be cast. The theme, *Second Chance*, catapulted the show into a new level of meta. Instead of avoiding talking about past seasons, now *all* we were talking about were past seasons—regrets players had, what they wanted to change. The pressure was on, not just because the players wanted to win for themselves, but because they wanted to win for the fans who voted them back in. The *RHAP* representative on the season was Stephen Fishbach. After his original season, Stephen started a weekly *Survivor* blog for *People* magazine where he'd analyze the episode and award a "Fishy" to the player of the week.† A few years after that, Stephen joined me on *RHAP* to start the *Know-It-Alls*, a weekly podcast recorded live immediately after a *Survivor* episode aired, breaking it all down. Suddenly, my co-host went from talking about *Survivor* on the *Know-It-Alls* to talking about the *Know-It-Alls* on *Survivor*. Stephen made a deep run before sadly being ruthlessly taken down by the new hotshot superfan on the block, Spencer. However, the main headline of *Second Chance* wasn't that we saw Stephen cry on TV; it was the evolution of the meta. It wasn't just that the show's strategy had evolved from sticking with an alliance from the start to having various voting blocs shifting from episode to episode—it was that this shift was openly discussed in the show itself. The show, and the superfans on the show, openly acknowledged the shift from the old-school shelter people who worked hard around camp and built long-term relationships, to

* And how the fans were *not* allowed to vote on whether I was *Survivor's* Sexiest Man.

† Though sometimes he decides to give out TWO Fishys, which, in my opinion, totally devalues the Fishy, rendering it completely meaningless.

the new-school beach people who scrambled around, constantly strategizing and running the numbers. Things that used to be only discussed on podcasts were now actually talked about on the show!

> "Like, if you had told me in whatever 2011 that I would soon be spending twenty minutes at a bar at a charity event in Florida hearing Neleh talk my ear off about how we need to form a pre-game alliance, I would have told you to take your pills."
>
> **—Spencer Reiman Bledsoe, February 3, 2016**

Each season, we got more and more new-school beach people, more Cochran sequels and spin-offs and reboots. Aubry Bracco, an original Brain tribe member like Spencer, was so beloved as the underdog superfan that they brought her back two more times in the 30s and once more for *50*. When introducing a challenge during her first outing in *Kaôh Rōng*, Jeff pointed out that the challenge was once won by Cochran himself. "You mean my boyfriend?" Aubry jokingly replied. Though she's happily married with children now, maybe we will see what this superfan power couple could've been if Dr. Strange ever joins the Cochran Cinematic Universe. Other entries in the CCU weren't quite as successful. Before Max Dawson went on the show, he actually taught a college class at Northwestern University *about* the show, but the *Survivor* professor did not make it past the swap in *Worlds Apart*. Though he wasn't eliminated before getting a chance to (mis)quote Malcolm's "hold up, bro" at tribal council, momentarily pretending he had an idol to Jeff's clear annoyance.

But Jeff wasn't always annoyed at the superfans. The first season shot after *Second Chance* was season 33, *Millennials vs. Gen X*,* and it felt like the superfan era had *arrived*. The cast was chock-full of superfans such as David Wright, Hannah Shapiro,

* Even though *Second Chance* aired as season 31 and *Kaôh Rōng* as 32, they were filmed the other way around.

Zeke Smith, Will Wahl, and Adam Klein. The eventual winner, Adam, might be the first cast member who was active on the *Survivor* subreddit (or at least the first one that had great success on the show). The Millennials grew up on *Survivor*. Like Bane, they were born in it, molded by it. Originally forbidden, it is now in the show's DNA to reference itself. As Jay Starrett emerges from the sea, Hannah Shapiro refers to him as Peruvian Ozzy. "I got naked on *Survivor*!" Bret LaBelle loudly celebrates after his shorts accidentally come off during a challenge—a callback all the way back to Richard Hatch in season 1, whose nudity was a major controversy then but is now recognized as iconic. Jeff really falls in love with this cast. He loves how well they know the show and that they're quick to make analogies. He loves that they're willing to change up alliances on the fly and play a fluid game—forget voting blocs, these youngsters are playing with trust clusters! He loves their sportsmanship—that they can blindside each other and still remain friends, understanding it's just a game.

> "I go to the Kama camp, and I knew, like, okay, you don't want to talk about *Survivor*, we don't want to get into the season 32 drama, we don't want to get into this and that. But I immediately realized that my plan of not talking about *Survivor* wasn't going to work, and that's because everyone wanted to talk about *Survivor*. Like, my favorite example is that we were sitting around the fire, Day 1 or 2, someone asked me a question about *Survivor* and someone else answered for me, and I was like, whoa, I didn't even know that about my damn game. Cool, man."
>
> **—Aubry Bracco, June 5, 2019**

The 30s continued with more and more fans getting their shot at playing. Season 35's turtleneck-wearing Ryan Ulrich seemed to have been genetically bred in a laboratory to be an ultimate superfan, able to spit out nonstop analogies to Jeff at tribal about what playing *Survivor* is like. He's never had a girlfriend, he tells Jeff unprompted (unclear if this has anything to do with the amount of time he's dedicated to watching and rewatching competitive reality television). The following season had Jacob Derwin, a fan who blogged about the show. He may not have made it as far as Ryan, but he did innovate the game with the emergent strategy of pouring the tribe's rice into his dirty sock in the hope of finding an idol. Christian Hubicki and Gabby Pascuzzi played in the sand together after watching so many others play in that very same sand before them.

The season's themes also grew in their meta nature. Season 34 could've been any all-star season, but it was titled *Game Changers*. By bringing back a cast full of players who (allegedly) changed the game, it implicitly drew attention to the fact that the players were there to change the show. They weren't playing within the vacuum of those specific thirty-nine days, but as part of a greater lineage that they themselves were instrumental in evolving. *Island of the Idols* reminded the new players (and the audience) that they were merely in the shadow of the greats like Rob and Sandra—both metaphorically and literally, as two giant statues of their heads were constructed.* The craziest theme to me was *Ghost Island*. It's one thing to bring back players for a second chance, but to bring back the props from the show of misplayed idols that are now haunting new players like a horror movie? "Will the newbies be doomed to repeat the mistakes of the past players?" we were asked every episode, as the show bombarded us with clips from previous seasons.

Ghost Island wasn't a very well-received season. It had an exciting start and even more exciting finish with the only ever tied jury vote, but the middle was a major drag due to the lopsided nature of the cast. There were definitely cast members like Dom and Wendell who knew what they were doing, along with Laurel Johnson, who (and please do reach out and correct me if I'm wrong) was the first patron of my podcast to make it onto the show. Laurel was able to combine all the knowledge Stephen and I espoused on the *Know-It-Alls* to become both a third placer and a losing finalist. But

* I'm not sure if those heads still stand in Fiji or are kept in Jeff Probst's backyard.

outside of the handful of players who understood what was going on, the majority of the cast felt like the earlier mactors—good-looking humans who were about as strategically savvy as the cast I played with on season 6. If you're not going to be good at *Survivor*, at the very least you should be entertaining on *Survivor*, and unfortunately, here, that only applied to the over-the-top Chris Noble. He may not have ever seen the show or had any bars, but this male model slash former baseball player swung for the proverbial fences* and the season took a nosedive once he struck out. *Ghost Island* may have been the nail in the coffin for recruits, and soon after, *Survivor* let go of its longtime casting director Lynne Spillman.

This era wrapped up with season 40, *Winners at War*. The premise of casting a season of winners isn't inherently more meta than casting all-stars, but this landmark season was a lot more self-celebratory. And it deserved to be. The show had been on for twenty years and was dripping in lore, rich in history. How can you bring back Boston Rob and Amber without acknowledging that, without *Survivor*, their four children would literally not exist? How can you bring back Tony and Sarah and ignore the Cops R Us trajectory of them starting off as adversaries trying to blindside each other to becoming incredibly close, unbreakable friends in real life? Excuse me, I meant to say Lacina, not Sarah. The fourth-wall-breaking joke Cochran made seventeen seasons prior about Jeff referring to his favorite players by their last name comes back into the conversation, but this time as a genuine discussion about gender bias when Jeff notices he's only done that with the male players. I don't know how accurate this was, however—apparently "Wentworth will not count" will not actually count.

The biggest change in the New Era was the sheer amount of new twists and trinkets being introduced. The hourglass, do-or-die, sweat-or-savvy, every vote potentially turning into a shot-in-the-dark. Jeff wasn't shying away from complicating the game mechanics; he loved when the strategy got complex—*Cambodia*'s final six vote was so convoluted that, during the live finale, Jeff brought out a freeze-frame of tribal council and drew on it with a marker, explaining the plays like he was prime John

* And he calls it Sammy Sosa.

Madden! The advantages have come a long way since Dan Foley got the vote-steal on season 30. The producers understood that the more they experimented with new gizmos and gadgets, the more they needed cast members who could wrap their heads around what these gizmos and gadgets could do. The game got so convoluted that it would become incredibly frustrating for the audience to see players have to learn the rules over and over again. You may have had a similar experience inviting someone not into complicated board games to your regular Blood on the Clocktower night.

The New Era began with an official diversity initiative but also an unofficial double-down on the superfan casting initiative. While my *Survivor* knowledge was once the anomaly, it is now the baseline. I wasn't allowed to talk about previous seasons on *The Amazon* and now there has been a literal challenge to place the previous seasons in chronological order! I'm sure every reader of this book was screaming at their screen as Hunter placed *Caramoan* between *Cook Islands* and *Tocantins*.

Dr. Evvie Jagoda, Brandon Donlon, Owen Knight . . . I'd run out of pages in the book if I listed every superfan cast on the show after season 40. Season 42 alone has Zach Wurtenberger, Omar Zaheer, and Daniel Strunk, and starts with soon-to-be-winner superfan Maryanne Oketch unable to contain her pure joy of being on *Survivor*. Season 47 had not only Andy Rueda, a longtime patron of my podcast, but winner-of-the-season Aysha Welch,* who is an actual podcaster on my network! Wednesday, September 18, 2024, marks the first (and likely last) time that the words "*Rob Has a Podcast*" have been uttered on *Survivor*. And Teeny Chirichillo happened to be a big enough superfan to recognize Aysha . . . purely from an audio medium! In the same episode, first boot Jon Lovett happens to tell his tribemates about *his* podcast, which no one seems aware of. This was the only possible data pool where *Rob Has a Podcast* was more popular than *Pod Save America*. Jon may have had former President Obama on his little show, but I've interviewed Peter Baggenstos, an emergency room doctor who kinda *looks* like former President Obama!

* My editor informs me that I unfortunately do have to admit Aysha did not win the season and it was actually Rachel LaMont—another mega superfan of the show.

Being so aware of the show, the players now come in fully formed, knowing exactly what their confessionals are supposed to sound like. But is this what we want? When Cochran made his first appearance, he struggled to fit into his tribe. Aubry, with similar social struggles, made the poignant analogy that *Survivor* often feels like high school. Aubry and Cochran and Spencer were fan favorites not just because they were funny, knew a lot about *Survivor*, and played well—but because they resonated with the audience, who also often had trouble finding their place in the world. Who doesn't root for the underdog? Now superfans are no longer the underdogs. They have become the top dog as the show has transitioned into an Oops! All Cochran© brand of casting. It's no longer a novelty to be obsessed with the show. Season 48's Shauhin Davari sits off to the side of the challenge, singing the tribal score they'll undoubtedly lay over the segment. Jeff himself joins in on the meta by doing his commercial-break "apply to *Survivor*!" call to action live on the beach.

> "It has to do with the caliber of player. So it's not that the game has gotten any easier. It's that the people that are playing the game just might not be as good at playing it as, you know, we were . . . I would say it just really depends on the personality. Like, you brought up Kathy Sleckman from season 16. She wasn't a great player, but she was a superfan of the show. Erik Reichenbach, also not a great player, but, you know, he gave us one of our greatest moments of the show. Huge fan, but a strategic mastermind? No, right? . . . I'd never even seen the show."
>
> **—Parvati Shallow, November 6, 2014**

Survivor began as an exploration of the human condition—specifically about the darkness of what people are willing to do to one another to get a million dollars. But as the show grew and evolved, the people making it seemed less interested in telling a story about what depths people are willing to reach to undermine each other and

more interested in telling the story of what people are able to get out of the experience of playing the game. And as they make the game more and more complicated, it becomes more about who is able to outmaneuver whom in this intricate Rube Goldberg machine. If I get you, it's really just because I operated the levers of the machine better than you did, not because I hate the person that you are. In older *Survivor*, with fewer levers and pulleys and buttons to press, interpersonal conflict was often the reason why you got voted out. So in a way, this advantage-laden superfan era has led to a kinder and gentler game . . . but maybe at the cost of the more compelling jagged edges that originally drew us in. The animosity between Ozzy and Cochran felt so personal; now, sure, we get more players who would be a delight to invite to a board game night, but are we missing the kind of personalities who would flip over the table when they're losing at Catan?

I often question if we've gone too far. And I wonder how responsible I am for this. Like Oppenheimer, I sit behind my microphone asking myself, "What have I created?" I lit a pilot light for the community which drew out the fans like moths to a flame, which eventually turned into a blazing inferno. When I had Kellyn Bechtold on my show after *Ghost Island*, I dug up all the times she had called into *RHAP*. I embarrassed her by playing the nearly identical voicemails she left week after week about Kelley Wentworth's run in *Cambodia*—sneaky, sneaky.* If we're already reaching back to World War II and comparing the fall of the Berlin Wall to the fall of *Survivor*'s fourth wall . . . it feels like I not only paved the way for the atomic bomb but for Carson Garrett.

I'm all for the diversity initiative CBS has implemented. I know that, in this day and age, a lot of people are scared to say what they really think, but I, Rob Cesternino, am willing to go on the record to state in no uncertain terms that racism is bad and racial diversity is good. What I do miss, however, is diversity in *Survivor* awareness. Not everyone on the show needs to be a superfan! Recruits get a bad rep, especially when a season like *48* flops hard, but recruits don't have to be gym-bro challenge beasts. The best recruits weren't necessarily mactors. Lynne Spillman found Jonny Fairplay while he was smoking a cigarette at a gas station and discovered Courtney Yates while she was serving her as a waitress. Amanda Kimmel, Earl Cole, Andrea Boehlke, and so many other favorites weren't necessarily fans of the show before they got cast on it. I'll let you in on a little secret:† Stephen Fishbach was a recruit! He has since put in his ten thousand superfan hours, but this *Know-It-All* began as a *Know-It-Nothing*! Not being a fan of the show doesn't mean you wouldn't do well on the show.

* Where she inexplicably greeted me with "Heyo, Robio."

† Not so secret if you read Stephen's foreword!

One self-aware Jamie Kennedy is fun in *Scream,* but the movie wouldn't have been a hit if it was all Jamie Kennedys. It works because of how balanced the cast is. *Scream* has heroes and villains, some brighter, some dimmer, leading to a very satisfying winner's arc. But as the *Scream* franchise goes on, each subsequent film gets more meta and more self-aware. Like *Survivor*, you can't put the toothpaste back into the tube—and you can't even bid on a regular tube of toothpaste at the auction without risking your vote. There's no going back to *Borneo*—we've seen the show, the players have seen the show, the show itself has seen the show. That may make the show more niche than the initial global phenomenon, but hey, I'm not complaining since I'm the exact niche they're trying to cater to. Some still remember me as a *Survivor* player, a few more might know me as a *Survivor* commentator, but above all else, I have always been and will always be a *Survivor* superfan.

WE QUIT!

CHAPTER 5

You Had to Be There

The Watercooler Watershed Moments

Back before everyone worked remotely on Zoom, there used to be a thing called "offices." These offices were conveniently located exactly one hour of heavy traffic away from wherever you lived where people like me managed computer systems for insurance companies, whatever that means. Offices were where you spent most of your life, navigating complicated social dynamics (like one would on *Survivor*) and pretending to be busy. But whenever you needed a break from the facade of working, there was a wonderful, aptly named area known as "the break room." The break room came with all sorts of amenities like a microwave, a fridge, a coffee maker, but most importantly . . . the water cooler. The water cooler ruled. It gave you free water in three different

settings: cold, room temperature, or hot.* Visiting the water cooler often meant running into co-workers who also operated in three different settings: complaining about the boss, gossiping about other co-workers, or chatting about what exciting thing happened on television the night before. If this sounds familiar, you're probably thinking of the television show *The Office* and, yes, it was like that. But back then, instead of endlessly binging *The Office* on Peacock, believe it or not, audiences used to have to wait until Thursday nights to all simultaneously experience *The Office* on NBC and then, if Michael Scott said something especially outrageous, they would go to work Friday mornings and incorrectly quote it to their co-workers by the water cooler. The bigger the show, and the bigger moment that happened on it, the bigger "water cooler moment" it would create.

When Mike Skupin fell into the fire during *The Australian Outback*, the cameras kept rolling. "I would've fired him on the spot," Mark Burnett later said about the camera operator if he had stopped filming to help Mike. "He would have been on the next plane out." Now, is this sort of prioritization of making great television over human safety something I personally endorse? Maybe not. Do I wish that the camera crew that was gleefully filming my camp burning down in *The Amazon* had just done me the solid and saved a few of my belongings? Sure. But I do understand we were all there to make a product that slid nicely in between commercial breaks and, if we didn't want the audience to switch over to see what shenanigans were happening on *Will & Grace*, then we had to give them something big to look forward to.

Survivor has no shortage of huge moments—the kind you'll never forget where you were when they happened. Fortunately, most of these do not involve someone getting badly injured or me losing all of my underwear in a fire. Many of these were passionately discussed amongst co-workers at water coolers around the world. These moments not only sparked conversation and sold CBS ad space but defined the eras of the show itself. These were monumental inflection points, sometimes creating ripple effects that changed how the game was played. Some are ceaselessly and fiercely debated to this very day on the internet—which is basically a virtual water cooler, if you really think about it.

* With an extra step to get the hot water so you don't accidentally burn yourself, forcing Mark Burnett to fire the receptionist who helps you with your burned hands.

The Golden Era

Seasons 1–8

These were the OG seasons, when we were all pioneers, figuring it out. Was the show at its best? That's what some purists would argue. It was definitely when the show was at its most popular. The biggest moments of this era came out of the social experiment of it all.

THE RATS AND SNAKES SPEECH

(*Borneo*, August 23, 2000)

Those of us who watched *Borneo* live had no idea how the finale was going to work. It was all new to us and the marketing team advertised it like the finale was going to be so exciting, they couldn't even show us one second of it! Luckily, it lived up to the hype. When Sue Hawk got up there and eviscerated poor Kelly Wiglesworth, comparing her to a rat being eaten by the snake Rich—when she said she wouldn't even give Kelly a sip of water if she was dying of thirst—television was changed forever. The trope of the scathing reality loser was born. It was so mean, so personal, and, frankly, so real. As manufactured as reality television can get, this proved that, in the right place and the right context, even a silly little game show can lay bare the visceral nature of a hurt human being. After the *Borneo* finale, fans had this speech memorized. I used to quote it regularly (and probably still can if anyone tries to test me). It was parodied relentlessly, and even though this was the not-meta era of *Survivor*, Mad Dog quoted it the following season when voting out Kel Gleason. As far as jury speeches go, it might still have never been topped, but I'd say Trish Hegarty and Reed Kelly came pretty close.

MIKE FALLS IN THE FIRE

(*The Australian Outback*, March 1, 2001)

If Sue Hawk demonstrated how emotionally raw the show could be, Mike Skupin (unintentionally) proved how physically dangerous it was. Nothing could match how real and intense *Survivor* was. Sure, you could switch over and watch *Friends* where you didn't know if Ross and Rachel would get together, but *Survivor* was a show where you really didn't know what could happen. During season 2, on Thursday night, I would buy a can of Foster's (Australian for beer) and take over the living room at my parents' house. The night Mike got burned, I was incredibly stressed since they had heavily promoted that something horrific was going to happen. Leading up to it, Mike was a really popular character.* He was a badass—he killed the boar! So if this wilderness guy wasn't safe from getting medically evacuated, no one was. When I was on the same tribe as Sue Hawk on *All-Stars*, one of the more annoying things I did was ask her to help me rate the most iconic moments of the show. I couldn't decide if it was her speech or Mike falling in the fire. Meanwhile, she couldn't decide if she was voting me out first or second, but my constant pestering her about former seasons helped her make that decision pretty quick.

COLBY TAKES TINA

(*The Australian Outback*, May 3, 2001)

I was so mad that I had to go to some boring insurance conference in Chicago during the *Australian Outback* finale. It's almost as if my job didn't care about which TV shows I was watching.† But on the actual finale night, I stood my ground and told my boss I wouldn't be going out to schmooze prospective clients. Instead, I would stay

* For some odd reason, he's lost popularity amongst the fans in recent years.

† Eventually, that would change for me.

at the hotel bar and watch *Survivor*. Ratings-wise, the second season was the biggest season they'd ever have. It seemed like there were only a dozen people in the entire United States not following the show. Unfortunately, all twelve of them were at that exact specific hotel bar. I couldn't get anyone to engage with me; nobody cared that the show was on. I couldn't really blame them, since it was a pretty snoozy finale. It seemed like it was going to be a runaway with the favorite Colby winning, but after winning the final immunity, Colby chose to eliminate the blowhard chef Keith Famie and lost the season to Tina Wesson. A bit of a knuckleheaded move, but it truly captured the era where Colby maybe cared more about seeming like a good guy on television, unwilling to betray a nice lady for *one million dollars*.

THE COCONUT CHOP CHALLENGE

(*Marquesas*, April 18, 2002)

A bit of an underreported story that many superfans aren't willing to admit is that early *Survivor* was starting to get boring. The back half of *The Australian Outback* was a bit of a slog and *Africa*, despite some great characters, got a little sleepy. *Marquesas* appeared to be going strategically like all the previous seasons—a majority alliance takes hold and steamrolls. In this case, that was the Rotu Four, led by John Carroll. Boston Rob, who was mounting a resistance, had just been voted out, so it seemed like the rest of the season was going to inevitably be Rotu Four domination. Then came the infamous coconut chop challenge. For the final nine immunity, the players had to answer true or false questions, with the kicker being that every time they got one right, they could chop one of the three ropes holding up someone else's bundle of coconuts. Once someone's coconuts dropped, they were out—so it wasn't a pure game of who could get the most trivia questions right, but a game within a game of showing your hand about who you wanted to eliminate, revealing your true alliances. The cocky and confident Rotu Four easily and unsurprisingly eliminated the three outsiders—Sean, Vecepia, and Kathy—but their mistake was then eliminating Neleh and Paschal, who thought they were in with the Rotu Four. Realizing they were at the bottom of a six-person alliance, Neleh and Paschal flipped to join the three outsiders (who also happened to be the fan favorites) and they voted out John. This moment fried my brain when it happened. Not only was it a thrilling, all-time great blindside, but it opened up the entire strategy of the show. We didn't have to live in a world where alliances just stuck together with the bigger one devouring the smaller;* we were free.

> "In my case, I overplayed. I was so eager and so excited to play that once the game was underfoot, I just overplayed it. I mean, I just got, I just did way too much, way too, too fast and didn't think one step ahead. . . . Almost everybody has a moment of combustibility and the key is, how do you react to it? Can you put yourself in that other person's shoes for a moment to try to understand like what's happening in that moment, and sometimes there's no ability to do that and sometimes things are moving so quickly that there isn't any way to fix those problems. I remember like when we were on our show when that coconut challenge came and after I got taken out first of our group and sitting there and watching them do the pecking order, it was such a helpless feeling because Tammy and the General were so blind to like what they were doing . . . There were only so many things that I could try to do and I didn't do enough."
>
> **—John Carroll, October 1, 2015**

* Although that's exactly what would happen the very next season.

CHOCOLATE AND PEANUT BUTTER

(*The Amazon*, March 26, 2003)

I can't remember exactly where Jenna and Heidi got the idea for what they did, but there was already a belief permeating amongst some of the women that after *Survivor*, they would get a chance to pose for *Playboy*, just like Jerri Manthey had. We knew there was very likely going to be an endurance challenge where Jeff tempts players with food to drop out. So when Jenna and Heidi were brainstorming offering to strip naked during that challenge if Jeff brought them their favorite dessert, I told them . . . "That is a great idea, you should definitely do that." Was it actually a great idea? It didn't totally make sense, right? If they're stripping for chocolate and peanut butter, why are they *also* giving up immunity? But within seven, eight months of that happening, they were on the cover of *Playboy*, so long-term, it worked flawlessly. Some people these days say this moment "did not age well," but let me tell you, at the time . . . it slapped, it ruled, everyone loved it. It was peak *Girls Gone Wild* era and the episode was even titled "Girls Gone Wilder." The blurred clip of them stripping got so much media coverage on the likes of *E!* and *Entertainment Tonight* that I got offended that all the funny and strategic stuff I was doing wasn't getting the same level of attention as two girls taking their clothes off. And I deeply regret not falling off into the water right after it happened so I'd be forever memorialized every time the clip got re-aired.

This is my wife's least favorite *Survivor* moment of all time. It doesn't matter to her that this was before we started dating or that, frankly, it was the least sexy thing that ever happened. No disrespect to Jenna or Heidi, both beautiful women, but this was twenty-one days into us living in the jungle and we hadn't showered in weeks. These were two starving, emaciated waifs, peeling off the disgusting bathing suits stuck to their unbathed bodies. I was much more focused on maintaining my balance on my perch than sneaking a peek at Jenna and Heidi performing the exact opposite of an erotic striptease. But for the sake of my marriage, I profusely apologize for my involvement with this piece of *Survivor* history.

> "The other one they got on me is that I get every week or every time I go somewhere: 'Butch, did you look when Heidi took her clothes off?' I said, 'I didn't look.' And they all start laughing. 'Yeah, right.' I said, 'I'm telling you, I didn't look.' And I didn't . . . Rob volunteered. Rob Cesternino, the greatest player but not to win, he did volunteer to take his clothes off for food. But Jeff didn't like that idea. Us guys wouldn't have liked it either."
>
> **—Butch Lockley, November 19, 2020**

THE ALEX AND CHRISTY BLINDSIDES

(*The Amazon*, April 24 and May 1, 2003)

Maybe you think it's a bit audacious for me to not only include two moments from my own season on this list, but to have this one be two blindsides in back-to-back episodes, but I do humbly believe this was a big deal in the evolution of the show. We had just voted out the great Deena Bennett and I was in the final seven, in a tight four with Jenna, Heidi, and Alex Bell. Now Alex was in a great position. He was a super likable guy, had real BDE, and the women loved him. Hell, *I* loved him. If he wanted to go to the end with me, I would've been so happy that such a cool guy liked me that I would've pulled a Colby and thrown my game away for him. But for some inexplicable reason, Alex decided to let me know that when we got to the final four, I'd be the next to go—which wasn't a plan I particularly jibed with. I figured I had a better chance to win with the bottom feeders than the cool kids group, so I rounded up Butch, Matthew, and Christy and flipped the vote on Alex.

When we got back to camp, Jenna and Heidi called me names I can't print in this book. That was fine—we had four votes to their two. Except now they were trying to pull Christy over, which I hadn't thought could be possible since they all hated each other so much. But suddenly, Christy was entertaining working with her evil stepsisters! Maybe she started enjoying the power and attention that came with being the swing vote. Unfortunately for her, back then, none of us knew what would happen in a potential three-three tie, so I went to Jenna and Heidi with a proposal that we all vote out Christy instead. After swearing on a certain appendage of mine, we made a pact to temporarily put our swords down and eliminate the uncertain variable. Christy did eventually decide to vote with my side but it was too late. All her hemming and hawing got her voted off. She may've been the first swing vote to catch the heat herself, but she certainly wasn't the last. Christy Smith walked so that Dolly Neely and Sarah Lacina could run—one back to her sheep farm, the other straight to the *Cagayan* jury.

In the Amazon, I was just making decisions moment to moment that seemed to best serve my game. It wasn't until I got back that I realized how it was perceived. *Marquesas* had one big flip, which did inspire me, but that just shifted from one Pagonging to a different Pagonging. This was different—from the Deena boot to the Alex boot to the Christy boot, for the first time, *Survivor* had an unpredictable post-merge. I'm so proud of what I was able to do and honored that I sometimes get credit for pushing forward strategic thinking in the show.

THE DEAD GRANDMA LIE

(*Pearl Islands*, November 26, 2003)

When Jonny Fairplay concocted a scheme that his friend Thunder D would come to the loved ones visit with fake news that his grandmother had passed away, this wasn't just the biggest lie in *Survivor* history—it was the biggest lie in reality TV history. This extended well past *Survivor* into a massive pop culture moment. Jonny Fairplay didn't just change *Survivor*; he permanently changed the television landscape. Thanks to him, countless aspiring reality show applicants strived to make a notorious name for themselves by playing a heel and being hated on national television. I missed this episode when it was airing because I had already shipped off to Panama to film *All-Stars*. I was in Patagonia after getting voted out and I snuck off to an internet café to catch up on all I had missed. I learned of the outcast twist, that Jenna Morasca's mother had sadly passed away, and that Jonny Fairplay's grandmother had shockingly not. Over two decades after the great lie, Jonny Fairplay's loving grandmother Ellen Jean Hauser has, for real this time, died of kidney failure.

Even though I missed this episode in real time, I was fortunate enough to get to watch it about four thousand times at Jonny Fairplay's apartment. He was the only friend I had when I moved to Los Angeles in 2004 and he helped me get an apartment around the corner from him, so I regularly came by like a sitcom character.* He was the unofficial mayor of reality stars—he knew who everyone was and where every party was happening, and introduced me to countless people. He constantly had women over, partied at the club all night long, and woke up at like six p.m. It was quite an incredible lifestyle and he had his big episode on loop in his apartment 24/7. Part of me wonders if he still does this to this very day.

ROB BETRAYS LEX

(*All-Stars*, April 8, 2004)

During *The Amazon*, my parents had so much fun throwing watch parties that they decided to run it back again for *All-Stars*. Then after I was voted out episode 4, I got so mad because they *still* kept inviting people every week. Hey, party's over! Go home, everyone! But they were enjoying watching the people who stabbed their firstborn son in the back too much. I wasn't particularly close with anyone who made it past

* Although I figure if this was a sitcom, Jonny Fairplay would be the Kramer-type neighbor who constantly barges in on me, not the other way around.

the merge so I actually didn't have the season spoiled for me. All I knew was that Lex was not happy with how things went down and the vibes were bad. Rob voting out Lex is probably the most significant vote in the history of the show. Rob's number one ally (and showmance and future mother of his four children) Amber was swapped unfavorably to the opposing tribe where she was outnumbered five to one. However, after the challenge, Rob ran over to his real-life close personal friend Lex with a plea that "if you take care of her, I'll take care of you." So Lex kept Amber around. But when merge came around and it was time for Rob to repay his debts, he instead stabbed Lex in the back, sending him to the jury in an unforgettable, rain-soaked, dramatic tribal council.

> "I have to hand it to players that are able to kind of completely turn the switch off and play without all of that kind of those handicaps that those of us that do sort of worry about kind of the human side of the equation, you know, we are handicapped. It's like running a marathon for us with a backpack full of cinder blocks. It's tougher when you want to try to go in there and be not just a player, but kind of retain your, you know, your humanity."
>
> **—Lex van den Berghe, April 2, 2010**

While turning on a friend of two years was highly controversial in season 8, by season 27, a different player would be celebrated for . . . voting out her own mother! If a Rob and Lex situation happened today, the only question would be if it was the *most optimal* game move for Rob. Out of the twenty thousand different *Survivor* podcasts out there, not a single one would question his character.

The Experimental Era

Seasons 9–18

The post-*All-Stars* era had the show willing to take big swings to avoid getting stagnant. We saw the introduction of the hidden immunity idol, the first appearance of Exile Island, and a new class of iconic players ready to push the game further creatively.

THE 3-2-1 VOTE

(*Panama*, April 27, 2006)

There were exciting vote-outs before Cirie, but the 3-2-1 was truly something special. It's one thing to pull someone over and win the vote; it's another to win the day without having the majority of votes. If you've taken advanced math in school, you may be able to quickly calculate that three votes is not more than half of six. So for Cirie to eliminate her target while avoiding a three-three tie, she needed to be damn sure where all the other votes were going. She nearly became the first boot of the season, but she was now so integrated with the tribe, having everyone's trust, that she knew Shane was voting for Danielle, Terry and Courtney were voting for Aras, and was able to steer Danielle and Aras to vote alongside her against Courtney. The 3-2-1 was groundshakingly brilliant. And it wasn't just the masterful social maneuvering Cirie did to win on a plurality. It was the choice target of Courtney who, with all due respect, was a goat taking up a spot in the final two. It was nothing new to target a threat on *Survivor*, but to strategically target a non-threat was super exciting to see. I had just moved into an apartment in West Hollywood, the first place I lived with my now-wife, and I was probably incessantly raving about this move. It took a new generation of fans to fully embrace the brilliance of what Cirie pulled off and now it's in the conversation for the best move of all time—a true watershed moment for the level of strategy the show would go on to see.

BILLY GARCIA FALLS IN LOVE

(*Cook Islands*, September 21, 2006)

Cook Islands gave us a lot. We got the first ever final three, a huge mutiny moment, the invention of the vote split, an extremely controversial theme of dividing the tribe by race,* and the first appearance of many multi-seasoned icons such as Parvati, Ozzy, Penner, Yul, and Candice. But Candice would've been a nobody one-time player if the second boot of the season hadn't put her on the map. Now, the second person voted out of a season is rarely too memorable. The first boot is at least a piece of trivia; they usually get some sympathy, with many fans clamoring for a season of a cast filled with just those who were eliminated first. The second player voted out is often sadly lost to time . . . but not Billy Garcia. Though Billy found himself on Aitutaki, the Hispanic tribe, he felt that he belonged more with the heavy metal community. So he

> "A lot of people don't know this—it didn't make the edit—but at the first challenge, I was set on fire. My shorts were set on fire. I was climbing up a ladder and Christina was the torchbearer for our team and the ladder was made up of pieces from our puzzle boat, and so it came undone. So that stopped me from going up. But she didn't see that. She kept going up, and her torch lit my butt . . . Jeff Probst was standing right there. And so he had to yell out to everybody, 'Billy's on fire, his ass is going up in flames!' And of course, I'm hearing this before I realized I'm on fire. So the first thing that comes out of my mouth is, 'That figures.' It was one of those cartoon moments where somebody tells me I'm on fire, I'm smelling smoke, I look down, then I feel the pain."
>
> **—Billy Garcia, May 8, 2010**

* I highly recommend looking up the *MadTV* parody of this.

appreciated the irony that the player trying hardest to get him voted out shared a first name with one of his idols, Ozzy Osbourne. After Aitutaki lost the second immunity challenge, Billy found himself standing on the mat next to Candice from Raro tribe. "I'm next," he whispers to her, correctly perceiving he was about to be voted out. "Aw, we love you," Candice replies compassionately, but, in one of the show's greatest misunderstandings, Billy hears this as "*I* love you." "I love you, too," Billy tells her back earnestly. At tribal, Billy announces to Jeff, his entire tribe, and the world that it doesn't matter that he isn't going to win the million dollars. His prize is falling in love with Candice. Nobody knew what to make of this, he was promptly voted out, and the Billy/Candice love story did not quite have the legs of the Rob/Amber love story. But it remains one of the strangest and most delightful moments of the show, the legend and meme of it growing larger by the day. Though he has not yet been invited back on the show, Billy stays somewhat active in the *Survivor* community and you may run into him at a fan event, where he'll still be wearing this patented red skull T-shirt like he's Bart Simpson who only owns one outfit.

THE CAR DEAL

(*Fiji*, May 13, 2007)

Even though *Fiji* came during the period of time where I took a personal break from watching *Survivor*, I still caught word about what happened with Dreamz and Yau-Man and that infamous 2008 Ford Super Duty truck. If you're relatively new to *Survivor*, when you think of a reward the players might win at a challenge, you're imagining a little snack at the *Survivor* sanctuary, like something you might get for free on a domestic flight. But back in the heyday, rewards used to be *rewards*. They would be feasts, once-in-a-lifetime helicopter trips over the Great Wall of China, and, sometimes, a brand-new car. The cars also came with a curse . . . the winner of the car would never go on to win the season.* This time around, the curse struck twice. At the final six, the beloved fan-favorite Yau-Man Chan won the truck but, rather than accept it, he decided to strike a deal with fellow contestant Dreamz Herd, who had been struggling with homelessness. In exchange for the truck, Yau-Man asked that, should Dreamz win immunity at the final four, he would give up the necklace to Yau-Man. Badly needing a vehicle, Dreamz took the deal, and thanks to the *Survivor* Gods, Dreamz also won the final four immunity. However, realizing he was going to be voted out if he gave up immunity, Dreamz chose to renege on the deal and sent Yau-Man to the jury. Dreamz got so much anger from the jury that he received zero jury votes. He got even more anger from the audience at large. It was so controversial that this

> “I went to a TV show to play a game for a million dollars . . . If I have to get in a fistfight with somebody, I'm doing that for a million dollars. . . . But all I had to do was renege on a deal to get me close to a million dollars. . . . You gotta remember, I don't know Yau-Man like that . . . If an extra pair of his pants and he had to fly home in his underwear was on the line, I would have tried to get that, too. . . . I think they painted me as, oh, this thug who would do anything for money instead of, you know, a kid from the projects, a kid who came from nothing, who didn't expect to end up on a TV show, who was willing to do whatever it took to get as far as he could, you know, to take care of his family. I think they could have painted that better.”
>
> **—Dreamz Herd, November 16, 2020**

* After twenty-two years, this curse was finally broken on an international season of the show. Also it's been argued that Amber technically beat the car curse when Boston Rob, who won a Chevrolet Colorado in the challenge, got to pick someone else to also receive a Chevrolet Malibu.

ended the car reward on *Survivor* (although I do think the Ford marketing team may've been a little shortsighted over how much attention it brought them). Over time, Dreamz's betrayal has been looked at much less harshly. First, we love it when players break promises to try to win the game. Second, with perspective, Yau-Man dangling a truck over someone desperate and struggling does feel slightly icky. Third, and most importantly, they filmed *Fiji* right after *Cook Islands*, so no one knew there was going to be a final three. When Dreamz struck the deal, he didn't realize the final four immunity would be the last immunity challenge. So, suddenly, he had a guaranteed spot to plead his case for a million dollars. No one can blame him for not throwing that away.

JAMES BLINDSIDED WITH TWO IDOLS

(*China*, November 29, 2007)

Fiji was the first season that had the "proper" idol rules (it had to be played before the votes were read) and the first season where the idol was played both "correctly" (with Yau-Man canceling four votes against him at the final six) and "incorrectly" (Mookie played his idol for Alex but Stacy made sure Edgardo was the one catching votes). It was a matter of time before somebody was sent home while in possession of an immunity idol they did not play. Little did we know that not only would it happen the following season, but that player getting sent home would be in possession of, not one, but *two* idols. *China* also fell under my break from watching the show live but I heard a lot about this incredible player Todd Herzog. After Todd's ally James got swapped unfavorably to the other side, Todd decided to slip James his idol for protection. Credit to James, he knew that Todd got the idol from the archway at the head of his former camp, so he decided to find the matching idol at his new camp. It was the final seven—an idol could be used for three more rounds, and there was

James sitting pretty with two of them. Or at least he thought he was sitting pretty. He may have had two idols, but Todd was two steps ahead, blindsiding James and sending him to the jury with two souvenirs. In the lore of *Survivor*, James not playing an idol is constantly referenced as one of the dumbest moves (or lack of a move) to have ever happened on the show. Fortunately for James, his blunder would soon be eclipsed by other players on his second and third times out.

THE EFFIN' STICK

(*Micronesia*, April 10, 2008)

Fake idols have a history just as long as real ones in *Survivor*. Though Yau-Man gets credit for constructing the first fake idol—a shell with "II" painted on it—the first fake idol was actually made in *Guatemala* by Gary Hogeboom, the first person to ever find a real idol. He took a piece of wood, carved a star in it, and buried it for someone to find. It was never found and never made the air. *Panama*'s Austin Carty also made a fake idol when he was out on Exile Island with Danielle DiLorenzo but changed his mind and didn't bluff with it. Whenever *Survivor* introduces a new element, players immediately try to hack it. So how could we expect anything less from a landmark season with a full tribe of returning favorites? I took a hiatus from my *Survivor* hiatus to drop back in for *Micronesia*. My pal Jonny Fairplay didn't make it too far, but fortunately there were others to root for. This was the pre–Russell Hantz era so nobody went out looking for idols. You had to wait to go to Exile Island and get a clue first. Ozzy was sent to exile multiple times and did the work, followed the clues, and found the hidden immunity idol. But before he went back to camp (to eventually get blindsided with it in his pocket), he took the Gary Hogeboom strategy, carved a smiley face into a stick, named it Igor, and buried it back where the idol was supposed to be, hoping to trick someone. And that someone was Jason Siska from the Fan tribe.

Jason came on the show wanting to be like Ozzy, compete physically like Ozzy, and I guess eventually also get blindsided with a real idol in his pocket like Ozzy. But before Jason got his hands on a real idol, he first ended up at Exile following the same clues Ozzy did to the smiley face stick. Jason wanted it to be true so badly that he ended up

fooling himself into believing that it was a real idol. At the merge, Eliza found herself targeted. Wanting to save his ally, Jason promised her his idol and when he finally gave it to her . . . we couldn't have asked for a better reaction. "It's a f—ing stick!" Eliza yells at the brokenhearted Jason, who is half in denial, half realizing his hero Ozzy had played him. Eliza helplessly got voted out and *Survivor* fell in love with fake idols. As the years went on, the hidden immunity idol became less and less cool looking, until it was just a string with some beads on it. Production's dream is to re-create this effin' stick moment where someone is this bamboozled, to the point that a fake idol making kit was offered as an advantage on a menu that Cochran presented to Debbie on *Game Changers*.

ERIK GIVES UP IMMUNITY

(*Micronesia*, May 8, 2008)

I got invited to an event soon after *Micronesia* ended where I can't remember if Parvati was throwing it or just attending it but I do remember she was there and had no idea who I was. I may have been on only eight seasons prior but it felt like a lifetime ago—I was officially old news. Other than not being recognized, it was a great party. I got free drinks and I met my lawyer Mikey Glazer there. We've worked together for many years since then and he's the one going through this book, making sure I don't get sued over saying something unsubstantiated or defamatory. Also at this party was Holly Hoffman, prior to her *Nicaragua* appearance, who got totally wasted and destroyed my $1,600 crocodile leather boots.

But what happened with Erik's necklace was so big, so insane, that I went from feeling left behind to just genuinely being excited by *Survivor* again. The final five had Erik Reichenbach up against four members of the Black Widow Brigade: Parvati, Cirie, Amanda, and Natalie. This all-women alliance was dominating the post-merge but there was one spanner in their works—the athletic Erik was good at winning challenges. Having won the final five immunity, Erik was safe and the Black Widows had to devour one of their own. Or did they? Cirie floated an idea to the girls . . . what if they got Erik to give up immunity? It should've been impossible, but the same could be said for that 3-2-1, yet Cirie pulled it off. Every girl played their part in what felt like a heist movie to convince (maybe even gaslight) poor Erik into believing that giving his immunity necklace to Natalie would give him a better chance of winning the jury vote at the very end. The second Erik gave up his necklace at tribal, James erupts into laughter from the jury. His record of having made the dumbest move ever

> "So I'm sitting there and [Erik] is giving his whole spiel. And, you know, people say, 'Oh, your facial reactions are so extreme, they seem like maybe they're exaggerated for the purposes of television.' Let me tell you, it was not exaggerated. Not even in the slightest. . . . This was so shocking to me. And, you know, if you've watched an entire episode, maybe you have seen the lead-up to something that happens at tribal council over the last three days of footage, et cetera, and the story is kind of taking you to this place. I've seen nothing. I'm getting to tribal council seeing absolutely nothing over the last three days. This is the first time I'm seeing any of it. And so I'm sitting there and Erik is like, 'You know, I want to prove my loyalty, and da, da, da.' And I'm like, no way. There's no way, he's not gonna do this. He just said at the last tribal council, 'I'd be an idiot to give this up.' You know, there's no way. And so my mouth is just dropping open, and then he takes it off and, I mean, James is cracking up. We are just, like, cannot believe that this happened. And of course the women were gonna vote him out. And what an idiot. And, you know, like Parv said, you will go down in *Survivor* as the dumbest contestant in the history of the show."
>
> **—Eliza Orlins, April 29, 2018**

was beaten just six months later. Every member of the Black Widow Brigade went up to the voting booth, wrote down Erik's name, dunked on him, and the editors decided to include every vote in the show. We didn't need any tension to see who got voted out; we were celebrating what they were able to pull over Erik. And all he could say after getting completely eaten alive by them was, "You guys drive me crazy." Erik's monumental f-up is up there with Sue Hawk's speech, Mike falling in the fire, and Fairplay's dead grandma lie on the Mount Rushmore of iconic *Survivor* moments. It made us realize that, even within the framework of the rules of the game show, absolutely anything could happen.

The Russell Hantz Era

Seasons 19–26

When CBS found Russell, they couldn't get enough. They started out just using Russell recreationally, which developed into a full-on Hantz addiction, and they needed an intervention. Within a four-year span, they had him on three times, had his nephew Brandon on twice, and even cast his brother Willie on *Big Brother 14*. The priority to replicate Russell with polarizing characters like NaOnka, Phillip, and Colton, rather than focusing on a strategically balanced cast, may've led to the more stagnant gameplay in seasons 21–24, known as the Dark Ages.

RUSSELL LOSES TO NATALIE

(*Samoa*, December 20, 2009)

Russell brought me back to watching *Survivor* live. He was electric, and we were all losing our minds watching him play. From burning socks to finding idols without a clue, it's hard to pinpoint the definitive Russell moment because *Samoa* was one long Russell moment. But what left the longest (still ongoing) discourse in its wake was Russell losing 7-2 to Natalie White. For the penultimate episode, I went to a viewing party in Jenn Lyon's honor at the Renaissance Hotel, dipping my toe back into the *Survivor* ecosystem. Russell was in attendance and he was walking around like a rock star. He truly was a phenomenon, the biggest star *Survivor* had seen in years. And believe it or not . . . he could be charming. He had the ability to turn it on and mesmerize everyone in the room. I don't know if he knew at this point that he hadn't won the season—the story goes that he played *Heroes vs. Villains* like he had just won and only Shambo told him soon before the *Samoa* finale that he had lost the game. If Russell plays poker, I hope his poker face is better than it was during the live reading of the votes. He could barely feign a smile as Jeff read out the two "Russell" votes, waiting for the inevitable barrage of "Natalie" votes to come in. The devastated Russell argued with Jeff and Natalie during the live reunion, even offering to buy the title of Sole Survivor from her as the zero-vote finalist Mick Trimming just sat there, being all feckless.

> "That was something that I can remember in pre-game interviews, you know, them asking me how I was going to play the game. . . . And I said, 'I'm going to be here to make friends.' And they kind of laughed at me, and they're like, 'You know what game you're playing, don't you?' And I said, 'Yeah, absolutely.'"
>
> **—Natalie White, May 15, 2010**

A lot of people were/are on Russell's side (even Jeff wrote him a note that he was robbed). You can't argue that Russell didn't have massive flaws in his social game and jury management, but his style of aggressive gameplay resonated so strongly with the audience that the show was forever changed. There may be some revisionist history going on nowadays, but at the time, Russell was the hands-down fan favorite and nobody was offended by him. Unfortunately for Russell, all of the anti-Russell sentiment happened to be sitting on that Samoan jury. Losing the jury vote (not to mention losing it the season right after) turned him into a martyr for this type of gameplay. Not to say he's a particularly sympathetic martyr—his behavior after the show and on social media definitely cost him more than a few fans—but Russell's loss was a line in the sand. Nobody cared to hear about honesty and integrity on the show after that.

PARVATI'S DOUBLE IDOL PLAY

(*Heroes vs. Villains*, April 22, 2010)

I started *Rob Has a Podcast* for *Heroes vs. Villains*. If it was a dud season, it's quite possible my podcast would've also completely flopped. I was so lucky that we got the best *Survivor* we could ever hope for for the first year of *RHAP*.* The show kept dropping banger after banger episode, the hype was building, and so many alumni were eager to come talk to me and share their takes. Parvati's double idol play at the merge was the climax for an incredible storyline that I'm not sure the greatest writers could even script.

It all started with J.T. on the Heroes tribe, coming off the perfect game in *Tocantins*, still eager to prove himself as a strategist. On the Villains tribe, he saw Parvati, whose reputation preceded her, and Russell, whose reputation was nonexistent (since *Samoa* had yet to air). When J.T. witnessed Tyson, Boston Rob, and Coach go out one after the other, he and the other heroes quite quickly jumped to the conclusion that Parvati was up to her old tricks banding the women together. Having found an idol, J.T. decided he was going to, after an immunity challenge, slip it to Russell, the player clearly on the bottom—the good ol' boy who had a trustworthy Southern accent just like his. This was like watching a slow-motion car wreck. It was impossible to look away as Russell and Parvati read and mocked the letter J.T. included with the idol, "teaching" Russell how to play it against Parvati. Russell gave the idol to Parvati, who had already found one Russell didn't know about, so Parvati headed into the merge with two.

The season started with ten heroes versus ten villains and now the merge whittled it down to five versus five. So Parvati had to play her idol(s) correctly to prevent the

* Which I had to karmically pay the price for the next few seasons.

vote from being deadlocked. She reasonably figured the heroes were either going to vote for "Parvati" or "not-Parvati," and after reading Amanda's lack of poker face, Parvati realized they were going the not-Parvati route. She deduced they weren't going to vote Russell since they incorrectly believed he might side with the heroes, so that left Sandra, Jerri, or Danielle. Mathematically speaking, two idols can't cover three people, but when Parvati found herself in a showdown against Danielle in the endurance immunity challenge, an opportunity presented itself. Parvati willingly stepped out, granting Danielle the immunity necklace and, at tribal, she dropped double bombshells by playing both her idols on fellow villainesses, Sandra and Jerri. The five hero votes for Jerri were negated and, in a twist of pure poetic perfection, the five villain votes landed on J.T.—the first player voted out, not with his idol, but by his own idol. Parvati's play and J.T.'s mistake are forever interlinked together as some of the smartest and dumbest moves in *Survivor* history.

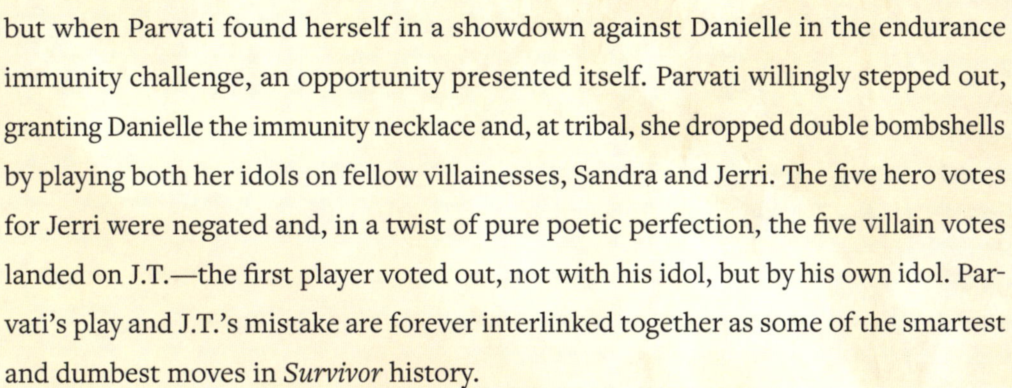

THE DOUBLE QUITS

(*Nicaragua*, December 1, 2010)

It's tough being the season following a big landmark returnee season.* *Vanuatu*, *Gabon*, *Nicaragua*, and *41* were all poorly received when they aired—*Kaôh Rōng* somehow evaded this fate (maybe because it was actually filmed prior to *Cambodia*). However, with the exception of *41*, all the others eventually became cult classics. Back before *Nicaragua* found its loyal fans, it was really disliked. A large part of this was due to the controversial NaOnka Mixon, who was edited as the star of the season. It's difficult to sum up NaOnka for those who haven't watched, but let's

* Good luck to everyone on *Survivor 51*!

just say she threatened to throw fellow castaway and amputee Kelly Bruno's fake leg into the ocean. But even that could be forgiven; what cannot be forgiven on *Survivor* is quitting. When someone quits, every superfan who has applied to the show countless times feels like the person who got their spot has squandered it. At the final nine, both NaOnka and her ally Kelly Shinn (known as Purple Kelly for the purple streaks in her hair) committed the greatest sin they could by laying down their torches and leaving the game. It was truly unfathomable. Not only was it Day 30, but NaOnka had an idol—with a little jury finessing, she could've won the whole damn thing! I can't tell you how upset people were about this.* I admit that because of the extreme outrage toward Kelly and NaOnka at the time, I maybe went harder on them in my exit interview than I should've, asking them if they were going to quit my podcast in the middle of recording it. Time was a little kinder to them. With perspective, it's clear that there was a strong racial component to the NaOnka backlash calling her ungrateful. As for Purple Kelly, she may've gotten barely any screen time (probably as retribution from production for quitting) but her legacy lives on forever: Underedited contestants are now referred to as being "purpled." The most notable purpled player since Kelly has probably been Chelsea Townsend. You may not have seen her on your TV screens but she was allegedly part of the *Ghost Island* cast.

* The show even changed their rules after this so that quitters wouldn't be allowed to serve on the jury.

THE THREE AMIGOS TRIBAL

(*Caramoan*, April 17, 2013)

During the second *Fans vs. Favorites* match-up, favorite Malcolm found himself on the outs with two "fans," Eddie Fox and Reynold Toepfer. This trio of friends, the "Three Amigos," were the rootable underdogs against the behemoth "Stealth R Us" alliance led by the Specialist Phillip Sheppard (or it might be more accurate to say the group allowed him to be the figurehead). At the final ten, the seven Stealth R Us members had the numbers to vote split on the Three Amigos, but Reynold won immunity and Malcolm had two hidden immunity idols. Rather than surprise everyone with his idols after the vote, Malcolm decided to bust them out in the middle of tribal, placing one around his neck and one around Eddie's. Chaos erupted—someone from the seven was about to go home. It was thrilling, exciting—not just for the audience but for the players, as well. "Whatever happens tonight, this is why I frickin' love *Survivor* after thirteen years," Cochran even said in his voting confessional. Unfortunately, the big flaw in Malcolm's plan was his announcement that the Three Amigos were putting their votes on Phillip, so the rest of Stealth R Us had no reason not to keep their votes the same and let Phillip take the bullet. Had their votes remained a mystery, maybe

> "And then the thing that happens there is he has to do what Malcolm did on *Caramoan* and basically play that thing every single tribal council. He has to both find it and play it every single tribal council because of the target it puts on you. . . . That's something I did in my strategy on pretty much every season. I never wanted to find the idol. It's a target. . . . To me, it was like a hot potato. . . . I'm sorry, I'm not Russell Hantz. I can't find it perfectly every time. I'm only going to be able to find it so much, and then my time's run out."
>
> **—Erik Reichenbach, October 31, 2013**

Stealth R Us could've fractured and sent votes flying at each other. The Three Amigos tribal didn't affect the trajectory of the season too much—all three were unceremoniously voted out soon after—but it did usher in an era of spectacle. It's fun to see deliberation happen in front of us when the vote is live (colloquially known as "live tribals"). Malcolm paved the way for such live tribals as the *Edge of Extinction*'s Pilots and Passengers tribal and, ironically, the *Game Changer* joint tribal council where J.T. unintentionally sent Malcolm himself packing.*

DAWN'S TEETH

(*Caramoan*, May 12, 2013)

Sue Hawk's speech was far from the last *biting* moment at final tribal council. Throughout *Caramoan*, Dawn Meehan emotionally leaned on her fellow tribemates. Rock bottom for her came on Day 26, when she lost her partial denture while washing it in the lagoon. Not wanting to appear on television with some of her bottom teeth missing, Dawn came close to quitting the show. However, in a moment that felt outside of the game, Brenda Lowe dove down and was able to retrieve the retainer, bringing Dawn from completely distraught to overwhelmingly grateful. Dawn and Brenda got so close that when Brenda won the loved ones challenge, she picked Dawn to go with her. But Jeff had a twist up his sleeve—giving Brenda the option to give up her (and thereby Dawn's) opportunity to spend time with her family and, instead, give the reward to the rest of the tribe. Brenda graciously gave up the reward, which sent Dawn into a spiral. She not only didn't get time with her husband but also got none of the credit for the rest of the tribe getting the reward. It didn't help that the reward went down on a barge within ear

* No spoilers, but the best live tribal council (and possibly tribal period) happens in the premerge of *Australian Survivor Heroes vs. Villains*. You'll know it when you get to it.

and eyeshot of the beach. This, combined with Brenda growing into a huge jury threat, led to Dawn and Cochran brutally blindsiding her.

When Dawn faced the jury, she caught a lot of flak for how emotionally she played the game. The brunt of this came from Brenda, who was genuinely heartbroken by Dawn's betrayal and demanded Dawn remove her teeth and let the world see her the way she was that day.

Dawn probably should've just pulled what Sherri did with Erik and told Brenda to sit back down, but after a tense back and forth, Dawn did remove her teeth. In retrospect, Brenda's request was somewhat messed up, though she may not have known that Dawn originally lost her teeth in a violent mugging. And it was a little messed up how hard Jeff forced Dawn to apologize at the reunion show for, checks notes, blindsiding someone on the show. But what's really messed up is that, after all that, Brenda still voted for Cochran! C'mon, Brenda, you publicly humiliated Dawn; the least you can do is throw her your jury vote.

The Big Movez Era

Seasons 27–34

The mostly stagnant gameplay of seasons 22–24 became the thing the show feared the most, leading us into an era of casting more dynamic players, creating the ethos that making the big move is the most important thing you can do on the show.

CIERA VOTES OUT HER MOM/ THE ROCK DRAW

(*Blood vs. Water*, November 20 and December 4, 2013)

Ciera Eastin, who would later appear on *Game Changers*, presents a curious case of making a completely non-game-changing move that did actually change the game in the greater meta of it all. In the post-merge of *Blood vs. Water*, the battle lines were drawn between the pairs of loved ones still in the game and the "singles." The singles, led by Tyson, were gearing up to vote out Ciera's mother, Laura Morett. Wanting to further herself in the game (and to the delight of Jeff), Ciera made the choice to vote out her own mom. I wasn't yet a full-time podcaster when this aired and I had to work late at the office that day. So I was cutting it very close to the *Know-It-Alls*, watching this episode while driving, over 4G on my phone through a Slingbox I had set up in my mom's* basement. Now, that's how you do it in 2013! What I remember thinking, while stuck in LA traffic, was that this vote-out was such a nothing burger. Ciera didn't flip on her mother—the votes to get Laura out were already there. Yet there couldn't be a more perfect emblem of the theme. Ciera became the poster child of playing hard, making the moves you need to make to get yourself further . . . even if those moves happen to embolden the existing power structure. However, a few episodes later, Ciera did have a wake-up call that she was just going along with the Tyson-Gervase-Monica faction and flipped over, at a live tribal, to the Hayden-Katie faction. Now this actually *was* a big move. It forced a tie and sent everyone to the first-ever rock draw in twenty-three seasons. Unlike voting out her mom, this totally (pun intended) rocked and actually did usher in the era of taking risks on the show. There's no real difference between fourth place or sixth. It paved the way for the incredible rock draw in *Millennials vs. Gen X* and established the general attitude that you gotta play like it's Sole Survivor or nothing.

WOO TAKES TONY

(*Cagayan*, May 21, 2014)

Top to bottom, everything about *Cagayan* was a real phenomenon. All of it was so cockamamy, it just didn't seem real. At the center of it all was Tony, a complete maniac, flipping and flopping, back and forth. He'd cut an ally, then rejoin his allies, then cut another ally, then rejoin his allies, over and over again. The best part—he kept not getting voted out! Tony became the living emblem of the Jesse Pinkman "he can't keep getting away with this!" meme. But surely, once Woo won the final three immunity, that was the end of the road for Tony. No more idols, no more shields. As the clear jury threat, Tony was going to be the third-place last juror fallen angel (not the worst

* Who I would never vote out—I've been put to the test playing the *Survivor* card game and I couldn't bear to pull a Ciera and vote out my own mother.

thing to be). Not to mention, as the season was airing, Tony was as active and combative on Twitter as a pre-merger desperate to stay in the limelight—there was no way someone tweeting like that could win! Woo had a choice between two doors: door #1, take Kass to the end and become Sole Survivor; door #2, take Tony to the end and go down in *Survivor* history as, hands down, the player that made the dumbest choice that's ever been made. Somehow, leaning on Woo's values about loyalty and honor and martial arts or whatever, Tony was able to convince Woo to make an unforced $900,000 error. Not since Colby taking Tina had there been such a surprise to the final two—maybe it's why this is the last time we've ever seen the final two; the producers probably believe they'll never get this lucky again and continue to hedge their bets on letting a player like Tony just barrel their way to a final three. Tony's game, even with his second win, may be unrepeatable, but it definitely set a high watermark of unpredictability and entertainment that the show would eagerly chase. More twists, more trinkets; let the maniacs fill their bags of tricks and havoc will reign.

"JACLYN, DID YOU VOTE FOR WHO I TOLD YOU TO VOTE FOR?"

(*San Juan del Sur*, December 17, 2014)

We've had many dominant winners and many under-the-radar winners, but Natalie Anderson is probably the best example of someone who played under-the-radar and then exploded into dominance, taking the W at the very end when it counted. I had a special fondness for Natalie going into the season because she and her twin sister Nadiya were both on *Amazing Race 21*, one of the first seasons I covered on the podcast. I had also done exit press with them for *Amazing Race: All-Stars*, where they were the first ones out. So they were already a little in the *RHAP* world, and Jessica Liese, our expert on all-things *Amazing Race*, gave them some *Survivor* pointers. Those pointers led Nadiya to being the first one booted off the season. Things got even worse for Natalie when her number one ally Jeremy Collins got blindsided in the early merge. Jeremy was such a star that the entire season was structured to be Natalie's revenge arc.

Instead of blowing up her own game, Natalie played masterfully, quietly plotting her payback. It was a joy for the fans to watch her infiltrate the dominant alliance, pulling off subtle moves like telling Jon to play his idol during the whole "stick to the plan" Keith Nale fiasco or "accidentally" flipping her vote to Alec in the split. Then at the final five, Natalie finally stepped out of the shadows to reveal to the entire cast who was actually running the game. "Did you vote for who I told you to vote for?" Natalie publicly asks Jaclyn, who was receiving the majority of the votes. After Jaclyn emphatically nods, Natalie plays the idol on her and coldly blindsides her own ally Baylor (who was there when she found the idol!). This thrust Natalie into a final three where the jury had to give it to her. As Jeremy eloquently put it, she balled out. While underappreciated at the time, *San Juan del Sur* (and Natalie specifically) has exploded in recent years as a beloved classic.

"WENTWORTH, WILL NOT COUNT."

(*Cambodia*, November 11, 2015)

Kelley Wentworth is a true *Survivor* underdog. Not only was she literally on the bottom during season 31, but it was wild she was on the season to begin with. Having been voted out pre-merge in *San Juan del Sur*, Kelley was a highly unlikely fan pick to be brought back, but against all odds, there she was. And she did not squander her second chance. Sneaky, sneaky, she was the first player to find an idol during a competition and waited for the right moment to play it. That moment came during the second vote into the merge. Kelley was part of the Witches' Coven alliance, targeted by the majority alliance led by Andrew Savage and Jeremy. The majority had more than enough votes to split, but there was so much distrust within the group that they decided to pile the votes on Kelley. And boy, were they in for a surprise when Kelley whipped that idol out of her bag and shattered the record for most votes negated. It seemed to go on forever: Jeff pulling vote after vote for Kelley, endlessly repeating "Wentworth, will not count." The fear and anticipation on everyone's faces was building . . . who had the Witches voted for? Regardless of who they'd picked, this would've been a legendary moment, but the cherry on top was that they voted for . . . Andrew Savage. Savage is a terrific character on the show partly because he's a bit full of himself. It's fun to see someone a little pompous about their position plummet. Additionally, he called Stephen Fishbach a "wimpy little non-leader," so the *RHAP* community was especially happy to see Savage topple. This also happened to air the night before my second son was born, so while it may have been the best moment of the season, it was only my second favorite moment that week. I got to slip in a very exciting *Know-It-Alls* episode that Wednesday (with Josh Wigler filling in for Stephen) before switching gears into husband and dad mode. I sadly had to skip doing an exit interview with Savage the next day, but fortunately got to do the first entrance interview with my son, Anthony.

> "But before we went to vote, I still had a good relationship with Keith, and I looked at Keith and I was like, 'Keith, who are you voting for tonight?' Because I knew that if Keith was voting for me or Joe was voting for me, then everyone was voting for me. And this is just classic Keith, right? Like, instead of keeping it to himself, he shared with me by writing in the sand; he started to write my name with his big, long walking stick. Like, he started to write 'Kelley.' And I just looked at him, and he looked at me, and we just kind of had this understanding."
>
> **—Kelley Wentworth, April 23, 2023**

ADVANTAGEGEDDON

(*Game Changers*, May 24, 2017)

The infamous "Advantagegeddon" was the tragic, inevitable conclusion of flooding the game with advantages. There were so many things in play during *Game Changers* that all came to a head at the final six. Brad had won individual immunity, Sarah had a legacy advantage keeping her immune, Troyzan played an idol on himself, and Tai played one on himself and one on Aubry, which left Cirie as the only player without safety. So even though no one had cast a vote for her (she pulled off yet another 3-2-1 on Sarah), Jeff explained she was the only one vulnerable in the revote and thus had to hit the road. Her consolation prize was Jeff letting her say his patented "the tribe has spoken" herself. This moment is a real crossroads in the show. If you were to ask Jeff, he'd describe it as an incredible, once-in-a-lifetime event. During his *On Fire* podcast, he compared it to the *Reservoir Dogs* scene where everyone had their guns pointed at one another. But if you were to ask a lot of fans, this moment is a real bummer. Cirie is such a fan favorite and she was getting so close to winning the game; it just felt . . . flat. No one necessarily outplayed her or pulled off some incredible blindside. It seemed like a bunch of deus ex machinas randomly happening to the player we were all rooting for. Until her announced return for *Australia vs. the World* and *50*, this felt like such an unsatisfying ending to the journey of a legend. A weird fluke at the time has now become somewhat standard in the New Era—small tribes with players constantly gaining and losing votes leads to all sorts of various advantagegeddons. We may be used to them now, but at the time, this was shocking. Cirie handled it, like many things, with great dignity. Much more dignified than how my son handled getting advantagegeddoned out of the *Survivor* card game when both my mom and brother played their idols at final three.

The Forever Fiji Era

Seasons 35–40

Sure, seasons 33 and 34 (and 14) were in Fiji, but it was after that filming cycle that the show decided to permanently settle into the Mamanuca Islands of Fiji. They lost new locations for budgetary reasons so they decided to up the ante in terms of themes and twists.

THE FIRE-MAKING TWIST

(*Heroes vs. Healers vs. Hustlers*, December 20, 2017)

Ben Driebergen was on an incredible idol-finding run. He had played from the top as King Ben but had toppled all the way to the bottom with no allies. So round after round he was the target, barely escaping elimination with his constant barrage of overly dramatic idol plays, much to the chagrin of his many enemies led by ally-turned-rival Chrissy Hofbeck. But then came the final four. Idols were no longer in play, so for Ben, it was win immunity or bust. He'd failed to win an individual challenge all season, but he was in the lead for this one, carefully placing letters on a wobbly platform to spell out the absurd theme of the season. Unfortunately, he placed his final tile upside down, spelling out "HՈSTLERS." Fixing the upside-down *U* cost him enough time for Chrissy to finish the challenge, tying the women's record for most challenge wins. This was sadly the end of the road for Ben—he got voted out in fourth place, making him a fan-favorite fallen angel.

Wait, record scratch—that's what *should've* happened. Instead, Chrissy's win came with an "advantage" in the form of information. It was revealed that instead of a traditional final four vote, from now on, the immunity challenge winner would pick two players to advance to the final three, while the remaining two would have to face off in a fire-making challenge. As Devon Pinto had said earlier in the season when his vote got taken away, "This is *not* an advantage." After probably cussing off-camera for a while, Chrissy ended up sending Devon to take down Ben in fire. Ben, however, made fire faster and advanced to the final three, where he was able to win the jury vote.

This latest twist was reported online before it happened, so there was plenty of time to debate it beforehand. The debate has yet to cease. The typical *Survivor* fan is never like, "Ooh, we're getting something new. Cool!" It's always the reaction that something is being taken from us. The "problem" this twist seemed to solve for production is that a lot of the favorites went out at the final voting round—most recently with David Wright on *Millennials vs. Gen X*. It's debatable if this solves the problem. The final three was introduced because they felt a lot of the favorites went out at three (can happen!) but that just led to the bigger threats getting voted out earlier; now with mandatory fire at the final four, the bigger threats tend to get taken out even earlier. But regardless of where one lands on this addition, it's undeniable it was pretty unfair in season 35. While everyone from season 36 on is aware there are no more "pure voting rounds" without idols or fire, none of the heroes, healers, or hustlers were privy to this. Their strategy of "beat Ben at immunity at final four and vote him out" should've worked. Ben's victory took him from a beloved underdog who couldn't quite make it to an unjustified winner amongst the superfans (I'm sure the million dollars helped wipe the tears away). Chrissy is coming back for *50* to try to take back what many believe is rightfully hers (though there is a strong contingent adamant that Devon was taking that final three).

> "They've sort of supercharged *Survivor.* It's like a sequel to a movie. . . . When you look at James Bond number one, *Dr. No*, you know, he kills three people . . . and by the time you get to the new one, they're blowing up the freaking world . . . and *Survivor*, there's, how many idols are there? How much craziness do they have to get in there? And it's, in some ways, a more fun show, but they have to keep adding a twist, and once they add it, they can't, like, take it away, you know? So they keep adding and adding and adding."
>
> —Jonathan Penner, April 16, 2010

JACKET-GATE

(*David vs. Goliath*, October 24, 2018)

David vs. Goliath was a season where everything worked. The theme, the gameplay, and the personalities all coalesced into a perfect storm. At the center of this storm was Angelina Keeley. It's one thing to be a star of a season, but it's a whole other thing when you're the supernova of a season already full of stars. Angelina had a relatively quiet start but Jacket-Gate put her on the map. The Goliaths had a favorable swap, gaining a three-two advantage on all three swapped beaches. The new Jabeni had Angelina, Mike White, and Natalie Cole against the two Davids, Nick Wilson and Lyrsa Torres. After they lost immunity, it should've been a simple vote, but there was already major tension between Natalie and Lyrsa over how to cook the eggs they won at reward. This was exacerbated by Angelina being rather cold and lacking a proper jacket. In order to help her tribemate, Natalie came to Nick and Lyrsa and not-very-subtly suggested that maybe one of them could be spared if they gave Angelina their jacket. While probably a lovely woman in the real world, within the show, Natalie often came off as rather abrasive. Nick and Lyrsa didn't take well to being blackmailed and caused a scene, and eventually, Mike and Angelina decided to flip on Natalie in order to build stronger David connections in the merge. This could've been a simple blindside, but Angelina concocted an additional scheme to vote *with* Natalie, appear shocked at tribal, and then ask Natalie for *her* very warm jacket. What resulted was an incredibly long and drawn out series of Angelina asking Natalie repeatedly for her jacket as the rest of the tribe stewed awkwardly and Natalie ignored her as her torch was snuffed. And Natalie proudly wears her jacket while giving her final words to camera.

Poker player Jason Somerville used to host this thing called Run It Up Reno. Since there are a lot of poker-playing *Survivor* alumni, we used to be part of the event. That year, there was a big group of players and fans at the Peppermill Resort and Casino and we had a huge screening for the episode. When Angelina asked for Natalie's jacket . . . the room exploded. No one could believe it. On top of this, by total coincidence, the woman of the night herself happened to be from Reno. So Angelina not only attended but brought like thirty of her family members. I'll never forget live streaming the podcast immediately after the episode and getting heckled by Angelina's family the whole time! This landmark moment proved that none of the twists and gameplay will ever take away what we truly love about *Survivor*: the clash of absolutely outlandish personalities. Plus they were both able to parlay it into a trip to *The White Lotus*.

CHRIS'S RETURN FROM THE EDGE

(*Edge of Extinction*, May 15, 2019)

I attended the live finale for *Edge of Extinction* and I remember seeing the third boot, Chris Underwood, really dressed to the nines. Noted. Maybe Chris is the player that gets back into the game? The controversial concept of the season was similar to Redemption Island—everyone voted out got to live on the Edge until there was a chance to get back in at the merge and at the final six. The fourth boot, Rick Devens, won his way back in at the merge and had been running the season with his antics. Then, at the top of the finale, Chris won the challenge and was back in the game as well. There were lots of downsides to being out on the Edge of Extinction—you had a lot less food and nothing to do but reflect on all the mistakes that led to getting voted out. There was one major upside, though: You had nothing but time to bond with the eventual jury, plot your possible revenge, and practice making fire. Chris returned with a plan and he executed it to perfection. He convinced Lauren to play an idol on him, then he played his own idol on himself. Most importantly, after winning final four immunity, he put *himself* into fire, taking out the big jury threat and audience favorite Rick Devens. He went on to win the jury vote against Gavin and

Julie, which is controversial, to say the least. While Gavin and Julie never got voted out, Chris ended up playing a total of only thirteen days of *Survivor* (having spent a New-Era-season-length twenty-six days on the Edge). But, as Wardog eloquently put it, the theme was not on trial, and the jury decided that the thirteen days Chris *did* play (well, more accurately, the five days he played at the end there) were deserving of the winning title. Those last few rounds were undeniably impressive and changed the ethos of what it means when Jeff says, "Now that's how you do it on *Survivor*!" We laughed when Erik gave up immunity in season 16, but now we applauded Chris for giving up his. The jury didn't give Mike White that much credit for making fire, but now they were suddenly blown away by Chris's ability to do so. As the days on *Survivor* decrease, the flashier you've gotta be with your time. To me, despite the impurity of the winner of a season getting voted out on Day 8, it was an incredibly exciting finale. My only complaint is that I wish Chris had won his way back in at the end of the penultimate episode so we could've had a week of analyzing and speculating about his path forward on the podcast.

> "I was really wishing that that had been on my season because I would have been able to at least try to get back in the game. . . . [Chris] was one of my favorites, in the very beginning! I really liked him and I was really glad to see him . . . but a lot of people that I know that I keep in touch with that are huge *Survivor* fans were not happy with Chris winning and it's because they didn't get to form a relationship with him. I mean, this guy was brilliant. And they're saying, 'Well, oh, it should have been Rick Devens.' Well, I'm thinking only because you saw Rick Devens more, you formed more of a relationship with Rick Devens. And I love Rick Devens, too. I would have loved to have seen a final two and those two go head-to-head."
>
> **—Helen Glover, May 30, 2019**

ADAM PLAYS THE PODIUM IDOL

(*Winners at War*, April 8, 2020)

We don't know when an era ends until a new one sneaks up on us. The players themselves on *Winners at War* didn't realize they were fighting the final battle of the Old Era. Adam Klein would always find himself on the bottom, often due to his own shenanigans backfiring. While he'd always manage to weasel his way out of trouble, it seemed to be the end of the line for him. But Adam had one more trick up his sleeve. He had noticed a fleur-de-lis on Jeff's podium at tribal—a similar design to the idols' that season. Now actually . . . that was just the art direction that season. But, being a creative player, and remembering that Palesa Tau took an idol from the tribal council podium in the sixth season of the South African version of *Survivor*, Adam decided his last stand was literally trying to play Jeff's podium as an idol.

It sadly didn't work, and Adam became the second player post-merge to be sent to the Edge of Extinction. The moment itself, from Adam standing up, to how long he tried to get the fleur-de-lis, to the back and forth with Jeff about it, was presented similarly to Jacket-Gate. The editors really let us painfully sit in the awkwardness. The difference was, despite it not working out, Adam became the poster child of the idea that anything is "worth a shot." And as funny as it was back then, was Adam really so ridiculous? Or was he just ahead of his time? Was he not just on the wavelength of what was ahead, where players had to publicly declare that trees looked like broccoli or use the tribe fire to melt their idol out of a wax totem? Adam Klein was the first casualty of the dangerous fun that was yet to come.

The New Era

Seasons 41 and Beyond

After taking a hiatus for Covid, *Survivor* returned with the New Era, defined by a shortened twenty-six-day game and balanced out with the tribes receiving less food and supplies. Jeff defines the era with a new brand of "dangerous fun," where players are hit with expedited gameplay and extreme experimental twists.

ERIKA BREAKS THE HOURGLASS

(41, October 27 and November 3, 2021)

The biggest twist of the New Era, and the most hated twist in the history of the show, came in the form of an hourglass. What used to be the merge has now become the "earn the merge" stage (colloquially known as "mergatory"). If you aren't already familiar, try to follow me here. The final twelve were combined into one tribe (but not merged!) and then split into two groups of five to compete in a challenge, with two players sitting out. The team of five that won would get their merge buff and officially be merged, allowing them to choose one of the two sit-outs to bring into the merge with them. These six would gain immunity, leaving the other five vulnerable to be voted out. And then the second sit-out that wasn't picked would be sent out to exile. Still following me? This exiled player ended up being Erika Casupanan, a purpled (and purple-haired) character we barely saw on the show. But here in exile, she was presented with an hourglass, a small hammer, and a twist to permanently change the game. Should she break the hourglass with the hammer, she would change the course of history and strip immunity from the winning six, giving it to the vulnerable six. She, of course, smashed the hourglass, resulting in Sydney Segal, who thought she had made the merge, going home. This did not go well with the audience, probably resulting in a 0 percent approval rating all around. It didn't sit well with the players, either. Danny McCray, who was part of the originally immune six and formerly a player on the Dallas Cowboys, actually reamed out Jeff over this. It's not a "twist," he

> "*Edge of Extinction* twist, not so bad now, huh? You know, I was joking with people that the twist, you know, 'it's not a merge, it's going to be them coming back from the *Edge of Extinction*' and everyone's like, groan, groan. And now they're like, 'I wish. If we could have Brad or JD back instead of this hourglass . . . ' It's still the greatest show, but, like, every week, I think all of us are just going, 'There can't be more. Like, there can't be more, right?' And there is. There just is. . . . I always think of *Project Runway*, like Tim Gunn, who I love, when he talks about accessorizing, he's like, put everything on and then take one thing off. And I feel like *Survivor* this season, they spent the whole quarantine making accessories, and then they just, like, kind of threw them all on there."
>
> **—Rick Devens, October 30, 2021**

argued, it's a straight up lie. It's just production lying to you when they say you have immunity. This was one of the few times where Jeff and production listened and they abandoned the hourglass twist (after trying a variation of it again in *42*).

To Erika's credit, she did play the hourglass perfectly, but this has always been a black stain on her win and the season as a whole. The tribal where Sydney goes home is actually exciting—that's when Liana plays her Knowledge is Power to try to steal Xander's idol but he gives her a fake*—and I think what soured everyone most on it, even more than they already were, is that they aired this as a two-part special. One week ended with the big cliffhanger

* What an insane sentence to read if you're a *Survivor* fan time traveling from the past with your own hourglass.

of "will Erika break the hourglass or not?" leaving us with a full, miserable week to wonder if she'd give herself immunity or let herself be vulnerable to be voted out. A minor complaint I've always had was that when Erika asked Jeff how much time she had to decide, he told her she had until tomorrow morning. Hey Jeff, you've got an hourglass prop right there! Turn it over!

KALEB HITS THE SHOT IN THE DARK

(*45*, November 1, 2023)

The Shot in the Dark isn't a successful twist because of how often it works; it's successful because of the *threat* of it working. If any player, at any time, can pull a Hail Mary, trade in their vote, and get a 16.67 percent chance at immunity . . . well, you'd better make sure their vote-out is a blindside! No more, "Hey, sorry, it's going to be you tonight." Every vote needed to be a big surprise. It was played a few times on seasons 41 through 43, but it never panned out. In season 44, Jaime successfully earned safety after playing her Shot in the Dark, but no one was voting for her anyway. Then came *45* where the Shot in the Dark destiny was truly fulfilled. Kaleb Gebrewold seemed to be in a great position: As a charming, personable guy, he was well liked by everyone. Then suddenly, at mergatory, everyone at once realized that everyone else liked Kaleb, too. Kaleb instantly went from being the most insulated to the number one target on the board. Sensing danger afoot, Kaleb used his Shot in the Dark to trade in his vote for one of the six scrolls. All the other eleven votes went on him, but when Jeff opened the scroll, it was . . . "SAFE!" Kaleb was immune, canceling out eleven votes and breaking Kelley Wentworth's record. We were lucky enough to be doing a live show at the Brea Improv for this episode. It was a sold-out show, a real rowdy, packed crowd of like 450 people. And when that Shot in the Dark hit, it was pandemonium. The room exploded, strangers were hugging, waiters who didn't even watch the show were high-fiving. Everyone went so berserk that it was frankly a little rude to J. Maya, the player who ended up going home, who also happened to be in attendance. Did this change the trajectory of the season? Not really; Kaleb was unceremoniously voted out the following round. But damn, was it fun when it happened.

LIZ DOESN'T GET APPLEBEE'S

(46, May 1, 2024)

A key feature of the New Era has been casting a lot of superfans. You can't recruit people out of gas stations anymore if you expect them to already be well versed in the nuanced strategy of how to delicately handle beware advantages. Fortunately for fans of big characters, *46* managed to smuggle in a bunch of wackadoos. From Jelinsky to Bhanu to Q, this was shaping up to be the *Gabon* of the New Era. Liz Wilcox was flying a bit under the radar, mostly with her strategy of pretending to be a millionaire in order to get taken to the end as a beatable goat. Things changed on Day 18 when the reward challenge was sponsored by Applebee's. Now, I like eating good in the neighborhood as much as the next guy, but something about Applebee's hits different when you're in Fiji. I understand craving the chicken fajita roll-up or the artichoke dip when you're starving, but on *Island of the Idols*, Karishma referred to Applebee's as her favorite sit-down restaurant.* Liz takes this Applebee's obsession to the next level. She unfortunately has a lot of food allergies, leaving her basically unable to eat anything but rice—which became a major problem when her tribe didn't have any. But despite all the foods her body has difficulty with, she is able to eat the Bourbon Street Mushroom Swiss Burger from Applebee's. On top of this, she has an incredible personal connection to Applebee's, with the tradition of taking her daughter there every Wednesday night to dine and watch *Survivor*.

> "Oh, I would *love* to go to Applebee's!"
> —Tina Wesson, June 4, 2024

Q was the first to finish the sandbag obstacle course, and he was allowed to bring three others with him to feast on Applebee's at the *Survivor* sanctuary. Unfortunately for Liz, despite her pleading, Q went with Kenzie, Maria, and Tiffany. This resulted in one of the most incredible *Survivor* meltdowns. "I'm pissed!" Liz erupts, before

* Implying that she prefers a fast-food one overall.

going on an explosive diatribe* about how Q messed up her game.

This whole time, Q keeps a straight face, reminding her that he doesn't owe her anything, as she had voted for him the night prior. This wasn't included in the edit, but we've since heard that both Kenzie and Maria offered to give up their spot, but Q shut it down. Eventually, Liz calms down, lets everyone know she feels better and appreciates the space to vent. Even though Liz lets it go (and actually ends up working with Q on the next vote), the fan base never will. Liz's tantrum was not only inadvertently the best advertising Applebee's could've hoped for, but also the most memorable moment of the New Era so far, proving that no matter how many evolutions the series goes through, the core of the franchise will always be human psychology. You can throw all sorts of twists and turns into the game, but what resonates the strongest is something that goes back to the early days of the show . . . somebody upset with somebody else for being left out of a reward.

The great tag on this debacle is in the following episode, when Maria wins a food reward; instead of taking Liz out of pity, she makes Liz and Q play rock-paper-scissors for it. Q goes paper, Liz goes rock.

OPERATION: ITALY

(47, December 4, 2024)

Operation: Italy continued a lucky streak I've had of the more exciting episodes coinciding with *RHAP* live shows. We were doing a show in Houston, Texas, for this one and it was an incredible blast to watch with a huge crowd. This was like *Ocean's 11*—well, more like *Andy's 3*: an episode structured around the underdogs pulling off an incredible heist. Similar to the Liz Wilcox Applebee's situation, Andy'd had a bit of a meltdown in the very first episode of the season. So even though he found himself in

* Would be a great monologue for an actor to use in their auditions.

an alliance of five at the final seven, he had enough social awareness to realize that he may not have enough cache with the jury. Meanwhile, top dogs Sam and Genevieve were now on the bottom. But when Sam won an Italian reward and brought Andy and Genevieve with him, Andy presented the underdogs with their only lifeline. The plan was rather simple: The majority five might be splitting their votes 3-2 on Sam and Genevieve, so if Andy swung over to their side, the votes would end up being 3-2-2 and they could send someone from the majority home. In execution, though, nearly anything could go wrong, and their plan could easily get sniffed out. However, with great social plays and some bluffing with a fake idol, they made the seemingly impossible possible. Their original target and eventual winner of the season, Rachel, won immunity, so they were forced to switch their plan over to Caroline. It didn't have quite the same impact on the season as a Rachel vote-out would've, but it was still a thrill and proved that, even in the trinket-and-luck-heavy era, interesting social and strategic gameplay can still emerge and win the day.

> "But it's like, so many people, too, in the New Era, where it's like, I gotta be under the radar . . . it's so boring to watch. So I appreciate, like, when stuff actually happens. . . . I like people eventually turning on their alliances. . . . I'll be real because I'm an emotional person and I watch for different reasons, and it's the truth, I like watching crazy and I like watching chaos."
>
> **—Carolyn Wiger, November 22, 2024**

I couldn't name more than ten people I went to high school with. And don't ask me the names of my kids' teachers. But I can recall these, and a thousand more *Survivor* moments, more vividly than I can memories from my own life. As long as the show keeps giving players room to maneuver, I'm sure they'll never cease to find ways to surprise us. I can't wait to see which iconic moment from *50* will push the Mets 2000 World Series roster out of my skull.

SIMMOTION
R.H.A.P.
R.H.A.P.
R.H.A.P.

CHAPTER 6

You've Got the Million-Dollar Check Written Already

The Ultimate *Survivor* Playbook

In *Caramoan*, at the tribal council where Corinne Kaplan was blindsided, she appropriately and ironically said, "Everybody's got a plan . . . until you get punched in the face." She was quoting Brett Clouser. Or maybe it was Mike Tyson, I always mix the two up. But whether it was said by the youngest heavyweight champion of the world or the youngest member of the Galu tribe of *Survivor: Samoa*, the point still stands. Everyone has a plan going into a season of *Survivor* until they get punched in the face . . . or knocked off a barge. Corinne had a good plan going into that tribal, but Dawn and Cochran ended up punching her in the face.

If there was only one "correct" way to play *Survivor*, it would be a rather boring show. We'd know what to expect and who would win every single time. Fortunately, it's a messy game with unexpected twists and even more unexpected choices made by fallible human players. In order to win, you need not only grit and cleverness but a whole lot of luck. Luck, however, as spoken-word artist Semhar once said, is when preparation meets opportunity. Or maybe that was Roman philosopher Seneca? Regardless of who said it, it's true. You can't account for every circumstance—but it never hurts to be a little prepared.

⚠ WARNING: NO REFUNDS ⚠

The second your gut tells you otherwise, trust your gut over me. I don't need you yelling on the podcast that my book sank your game. Plus, my publisher told me there's no special refund policy if my book's advice gets you kicked off the show.

Getting on the Show

Before you get a chance to make a fool of yourself in Fiji,* you'll first have to get *invited* to Fiji. That starts with your casting video. Over the years, I've watched a lot of tapes, and let me tell you, most videos—and I say this with love—are very bad. But here are a few ways to make them less bad:

Show your personality. Be yourself. This is cliche, but it's true. "Huge fan of *Survivor*" is not a personality.† Yes, they're looking for superfans, but be sure to highlight who you are outside of your obsession with this TV show. If you're naturally funny, be funny. If you're naturally a lunatic, go off.

* Or maybe win!

† Unlike "podcaster of *Survivor*," which is.

Show, don't tell. Don't just tell us you constantly manipulate your boss at work, give examples of *how* you manipulate your boss. Describe *how* you get that barista to give you a free coffee. Go into great detail about *how* you were able to smuggle drugs and contraband into this country.*

Off the cuff is better than overprepared. It's always going to feel better if the video comes across as, "Hey, I'm at work right now, but I have a few minutes to tell you about myself," rather than too scripted and rehearsed. Think of this video as a pilot for your confessionals out on the island—they wanna see if the way you naturally speak can hold the attention of the viewer.

Tell us your superpower (and kryptonite). Get specific. What unique skill do you have that you'll use to cut through the game? Which former players do you think you'll play like? But also tell us your weaknesses. They aren't just casting players they can see winning; they want flawed humans who can make fun mistakes out there.

> "I read in a book somewhere that it said, whatever you do, be memorable. . . . So before I flew to LA, I bought a red Speedo that was like two sizes too small. And every day at pool time, I'd go out to the pool wearing this red Speedo with about three inches of my crack showing. . . . And I get up on the diving board with my red Speedo and start stretching and doing yoga poses and stuff. And I look up at the hotel and there's like people on the eighth floor with their walkie-talkies. . . . And I'd see curtains being pulled, and they'd be looking, and I pretended to be oblivious to it and just continue my stretching. And yeah, a couple days later, meeting with Probst and Mark, they said, 'Did you really wear a red Speedo to the pool?' And I said, 'Yeah, I don't know, I just put on one of my swimsuits. Not sure what color.' Just playing dumb. Anyway, I owned them."
>
> **—Randy Bailey, August 8, 2020**

* This book is not legal advice.

Why now? What are you currently wrestling with in your life that *Survivor* will help you accomplish? It used to be that producers only cast people that were interesting. They never asked, "What makes Jonny Fairplay an asshole?" but just presented an asshole for the others to contend with. Now, they are looking for people with a built-in story. They want eighteen protagonists who are there for the right reasons.

No fancy video editing necessary. Nobody will be impressed by your cutting abilities so leave the bells and whistles for the *Survivor* editing department (you'll never top the "Genevieve thinking about blindsiding Kishan" sequence anyway).

Forget friends and family. No need to have your co-worker or your wife talk about why you'll be great (or a disaster). They're not going to be the ones on the show. . . . especially since they don't have the loved ones visits anymore.

Keep it short.

Prepping for the Show

Congratulations, you've been cast on *Survivor: 58*! Now, the real work begins. You probably have a few months (or maybe over a year if you're an alternate who gets bumped to the next season) so get to work.

Learn to make fire. We're fifty seasons in; I shouldn't need to tell you that in this game, fire doesn't just represent your life, it is literally used for warmth and to cook your meals. Not to mention, there's now a mandatory fire-making challenge every season.* You wanna end up like Sam in 47? Sure, he got extremely lucky with the wind, but he was the first to admit it's completely insane he came out there unprepared to make fire. Go find a safe place to practice, get some flint, get some husk, get a knife,† and get to striking.

* Unless that vote goes your way . . .

† You might use a machete around camp, but, at final four, you get a knife.

Hit the gym. If you're already a gym rat, great. Otherwise, you don't need to get swole, you don't need to take steroids, but you don't want to get voted out first because you were the least helpful at pushing something heavy during a challenge. Don't skip leg day and definitely don't skip any yoga or Pilates classes for the endurance and balance challenges that happen later in the game.

Hit the water. If you've never learned to swim, there's no time better than right now. And if you do know how to swim, find a pool to regularly do laps in. You don't need to be a human dolphin like Ozzy, but you might not have Jonathan Young on your tribe to single-handedly pull you through the ocean.

Work on your grip strength. Charlie Davis had the brilliant insight that grip strength is a highly underrated skill for the challenges. Doesn't matter how strong your arms are if your sweaty hands can't hold on to the end of a rope. Buy a couple of those hand-grip-exercise-thingies and start squeezing while you do the following step:

Watch and rewatch a lot of *Survivor*. Pay extra close attention to what players do right or wrong. Sorry for the shameless cross-promotion, but you can listen to a lot of in-depth postgame interviews on RobHasAWebsite.com/PostSeason for all the small minutiae that made an impact on the game but were too complicated to make the edited show.* When you run out of all of those, watch any other social strategy show—*Big Brother, The Circle,* hell, even *Million Dollar Secret*. Who knows where gameplay inspiration might strike you.

Study the puzzles. Start obsessively playing with a slide puzzle app on your phone. Order some makeshift *Survivor* puzzles. The show almost always has the same type of hanging jigsaw puzzle. A quick YouTube search will also get you on your way to strategies for solving the complex puzzles, such as the one where you have to stack four multicolored cubes without duplicating any colors on any side—I guess the trick is to first look for opposite sides on the cubes that have the same color? I don't know. You're the one going out there, you figure it out.

* Or this book!

Go in a little heavy. I know you're about to be shirtless on national television, but when dealing with starvation, you're probably better off carrying a few extra pounds than showing off those perfect abs. Conversely, if you consume *a lot* of daily calories, now might be the best time to cut down and start preparing your body for an unexpected number of calories at unexpected times of day.

Read some Robert Greene. *The 48 Laws of Power*, *The Art of Seduction*, *Mastery*—you won't go wrong reading some of Robert Greene's work (or listening to an audiobook version while hitting the gym). I know most of this list is how to brace yourself physically, but the real work is preparing yourself mentally for war. Additionally, you'll definitely want to check out Dale Carnegie's classic *How to Win Friends and Influence People* and FBI hostage negotiator Chris Voss's book *Never Split the Difference* to learn about his negotiation approach of "tactical empathy."

Ask your friends and family about yourself. Find out if you naturally come across as trustworthy, annoying, sneaky, smart, stupid, whatever. If you have people in your life willing to be truthful and give you tough-love feedback, being self-aware about how others see you could prove very useful when you're on *Survivor*.

Build a game plan around your strong suits. If you're already fit, work on your balance. If you're already social, bulk up a little. You can only do so much, so find the right combo of supercharging your superpower and shoring up your weak points.

Pre-Game Ponderosa

So you've made it to Ponderosa, the hotel where they hold you before and after the game. You'll see the rest of your cast, but no one is allowed to speak to one another until the show officially starts. When you can't speak, everything is amplified. Others will read into what you're wearing, what you're doing, and especially what you're reading. That means don't whip out *The 48 Laws of Power* in public. Also, journal in private. Nobody likes it when it looks like you're taking notes on them.

Be friendly but not too friendly. Kaleb in *45* apparently entered the game a massive threat because he was seen as making too much eye contact, trying to get on everyone's good side. And while you'll naturally start to prejudge people, make sure you remain open-minded. Don't rule out working with someone just because they're wearing a Yankees jersey (although I might).

The Opening Mat Chat

You've been applying to the show for years, spent months bulking up and crunching puzzles, and were quarantined in silence for days—now it's time to go live. All the cameras and microphones are on and the real-life Jeff Probst is asking you questions. You're more than ready to explode. But please do not explode.

The only thing to remember about this opening mat chat is that you cannot win the game here—but you can certainly screw it up. All you need to say is you're excited to be there and you love your entire group. *That's it.* Just answer Jeff's questions and shut your mouth, homie g. You don't want any heat on yourself.

Christine Markowski and Francesca Hogi didn't make it far past the mat after speaking out about Coach and Boston Rob, respectively. Domenick Abbate and financial analyst Emily Flippen fared a little better after their initial mat chat mishaps, but *Survivor*'s hard enough—why add to your problems?

Although if you end up winning, they'll almost definitely show whatever you say here, so try to say at least one memorable thing.

First Days on the Beach

All right, you were perfectly pleasant on the mat, you got your tribe, you're at your beach. Now the real work begins.

Prioritize shelter, fire, and food, in that order. Night is coming. You need a bed. Pray that it won't rain. When you've got a shelter, then you can focus on starting a fire for warmth. Only then can you finally scrounge around for some coconuts.

Build your shelter off the ground. You definitely do not want to sleep on the damn ground, man. There's lots of creepy crawlies out there and you don't need them crawling all over you when you're trying to sleep.

Match the vibe of your tribe. If you're on a tribe of workers, work. If you're on a tribe of slackers, slack. If people are talking a lot of game, talk a lot of game. And if they aren't, zip it. Don't be the one standing out.

Don't be bossy (even if you're right). Everyone is there to have an adventure, not to be yelled at by their mom to clean up their room. Players that come across as bossy don't tend to do well—rewatch my season and see how it goes for Roger.

Do not isolate. Especially if they return to bigger tribes, don't be going off with just the three of you. Always be part of the bigger group.

Do not go on a journey. You do not want to get on that boat and be carted off to Shipwheel Island. Not only will you paint a target on your back as someone who might have an advantage, but you'll also miss some prime socializing time in a fast-paced game.

Focus on relationships, not alliances. Have conversations. Open up about yourself, but be sure to ask others about themselves, too. It will be easier to build alliances with people you genuinely connect with. When you find the people you feel best about, there's no need to be the first to throw out names; just gently open the door with soft alliance questions. "Are you feeling how I'm feeling?," "Am I crazy or should we maybe consider working together?"

But if you haven't been asked to be in any four-person alliance by Day 3, you might need to **pursue an alliance a bit more aggressively** before it's too late.

Say yes to everything and everyone. Yes, you love that idea. Yes, you want to work together. Yes, you also think you should bring Jane Doe into your alliance. Yes, of course Jane Doe should be the next to go. You wanna come across as agreeable. If Sai sits you down and wants to work together, do you really want to come off as wishy-washy?

Look for the idol without looking like you're looking for the idol. Everything you're doing—collecting bamboo, gathering firewood—is done against the backdrop of looking for the hidden immunity idol. You definitely *do not* want to be spotted idol hunting,* but when you're going to the well to fill up canteens . . . keep your eyes open, turn over a few rocks, stick your hand in some tree trunks.

Giving Confessionals

There's no real trick to being great at confessionals. Either you have the gift of gab or you don't. Since you've been cast on the show, it's safe to assume someone saw a video of you talking to the camera and wanted to put that on TV, so you must have something going for you. No need to overthink anything; just tell your story and have fun. If it's in your personality to tell it in a colorful way, by all means do.

⚠ WARNING ⚠

Be careful when you say something akin to "I feel safe tonight." You might say that in a dozen confessionals they never use, but the second you're blindsided, believe me, they'll drop that clip into the editing timeline before Jeff has even snuffed your torch.

* Counterpoint, on small tribes, having an idol kind of makes you bulletproof. So maybe who cares if anyone catches you looking . . . as long as you actually find it!

> "Everyone on *Survivor* thinks that all of their confessionals are going to be shown. They're like, 'I can't believe they didn't talk about that time that I was in sixth grade and talked about this.' Everyone thinks all of their confessionals are gold, everyone thinks they're the main character. But yeah, maybe that is a meta strategy. People in the future, players should be like, 'I want to be in an alliance with like the two more soft-spoken people and not the two wacky people because they're going to overshadow me.'"
>
> **—Gabby Pascuzzi, March 8, 2023**

You don't have to be funnier or more confident than you are, but if you don't want to risk getting purpled by production, you need to be as authentic as you are. You have to be both emotionally honest and literally honest. Lie all you want to the other players, but not to the audience watching at home. We fans will forgive a lot of things, but we won't forgive you trying to trick us.

OVERUSED CONFESSIONAL LINES TO AVOID

- ✕ "I don't trust them as far as I can throw them!"
- ✕ "Anything can happen tonight at tribal!"
- ✕ "We need to cut the head off the snake!"

★ BONUS POINTS ★

If you've read this book and are out there giving confessionals . . . see if you can slip in the phrase "Houston, we have multiple problems!" as a code to signal to me that I can take full credit for how well/poorly you end up doing.

How to Lie

If we really break down what "playing the game" entails, it's like 3 percent carnival-type games where you try to roll a little ball through a snake maze and 97 percent lying to people's faces with the intention of crushing all of their hopes and dreams.

Don't lie if you can avoid it. Even in the real world, unless you're a sociopath who doesn't need to read about "How to Lie" to begin with, lying can be incredibly taxing. Think about budgeting your emotional energy. Lying is going to burn calories and you are already in short supply there. If you lie about a million stupid things, you'll spend the whole game trying to keep those lies up!

Small lies are better than big lies. How many shocking big lies do you remember truly working on *Survivor*? The dead grandma lie?* The best players plant seeds, telling little lies that subtly influence others. Even better, make sure to mix truths in with your lie. Don't make up a conversation you had with someone—distort it. Brew a little half-truth concoction that'll make it incredibly difficult for someone to deny. Once you've built enough trust with people, you can probably get away with one big lie.

Lies of omission are probably better than making something up. Other players are sharp and are looking to poke holes in your story. Can't poke a hole in nothing, though.

Be specific but not too specific. You don't want to be too vague because then it seems like you're making up something you haven't thought through, but you don't want to give too many unnecessary details because then it seems like you're over-selling a made-up story.

Make yourself look bad. When telling a fake story, paint yourself (a little) unfavorably in it. If that was a lie, why would you include the embarrassing part where you got diarrhea? If you acknowledge something where you don't look good, like

* And even that mostly got him one reward challenge win.

maybe you were planning to steal something but got scared and overheard something you shouldn't have . . . it could be more plausible because you admitted something (slightly) damning about yourself, as well.

Commit to the lie. Once you've decided to lie, stick with it. That's your story. As George Costanza would say, it's not a lie if you believe it.* If you're Amanda Kimmel of *Survivor: China*, *Survivor: Micronesia—Fans vs. Favorites*, and *Survivor: Heroes vs. Villains* fame, and you decide you're going to lie to your former friend Parvati and tell her that she needs to play the idol on herself . . . convince her that she needs to play the idol on herself! Swear to God, on your family, whatever you have to do. What you don't want to do is stammer around uncommitted to the point where Parvati sees right through you and ends your entire game.

THE FAKE PLAN

For every real plan you put together, you'd better have a fake plan or two ready to go. You can't say you haven't thought about it when your target asks you who you're voting for. Of course you've thought about it. It's all anyone's thinking about!

Creating a fake plan is a very delicate matter, because odds are, the fake name you're floating around as the person to be voted out will catch wind of it and, odds are, they won't love it! In *Blood vs. Water*, Brad Culpepper suggested voting out Caleb to Ciera—and it didn't matter that he was lying to Ciera's face, once Caleb heard Brad saying his name, he flipped on Brad faster than Marissa could say, "F— you, Brad Culpepper!" So before you put any names out there, you first need to do a calculation to judge who can handle it. If one of your allies is a volatile personality, probably best not to use that name. Or at the very least, don't let it be traced back to you. Pro tip: Always blame the person you want to vote out as the one who threw the name out.

* While George would naturally be a first boot on any season, I do believe he could actually win the game if he did the opposite of all of his instincts. "My name is George, I don't have a vote, and I'm lying to everyone."

But what happens when you hear that your name is the fake name going around? Well, try not to immediately panic. Seeming unstable to your allies could mold that fake plan into a real one. Then, do a vibe check. What are the odds this fake plan is real? How many people actually believe they should be writing your name down? What are the odds the real target has an idol? If allegedly only the target is writing your name down, you can always offset that by throwing your vote on someone else, like Devon saving his butt by throwing a rogue vote on Dr. Mike at the final five of *HHH*.

> "And the worst part of that is when you're at camp and you're with the person you're working with and the person that you're not working with, but you've got to speak to the person you're not working with, and then you're wondering, well, is this person now thinking that I'm really doing that? And you feel like you have to reconnect and reset up the plan. It's a stressful game."
>
> —David Wright, March 29, 2017

But even if your name *is* just the fake plan, this is a bad sign. Clearly, you lack social capital right now if people aren't afraid to throw your name around. Again, don't panic, but perform an audit on how you can improve things. Lastly, never suggest your own name for the fake plan. There's situations where you become the fake plan and there's nothing you can do about it, but I would never co-sign you originating that idea. I don't care if you're on the outs and trying to build some trust; once your name is out there, it'll reinforce how disposable you are.

WHAT IF I FEEL BAD LYING?

While you may fantasize about going on *Survivor* and cutting through people left and right, you're fantasizing about cutting through faceless avatars. Once you get out there, they'll suddenly get faces and names, and you'll learn about their families and children and passions and favorite Pokémon and, before you know it, you like them! So if you feel bad lying to their faces . . . good, it means you're human. Just remind yourself that lying (and getting lied to) is the price of doing business. Try to remember who you're coming home to. Imagine explaining to your husband or wife or co-workers or dog that you're returning without a million dollars because you felt bad lying to someone you've known for two weeks.

SHOULD I LIE ABOUT MY JOB?

Everyone seems especially scared to admit that they're either a lawyer or a cop. But here's the rub: There's no job that inherently makes you great at *Survivor*. Some police officers have done well; others, not so much. Poker players always seem like a threat, but they often end up flopping. If you still really feel the need to hide your profession, go for it. But at least change it to something that is close to what you do, like Domenick saying he worked in construction while not admitting he was actually a construction supervisor.*

Counterpoint, be like *Nicaragua*'s Marty Piombo and claim to be a chess grandmaster. Why not?

> “I said something to the effect of, 'Yeah, I think we got the votes, I think someone told Liz and Kenzie,' so it was intentionally a shaky answer to make her feel like, you know, I didn't actually have the votes . . . but it was also sort of a test. . . . If she was actually voting Q, she would be alarmed by my answer because she'd be like, 'Whoa, we don't have the votes.' And then I gave a wicked look to the camera because I knew at that point that it was Maria and Q writing my name.”
>
> **—Charlie Davis, June 15, 2024**

* As if someone would be incredibly threatened by a supervisor. “We gotta get Dom out, he might not approve our vacation days!”

HOW CAN I TELL IF SOMEONE IS LYING TO ME?

Of course, the flipside of running around and lying to everyone is that some of those people might be lying back to you. Those bastards, how dare they?! Here's a few things to consider if you're suspicious that someone has the unmitigated gall to try to deceive you:

Is their story inconsistent? Does their story change when you hear it again? Do they tell different people different versions?

Do they not want to talk about it? When people lie, they tend to be cagey; they want to change the subject and move on to the next thing. If they avoid you completely or you've noticed any shift in your relationship, take that as a real bad sign.

Are they pandering? When you talk to them, are they actually contributing to the conversation or are they just saying yes to get you off their back? If someone truly wants to work with you, they'll push back on bad ideas. Suggest a terrible alliance name. If they say, "Yeah, sure, okay," and walk off, maybe they don't actually intend to work with you. But if they are serious about an alliance with you, they might say something like, "No, I don't want to call our alliance the Foot Fetish Five."

How to Act at Tribal Council

All the hard work you're putting into the game culminates into voting somebody out. But before you get to write someone's name, you'll still have to participate in the tense, sacred ritual of tribal council.

ARRIVING

The first time your tribe shows up at tribal council, you must dip your torch in the flame and place it into a little hole behind where you sit. Jeff is going to remind you so I'm not even sure why I included this part in the book. But if you're having trouble placing it into the little hole, see if Ben is around to help you.

TALKING TO JEFF

An unfortunate important part of tribal council is answering Jeff's questions. You're there playing a game; he's there making a TV show. If you try to punt on any questions, Jeff's going to keep badgering you until you give him something he likes. Similar to the mat chat, you won't be able to win the game here, but you can certainly lose it. But just because you have to answer Jeff's questions, doesn't mean you have to tell him the truth, the whole truth, and nothing but the truth . . .

Keep your stories straight. Tribal council is theater. And the performance you'll have to pull off is a delicate high-wire act. You can't tell Jeff exactly what you're planning because you want it to be a surprise to the person you're voting out; they might have an idol and they definitely have a Shot in the Dark. So stick to answering as if your reality is the fake reality you agreed upon with the person you're betraying. But when you do agree on a fake plan with the person who thinks it's a real plan, you might also agree to put up a fake charade at tribal council. So you also have to make sure your real allies know ahead of time what you're actually going to do, what you're going to be pretending to do, and what they should be doing and pretending to do, as well.

Confusing? Yeah, good luck. Just stick to the plan and you should be fine. But maybe don't announce you're sticking to the plan to the players no one else knows you're secretly working with. If you're stuck and don't want to answer what's being asked, try the following to get Jeff to say "wow" and move on to someone else:

Keep it vague and general. You're "balancing thinking about your short game and your long game." You're "trying to figure out who you can trust." Say stuff that is technically true yet reveals nothing.

Compliment the show. You "weren't expecting how tricky and complicated it would be to play *Survivor*." It's "so much harder than it seems on TV." All the new twists are "so cool and add an incredible layer of complexity." Watch Jeff beam as you sell how much you love the show.

Lean on your personal growth. Scheming on *Survivor* is "pushing you out of your comfort zone and helping you come out of your shell." Let's not worry about who you're scheming with or against, Jeff, let's worry about getting that inspirational music playing under me as I come out of my shell.

Drop a metaphor.* A metaphor on *Survivor* is like a Picasso painting. It may be aesthetically pleasing, but the closer you look at one, the less sense it actually makes. Nothing will please Jeff more than an appropriate metaphor about how looking for an alliance is like choosing which table to sit at in the high school cafeteria or that people taking turns steering a vote is like taking turns driving a car. You can take Ryan Ulrich's birthday party metaphor and hang it in a museum next to *Guernica.*

> "Jeff did ask me for a metaphor during one of the tribal councils and I literally said I can't give you one because I'm not that quick-witted. And anyone that is that quick-witted is such a red flag."
>
> **—Emily Flippen, April 9, 2025**

If your season happens to have a theme, reference it. If you're on *Real Estate Agents vs. Scuba Instructors*, get ready to talk about how you're trying to close deals or not come up too fast for air.

SHOULD I GET UP AND START A LIVE TRIBAL?

General rule of thumb is that if you're in power, you want things to stay the course. But if you're in trouble, all chaos helps you. So if you're really worried about getting sent home, why not get up, start whispering, and try to shake things up? Odds are you won't be able to change the vote, but who knows? Rick Devens didn't go from being a passenger to a pilot by sitting silently with his seat belt on and his tray table up.

* Most of what is referred to as a "metaphor" on *Survivor* is technically a "simile" or an "analogy," but another piece of advice for winning the game is to not go around correcting people's grammar.

WHAT DO I DO IF A LIVE TRIBAL STARTS AROUND ME?

If a live tribal breaks out and everyone jumps up and starts having little side conversations . . . don't be a bump on a log, join them! Do your best to keep up with what's going on, trust your allies, and definitely pitch a name hard if you're hearing your own. If you've been sitting on a juicy piece of pertinent information (like someone told you something they shouldn't have about someone else having an idol), a live tribal might be just the time to reveal that piece of information.

SHOULD I SIT IN JEFF'S CHAIR?

Probably not. If he even offers, it might not be a great sign for your chances of surviving tribal.

VOTING CONFESSIONAL

"The fact that you're a nuclear engineer is genuinely, genuinely scary." "Put the pen down, bro. Use an eraser." "You are a 100 percent, grade-A dirt-squirrel." This is your chance to drop an iconic line, don't squander the opportunity!

Never forget that the following legendary voting confessionals all came from the *same* tribal council in *Survivor: Gabon*:

"This vote is not strategic, it's strictly personal."

"You are a disgusting, old, hot-headed, chauvinistic, alcoholic bigot, and you need to grow up before you die alone . . . loser!"

"You have made my life hell from day one! Forget you, go home, goodbye!"

This is what you're aiming for! Crystal Cox isn't just a gold-medal-winning Olympian, she is the gold standard of how you want to be in the voting booth.

IF YOU'RE BLINDSIDED . . .

As much as you don't want to believe it, it might be time for you to go. It sucks, but there's not much you can do but express your genuine reaction. Don't do a bit, don't do a De Niro impression. If you're mad, be mad. If you're heartbroken, be heartbroken. If you think the rest of your tribemates are scumbags and you hope they all get bitten by a freakin' crocodile, please be sure to vocalize that. You don't need to fake being overly upset, but definitely don't fake being overly okay with it. Who's that fun for? I mean, they just ended your *Survivor* journey—what the hell, guys?!

★ BONUS POINTS ★

There is no real strategic reason to do this and you have to start planning this long before tribal, but if you manage to make it so the real target and the decoy target share the same first letter of their name . . . the editors will love you forever.

The Pre-Merge

The pre-merge is all about finding your footing and setting up the rest of your game. Mistakes you make here might be easily fixable later as you go on to win the game, or might get you instantly voted out, forgotten forever. So it's simultaneously the least and most important part of the game. Good luck.

Gauge trust versus challenge prowess. From the dawn of *Survivor*, the question has been if you should vote based on who does best in challenges or who you trust the most. The most-often correct answer is to prioritize keeping the tribe strong at first and de-prioritize closer to the merge. Focus more on protecting people you want around, but if the Yanu tribe had kept Jelinksy, maybe they could've won several challenges. Instead, they seemed to have made, as Q would say, a big mistake.*

* Though one of them ended up winning a million dollars, so who knows?

Don't worry about final tribal yet. *Survivor* requires planning ahead, while not missing what's right in front of you. It's way too early to worry about your jury speech right now. You can (most likely) change perceptions later, so there's no need to assert yourself as a threat just yet.

Of all the rewards, the tarp is most important. Don't worry about the fishing gear, don't worry about the tool kit; what you want the most is that dang tarp. It doesn't seem that important . . . until the second it starts raining. The rain is the worst part of *Survivor* and I bet I could do a thousand days out there if I was guaranteed no rain. Since you're allowed to trade any rewards won for any of the previous rewards (since when?!), trade anything you get for that tarp.

If you're going to scumbag someone, do it now. I told Ryan Aiken I was voting with him and then I had no problem sending him out the door knowing I wouldn't have to see him again for eight months. Now that the live reunion is gone, you might never see any of these pre-mergers again. So if you got the devil in you and wanna really snake somebody . . . do it before the merge.

DO I NEED A NUMBER ONE?

I've personally never had a ride-or-die, but I've also never won. Finding a super close ally to lean on will generally help you, both strategically and emotionally. Ideally, you'll keep your relationship under wraps like Kyle and Kamilla, rather than painting a double target on both of your backs. In a perfect world, your number one would shield you as a bigger threat so, through no fault of your own, they get taken out by others and then stump for you on the jury.

> "If you go and play *Survivor*, you can have multiple number ones; just like, use slightly different language with all of them so they can't match it up."
>
> **—Genevieve Mushaluk, January 22, 2025**

SHOULD I EVER THROW A CHALLENGE?

Unless you're basically a badass and manipulator of the game, you should probably avoid it. If you really, really think you should throw a challenge, there's an 80 percent chance you still shouldn't. There's so much uncertainty now, especially on smaller tribes with dozens of advantages floating around. So much can quickly go sideways. However, throwing happens more often than we know and often gets left on the cutting room floor.* In *Ghost Island*, the new-new-Naviti lost a challenge on purpose to get rid of Bradley Kleihege, but the typical uncultured audience member who doesn't consume supplemental *Survivor* material probably doesn't know that.

SHOULD I DO AN INTENTIONAL MATSING?

The *un*intentional Matsing is what happened to the Matsing tribe in *Survivor: Philippines*. They lost every single challenge and entered the merge with just Denise and Malcolm remaining. No one considered them as too much of a threat, so they kept slipping by until suddenly Denise was cashing her million-dollar check. Since then, it's been a meme idea floating around to intentionally try to Matsing your own tribe and come into the merge at a much lower threat level.

So should you try it? Absolutely not. Yes, Yam Yam was able to win *44* by entering the merge from the most decimated tribe, but statistically speaking you're better off keeping more people around. However, if it's already happening and you can't win a challenge to save your life, lean into it. You're going to get all the confessionals and be a fan favorite, so play it up and ride that crashing wave.

* In general, they prioritize keeping the tension in who will win the challenge rather than giving us the answer ahead of time (as interesting strategically as it may be to a small number of us).

The Swap

You work so hard, you build lasting alliances, you have a flawless plan on how to get to the end—and now you have to stick your hand into a bag and let your fate be dictated by the color buff you pull. The good news for you is they usually don't swap the tribes anymore. Bad news is, sometimes they do. So brace yourself.

WHAT IF I SWAP FAVORABLY?

Congratulations, you and your original tribemates have swapped into the majority. Now you can lay in your hammock and take a nap. Actually, no—you still have some work ahead of you.

Don't be a jerk. Don't gloat, don't boss people around, and don't try to blackmail someone in the minority to give up their jacket (or fire tokens) in exchange for your vote. You might have the upper hand now, but some of these players in the minority might still be around later on.

Really weigh your options. Before you get antsy and flip on your original tribe, do an honest assessment. If you hadn't swapped and your tribe went back to tribal, who would your target have been? Is this an opportunity to take out somebody you were going to already? Is this an opportunity to forge a new alliance moving forward? Would there be major ramifications from your original tribe if you flipped?

Seriously, don't flip on your allies just because it's fun. Do we love Michaela's "Whaaaaaaaaat?!" in *Millennials vs. Gen X* when she gets savagely blindsided? Do we love Natalia's, "Don't be sorry, shut up. Why are you smiling? Oh my God, I can't handle you right now," in *David vs. Goliath* when she is betrayed? Absolutely. Incredible television. But did Jay or Alec benefit even slightly from those moves? I really can't say that they did.

Maybe, just maybe, you can consider throwing a challenge. I know I said not to, but if there was ever a time for a calculated risk, it would be now. If you're very confident, this could be the golden opportunity to take out a threat from the opposing alliance *and* possibly protect one of your allies on the other side.

Watch out for idols and advantages. Split the vote, don't reveal your real target, and do whatever you can to be safe from whatever hijinks are out there.

WHAT IF I SWAP UNFAVORABLY?

Whoops, you've been swap screwed. Kelley Wentworth, Stephanie Johnson, and the beloved Anna Khait are a few examples of fan favorites who fell here through no real fault of their own. It's not looking good if you're outnumbered by the enemy alliance, but don't lose hope yet.

Ask Jeff if you can re-draw buffs. This has never happened before and is probably not allowed . . . but you never know until you ask.

Don't signal for help to the other tribe. Bubba in *Vanuatu* and Varner in *Cambodia* both got busted signaling for help from their allies on the other side. What can they even do to help you? The only thing they could try is to throw a challenge; don't worry, they'll decide that on their own.

Act as if you've been rescued. I don't care how well you were set up on the other side; if anyone asks, you hated it over there, you hated your tribe, and thank God you're here now. There are some situations where having solid allies on the other side will seem fruitful to those in power,* but, most likely, you want to be helpless and seem pick-up-able. Identify who is in power and appeal to their interests. Carson is a great example of doing this correctly in *44*—everyone wanted to use him for themselves, functionally making him everyone's ally.

* Worked out pretty good for Amber.

Get creative with your advantages. If you haven't shared your idol or advantage with your allies who are now on the bottom with you, it's probably a good time to do it now. Maybe you're not as powerless as you thought. If the majority doesn't have enough to split, you definitely have a great shot of striking correctly with the idol. Just ask Kyle and Kamilla. You may also consider using your idol as a threat to find cracks in the majority. In *Australian Survivor: Brains vs. Brawn*, Brains tribe's Hayley Leake was swapped to a majority Brawn tribe. However, after calmly showing them her idol she was planning on playing for either herself or her fellow Brain, the Brawn tribe instantly crumbled, throwing each other under the bus. She ended up not even playing her idol and made it rather far in the season.

Throw your allies under the bus. At some point, it's just about making it one more day. It doesn't matter if you get along with them; they're not you, therefore, they are more of a threat, have more allies, and are a pain in the ass around camp. Say whatever you gotta say to convince others you're willing to put your ally's name down and vote them out. Just be careful about revealing if your ally has an idol—it might influence them to vote for someone who definitely doesn't have the idol: you.

WHAT IF I SWAP TO AN EVEN SPLIT?

All right, you're like me during *The Amazon* and you've swapped with equal numbers from your tribe and their tribe. Take a beat and assess your situation. Were you on the outs with your old tribe? Is it worth taking a shot at an original tribemate now? Be extra cautious before you let go of one of your own. "I'll give you one of mine if next time you'll give me one of yours" is a great deal for the person who has to give up one of their own second . . . weirdly, they never seem to get around to that part of the deal.

> "In exit interviews, [Tony] would talk about how he'd work with production specifically to make the spy shack work, which is that he would basically, like, make a deal with his producers on the island to say, like, 'Hey, you let me hide in here and don't have a camera on me because that'll blow it, obviously, if there's a camera pointed at a random shrub.' And he would say, 'If you let me do this for a few hours, I will come back with you and get the footage you need.' And that's something that I think for any future *Survivor* players, like work with production in that way; their focus is getting a good show, you know? So, if you want to do these wacky schemes, they will play along with it if they can."
>
> —Zach Wurtenberger, June 12, 2025

Idols and Advantages

Now, I've never played in an era where idols or advantages existed so I may be the wrong person to ask, but here's the info I've gathered about all these dangerous little trinkets floating around out there.

HOW DO I FIND AN IDOL/ADVANTAGE?

You look. A lot. Here's what could help you while looking:

Start with the landmarks. Check any unusual-looking trees or rock formations, anything that really stands out. Put yourself in the shoes of Jeff (or some PA) when he's hiding the idols. What is a place they could put it where that would be memorable enough that they could return to it themselves if they had to?

Employ a breadth-first search. Articulated by Dr. Christian Hubicki on *David vs. Goliath,* it's a simple concept of searching a lot of different places for a little bit, instead of a few places a lot. Cover more ground.

Look for unnatural colors. As Ben taught Denise on *Winners at War,* you want to keep an eye out for colors like blue or purple that don't naturally show up in nature—keep an extra eye out for the color matching your own buff. What you find could be string leading to an idol. Noura on *Island of the Idols* talks about using a "reticular activating system," where if you tell your brain "blue, blue, blue" over and over again, your brain will be better at finding blue. Noura didn't end up finding an idol, but Denise did . . . take from that what you will.

Look for clues in and at every reward. Don't be too obvious about it, but, when you get something like a tool kit, there's going to be a little note slipped in there somewhere. When you all get to pick a seat at a table with fancy folded napkins, someone's going to have something folded in those napkins, so watch everyone carefully.* If you get the kind of reward where you choose the order of who goes to eat first, try to make sure you or your trusted ally goes first . . . then tear the whole place apart looking for the clue.

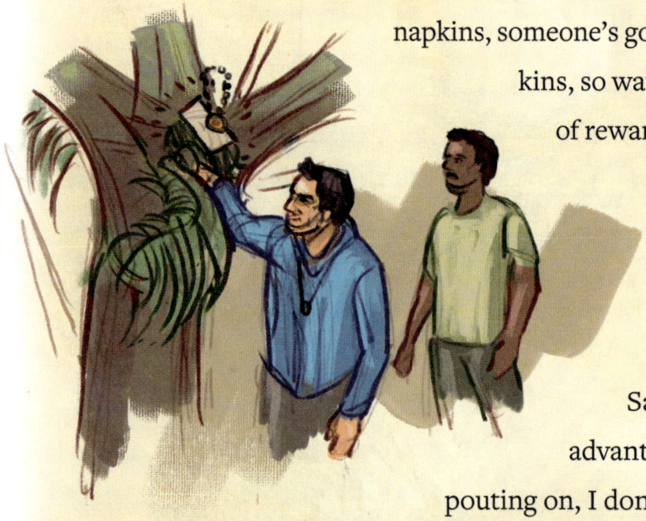

Check under the sit-out bench. After Sarah Lacina so memorably snagged the advantage under the sit-out bench Michaela was pouting on, I don't know how likely it'll be that they'll ever put another one there. But you can always tell who a real superfan is if you see them searching under the sit-out bench while a challenge is happening. Anytime there's a random draw to isolate a person, there could be a clue or something planted there for that person.

* Especially watch the winner of the challenge if there are assigned seats.

Watch the camera people. Russell's idol-finding trick was keeping tabs on how many camera people would follow him. They don't want to miss catching you finding an idol on camera, so the more that are on you, the closer you probably are.

WHERE SHOULD I STASH MY IDOL?

I'll tell you where you *shouldn't*: in your bag, unattended. If it's small enough, depending on what you wear, you can keep it on your person. Or bury it somewhere no one else will find, as long as you remember where.

SHOULD I TELL ANYONE ABOUT MY IDOL/ADVANTAGE?

As a general rule of thumb, I'd say *no*. Information is the most valuable thing out there and players who have kept their idols secret have often been able to use them to great effect. But there are a few exceptions:

If people know or highly suspect you have gotten something. For example, after you go on a journey, you risk them thinking you have something much more powerful than you actually do. Rachel (correctly) told her allies in *47* about her vote block. This made everyone less suspicious about what she got and she was able to keep her immunity idol a secret.

If you make the calculated risk to build trust with someone. Showing someone you have something is a great way to forge a connection. You're giving them ammunition to target you, but you're also opening up a path for them to trust you. Tyson (correctly) shared his idol with Monica in *Blood vs. Water* and was able to lock her in as a solid number.

If you want to use it as a threat. If you want to play aggressively, go ahead and let people know you have it. Wear it around your neck at tribal. General rule of thumb is not to flaunt your idol until you're ready to play it, but it could give you implicit immunity for a bit if everyone is scared to vote for you.

If you're going to be like Malcolm or Mike Holloway and publicly announce you're playing your idol at tribal so the majority alliance is forced to pick a new target . . . **don't tell them who you're voting for**. Once Malcom revealed the Amigos had Phillip in their crosshairs, the rest of the tribe realized they could still vote Malcolm. Even if he did play his idol, it was Phillip's neck on the line, not theirs.

SHOULD I MAKE A FAKE IDOL?

Long gone are the days where Bob had to make a true masterpiece in *Gabon*; now anyone can do it with a couple beads off Tree Mail. It's usually more fun TV than it is strategically useful, but here are a couple pointers:

Don't be obvious about it. If someone catches wind of you trying to make a fake idol, you'll seem even less trustworthy than if they catch you finding a real one.

See if you can get a note from a real idol. A real note is more valuable than a fake idol because the note is harder to fake. Contrary to what some believe, you do not have access to a printer out there. Not even the *Survivor* sanctuary has a business center.

Don't go overboard. The harder you claim you're going to play an idol, the more obvious it is you don't intend to play it. The best fake idol play is still Rupert putting a rock in his pocket.

The reverse is true if you want to suss out if someone's idol is fake. How hard are they claiming you'll see their idol tonight? Did they show you a note? Usually when someone has a fake idol, they have a terrible excuse about what they did with the note. "I ate the note." Okay . . . why?

HOW CAN I TELL IF SOMEONE ELSE HAS AN IDOL?

This is where the poker part of *Survivor* kicks in—gauging who's bluffing, double bluffing, or triple bluffing their double fluff. Do they seem overly comfortable when their position dictates they shouldn't be? Are they not looking as much as you'd expect them to? Are they casually dropping hints that they're ready to go home but just wanna know where the votes are going so they aren't surprised? It's a gut call.

SHOULD I LOOK THROUGH PEOPLE'S BAGS?

If you have reason to believe someone has an idol—or even just a shadow of a reason to believe—go for it. But be sure to do it privately or with a trusted ally as your lookout. You don't want to do it out in the open. It'll get back to the person whose bag you checked. The audience at home might not love it, but all's fair in love and *Survivor*.

SHOULD I PLAY MY IDOL?

If you're already asking yourself, "Should I play my idol?" I would definitely lean toward yes. The *Survivor* graveyard is littered with players who felt something was off but didn't do anything about it.* So if something doesn't sit right with you, don't be a hero; play that thing. Don't worry about looking dumb by playing an idol unnecessarily. Lots of winners have done that. You're clearly good at finding idols, so you can find another one tomorrow.

If you really want, you can try to gauge everyone's reactions before you play your idol—like Tony "validating" his or Rachel playing her Shot in the Dark first—but it's hard to do while you've got a ton of adrenaline surging through your system. "Hold up, Reynold"† might've been a thrilling moment, but Malcolm did read the room wrong.

Finally, if you've got a public idol everyone knows about, it's often better to just burn it and move on.

SHOULD I PLAY MY IDOL ON AN ALLY?

If you have good intel and you think it'll put you in a better position tomorrow, absolutely.

* That graveyard has a special section for season 46. And an extra special section for James, Kellee, and Australian Simon for going home with two.

† Often misquoted as "hold up, bro," but go back and rewatch it. He says "Reynold"!

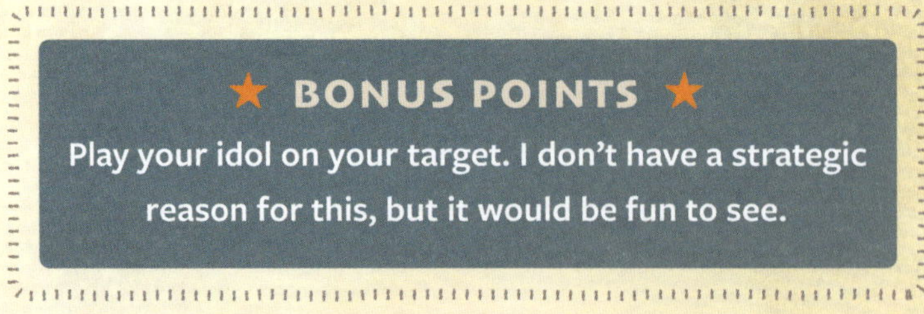

SHOULD I TAKE A BEWARE ADVANTAGE?

Yeah, do it. Getting an advantage in exchange for losing your vote until you complete some mission does sound pretty dicey, but the mechanisms for getting your vote back have gotten more contained and easier to accomplish.

Also, as scary as it is to lose your vote, it often makes you less threatening. It's more likely that your *ally* goes home as a result of your lost vote. Not ideal, but survivable. Sometimes, not having a vote could even be an advantage. Players like Omar and Jesse utilized not having to write someone's name down and continued to play the middle.

But if you do lose your vote, definitely *do not* tell Cedrek. Wait . . . in Justin's case, he *should've* told Cedrek. I guess I highly, highly recommend not ending up on a tribe with Cedrek.

SHOULD I GO ON A JOURNEY?

Short answer, no. Unless you're clearly on the bottom and need something or want to prevent someone on the bottom from getting something, there's very little upside. Even if you do get something, everyone will suspect that you found something potentially more powerful and threatening than what you actually have. But if you do go:

Your priority is the social element of the journey. Get to know your fellow journeymen. Don't pretend they're not there like Brandon and Danny did to Carolyn. See if there's an opportunity to work together in the future. Brendan formed the Exile Alliance in *Tocantins*, just as Q formed the Journey Six in *46*. Neither worked out, but yours might.

Don't spill the beans. Focus on getting information about the other tribe(s) instead. Don't be too cagey, because it could come across as untrustworthy. You wanna reveal just enough and in a way that paints you as a bit on the outs and a number they can later pick up.

Yes, losing your vote isn't the end all be all. But if you are going to tribal that night and you know you *need* your vote . . . **don't risk it**!*

Amulets are not worth it. As Rome explained from Jeff's seat, getting this "advantage" that you have to share with two others from different tribes isn't an advantage at all. Not only will it not stay secret, but it'll also instantly make you a target of the two other amulet holders. I'm sure Austin will agree with me here when I say if you ever have a choice between an amulet or a sandwich, take the sandwich. And I'm sure Christian Hubicki will agree that ideally, that sandwich would be a Reuben.

SHOT IN THE DARKS (OR IS IT SHOTS IN THE DARK?)

The primary production purpose for the Shot in the Dark is to encourage a blindside. If any player can trade their vote for a 1-in-6 shot at immunity, you wanna be extra careful to keep the real plan from them. So it probably doesn't really matter to producers if the SITD ever hits. Don't get me wrong—I bet they were jumping with joy for Kaleb or Mary, but that's just icing on the cake.

If you're out of options, definitely play it, but only as a last resort. Instead, you need to get creative about how to use that little die (that they inexplicably don't make you roll). Maybe you wanna give it to someone as a show of trust or trade it with Jeff for rice. Rachel got more out of reading the room than its intended safety.

To defend against SITDs, sell your target on a fake plan. If they ain't buying it or if the fake plan involves really straining your relationship with an ally . . . screw it. Roll the metaphorical die. They only have a 17 percent chance—pardon me, a *16.7 percent* chance, per David Voce—of foiling your plan. Sometimes bending over backward to avoid something creates more problems than the thing you were initially trying to avoid.

* If you even have a choice.

The Merge

Holy crap! This guide actually worked and you've made the merge. You are officially dateable. Now, the individual portion of the game can—wait, I'm sorry, one moment, I'm getting a call from my . . . uh-huh, uh-huh, okay, yes, I understand, I will let them know. Okay, my mistake; you are all on the same beach and voting together, but you are *not* yet merged. You do not have a buff yet, which you will have to earn. You are currently between the pre-merge and the merge, in . . .

MERGE-ATORY

So you've *not* made the merge and you've been split into two teams, one of which will be immune. Shii Ann is having PTSD fake-merge flashbacks. Here's what you gotta do to "earn the merge":

Win the challenge. Be immune here, best strategy.

If there's an hourglass around, smash it. Smash any hourglasses you see. The hourglass twist of reversing who gets immunity might be the most universally despised twist the show has ever tried, but you know who doesn't hate it? Erika.

If you are one of the vulnerable people who can be voted for, do not throw out names. I generally advocate for players to be proactive, but this is the big exception. The six who won immunity are going to decide amongst themselves who the target is, so all you can do is plead your case to any allies you've got in that six. Players like Ellie, Lydia, Josh, and Rome threw names in this position and the vote boomeranged back on them.

THE ACTUAL MERGE

Now that you've earned the *actual* merge, the individual portion of the game can begin. The end is in sight.

Now's a great time for an evaluation. I know I've labeled a few other times as great times for evaluation, but so what? Do an evaluation every day. How are you feeling within your alliance coming from the pre-merge? Do you have trust in your group to pull it off, or are you open for business looking for potential new allies? Can you pinpoint who is on the bottom of the other alliances? Identify these squeaky wheels and maybe they can be useful allies to you . . . or at least useful idiots for a vote or two.

Options are your most valuable currency. Kim Spradlin is probably the best illustration of the fact that the more paths you have to the end, the better! Be open to working with everyone. Even if you're stringing people along for a few votes, maybe your backup alliance will prove more fruitful than your primary one. If anyone wants to take you to the end, great—even if it's because they think they can beat you. That's for you to worry about in the endgame. In the meantime, any additional path to the end is good news.

Conversely, **you want your allies to have the *fewest* number of options**. The grass can't be greener on the other side if you burn your neighbor's house down. Tony sniping Sophie was the perfect move not because she's a strategic force of nature or secretly had an idol, but because she was working so closely with his number one ally Sarah. Was Sarah plotting to use Sophie to blindside Tony? Maybe she wasn't yet . . . but one way to guarantee she never would was to ensure Sophie wasn't around anymore. As pissed as Officer Sarah may have gotten, the Cops R Us alliance was her only remaining option so she stuck to it.

Be conscious of your threat level. If you don't think you're a threat to win, target the threats. But if you are a threat, keep other jury threats around, aka the "meat shield strategy" coined by Jeremy. Being aware of everyone's perceptions of everyone else's threat levels is one of the most valuable skills to have. Adam may not have been the biggest threat in *Millennials vs. Gen X*, but he correctly assessed three bigger threats than himself and made sure to keep them around until the final six. When they toppled one after the other, Adam easily swept the final three. However, if you've been coined a challenge threat, there's not much you can do except win out every single f—ing challenge. Better lock in.

WHO SHOULD I TAKE ON REWARD?

Rewards are great. Depending on the season and budget, they could range from an amazing overnight luxury hotel stay to eating a whole Costco chicken off the ground without utensils or condiments. Regardless, you'll get fed, you may get to wash up, and you'll have some crucial alone time with a select group of people to strategize with. But realize that, for every player getting to partake in the reward, there's another fuming back at camp that they didn't get to go. So if you win the reward and get to take others along, choose wisely. The history of *Survivor* is riddled with players who made the wrong choice and it bit them in the ass.

Prioritize the swing votes or the person you're most worried about flipping. If someone just flipped over to your side, definitely take them so they don't feel used.

Leave your closest ally behind. As tough as it may be, even though you may really wanna party it up with your best bud, it's probably smartest to leave trusted ears behind to keep tabs on everything. Burton probably lost *Pearl Islands* because he couldn't stand being around Lill any longer and just wanted an easy reward with his boy Jonny Fairplay.

If it's a reward involving loved ones, consider not winning it. People (understandably) get very emotional when it comes to their family. A grudge about not getting to eat a plain, dry hot dog is nothing compared to a grudge about not getting a letter from your sister that you can reread over and over again every time things get tough. Just ask Charlie, who followed the previous suggestion and left his number one Maria out of getting her letter.

Don't feed the challenge threat. If you're trying to beat someone at the endurance challenge tomorrow, better try to keep their tank empty today.

If you get the option to give up your reward to everyone else, don't feel obligated to give it up. The same players who might target you for *not* giving it up are the exact same ones who will target you *for* giving it up (and raising your jury threat level). It's a lose-lose situation by design so you may as well enjoy the reward you earned.

Have reasons ready for your choices. Regardless of who you pick and why, be ready to explain in the least-threatening way possible. You already promised someone; they haven't eaten in a while; it's their birthday. Have something prepared and don't make anyone play rock-paper-scissors for it.

And if you're the one not chosen for a reward, don't fret, don't throw a tantrum. Enjoy the time back at camp to search for idols and bond with the other unpicked losers. Cook extra rice to commiserate. If anyone is upset about not getting picked, fan that flame.

SHOULD I SPLIT THE VOTE?

In *Cook Islands*, Cao Boi had a dream about a shaman lady who asked him for multiple American Express credit cards and he awoke with the idea for Plan Voodoo: If they split the votes across multiple targets, they don't have to worry about the hidden immunity idol. Even though Cao Boi instantly got voted out because he shared his idea with Yul, the player who secretly had the idol, his revolutionary idea became a staple of strategy.

But splitting the vote is always a risk, which comes with one pro (you protect against the idol) and a lot of cons. So before you split, you need to ask yourself a few questions.

Do you have enough votes to split? If your coalition doesn't have *at least* twice as many votes as the other side, then you don't have enough. Assuming they play their hypothetical idol correctly on your *primary* target (who gets the majority of votes), you need to have at least enough votes on your *secondary* target to force a revote. If you don't have enough to split, then just dump all your votes on who you feel is least likely to have an idol or have an idol played on them.

Do you trust everyone in your alliance? Splitting the vote creates an opportunity for someone on your side to flip and gain the plurality* of votes. In *Cambodia*, at first, it was a mistake for the alliance not to split the vote on Wentworth, and then it became

* Plurality is when the highest number of votes aren't the majority. Four votes is clearly not the majority in a tribe of nine so in a typical five to four vote, the four obviously loses. But four votes becomes the (winning) plurality when the votes are split four to three to two.

a mistake for Stephen *to* split the votes on Joe. He trusted Spencer who took the opportunity to flip his vote on Stephen—he didn't have the majority but he won the day on a plurality.

Is anyone TOO eager to split the vote? A clear sign someone is trying to swap their vote and get a plurality is if they are not only pushing a vote split, but pushing to be on the primary side of the votes. In *Australian Survivor: Heroes vs. Villains*, George instantly sniffed out Simon's transparent ploy and stopped the split, but in *47*, the tribe let Operation: Italy happen despite how pushy Andy was about it. The person most amped up to split the vote should always be on the secondary target.

Who would you be splitting the vote on? If you're splitting against a known alliance, then it's pretty obvious who to split on. Otherwise, be wary; splitting on someone is publicly declaring that you do not care if they get sent out of the game. The risk of losing an ally might outweigh the risk of an idol bouncing back on you. The Goliaths permanently lost Angelina when they split a few votes her way.

SHOULD I BLINDSIDE MY ALLY?

- Is your ally planning to blindside you? If yes, blindside them.
- Is your ally going to beat you at the end? If yes, blindside them. But make sure the time is right.
- Is your ally shielding you from being voted out? If yes, don't blindside them (yet).
- Are you considering voting out your ally just to pad your *Survivor* résumé? If yes, don't blindside them (see the next chapter for more on this résumé nonsense).

- Are you only considering it because you think it'll make fun television? If yes, then probably don't do it. The reason the most tedious seasons tend to have the most dominant winners (Kim, Rob, South African Rob) is because the smartest move is often boring. But winning isn't everything, so if you want to give me something juicy to podcast about, by all means, don't let me stop you. Taking wild swings could hurt your chances of winning but increase your chances of being brought back.

SHOULD I GO TO ROCKS?

Forcing a tribal council tie and leaving your life in the game to chance is not a decision to be taken lightly. Earlier in the game, I'd say you should almost definitely avoid it. Later in the game is a different question. It was perfectly done in *Blood vs. Water* at the final six, but it probably didn't need to happen in *Millennials vs. Gen X* at the final ten. There's usually another creative play, but if you don't see any other path forward for you and your allies to combat the other side, then yes, you've gotta do it. Don't just sit there, getting picked off one by one.

Dealing with the Bad Stuff

If you organize a typical *Survivor* experience in a pie chart of good/bad/ugly, the bad and the ugly will probably outweigh the good, so you'll need to be ready for that, too.

HOW DO I HANDLE MY PARANOIA?

You see two people chitchatting and you wonder . . . is it about you? Are you next to go? Is everything everyone has ever told you a complete fabrication and everyone is just laughing and laughing at how utterly stupid you are for believing a single word? Paranoia and self-doubt can be powerful tools. In the *Caramoan* final tribal council, Cochran even talked about how his deep-seated insecurity manifested itself in a healthy way and led to him taking out threats before they got to take him out.

So where do you draw the line? Paranoia is going to keep you alive, but you don't want to get into a cycle where your allies aren't trusting you because you're not trusting them. If you're starting to go down a paranoid spiral, ask yourself this:

How many things feel off? If it's only one weird conversation, you could be fine. There are a million reasons why someone might seem off—they could feel sick, they could be missing someone. Is it just the one thing or are there other red flags around?

Can you identify two or three other things that are consistent with your concern? If what you're worried about is true, which other things must also be true? And are those things happening?

What is the best move for everyone? If you aren't trusting someone, you can try to trust in their self-interest in winning the game. If you were them, would you betray you? Don't just take people for their word, take them for their motivation.

HOW DO I RECOVER AFTER BEING BETRAYED?

So you walked into tribal council with a brilliant plan but walked out with your number one ally blindsided and your head on the chopping block. Not a great night, but the game's not over yet.

Do not explode. Bro, I know emotions are high, but you can't just go, "Screw you, dude," and blow up on everyone. Show a little emotion, admit you've been caught off guard. What you want is some sympathy; what you don't want is to get into a screaming match. Don't give them another reason to vote you out next. Do not be like Ozzy, announcing you're now a free agent. Be like Natalie Anderson, playing it cool while saving your ire for the confessionals.

Don't be super phony. You don't want to be too angry, but you also don't wanna be too chill. If your attitude is "thank you, sir, may I have another?" they *will* serve you another. If you come across as a doormat, they will continue to walk all over you and the jury may not respect someone covered in everyone else's footprints.

Mend your relationships. Figure out why this happened. Did the numbers just not fall your way or did you take an ally for granted? Even if it's not your fault, see if there's a way to repair that bond. Don't come into that conversation with the attitude that they made a massive blunder—people dig in their heels when told they're wrong. Instead, just own your side of the street and leave the door open for reconciliation.

Be a tool. Not a jerk, but a useful tool. Go to who you perceive to be in power and offer yourself up as someone they can use. *Survivor* players are mostly motivated by two things—fear and greed. Since you've been blindsided, you're basically defanged . . . you are not someone to be feared. But to the greedy player in power, basking in their brilliant blindside, present yourself as a number they can use for their next conquest.

Do not throw out names. You're on the bottom; you don't get the luxury of picking targets. Even if someone is already thinking about voting someone out, if you say it first, it might seem like it's your idea. No one cares about building up your reputation. Be open, be flexible, wait for someone else to suggest a name and you love that name—you know how to spell it and you can't wait to write it down.

WHAT SHOULD I DO IF I'M ON SOME SORT OF EDGE OF EXTINCTION/REDEMPTION ISLAND TYPE THING?

Sorry you've been voted out, but, congratulations, there is a twist that allows you a chance to re-enter the game. The fans might be livid but it's terrific news for you. So how do you avoid squandering this second chance?

Win the challenges. That's pretty much it. Hope you're good at all the carnival games.

Free jury management. Ozzy had the right idea—he made a fish dinner for every visitor and sent them merrily on their way. It's truly an incredible opportunity to make friends with the jury because you no longer have to lie to anyone. Look at the two Edge-returnees, Chris Underwood and Natalie Anderson. One was friendly with everyone and the other stuck to an exclusive cool-kids clique. Who did better with the jury?

SHOULD I EVER QUIT?

- Are you on the Edge of Extinction and are completely uncompetitive in the challenges? If yes, then go ahead and pull the white flag. I don't even consider that quitting.
- Do you have a family emergency back home like Jenna Morasca or Terry Deitz? If yes, then, of course, leave the game. Also not quitting.
- Are you dealing with a medical issue like *David vs. Goliath*'s Bi or *44*'s Matthew but aren't being pulled by the medical team? If yes, then it's up to you. I can't judge you for erring on the side of caution. But I can judge you for climbing a rock for no reason or not slipping an ally your hidden immunity idol on your way out.
- In every other scenario, no, you should not quit. Quitting won't be fun for anyone—not the audience, not your allies, and I do think, one day, you'll regret it, too. If you're truly struggling out there, take a deep breath and just try to go moment by moment. On *The Social Game* podcast, Michele Fitzgerald said that, when she was out there, she calculated that a million dollars over thirty-nine days comes out to something like twenty dollars a minute. So whenever things got hard, she'd remind herself that another minute was an extra twenty dollars. On a twenty-six-day season, each minute is worth even more! So you can't afford to quit. Just ride it out; you never know what could happen. Courtney Yates came on the show fully expecting to be the first person voted out, just for a free vacation. Yet she ended a beloved fan favorite and was two votes shy of winning it all.

Now if you're really, really struggling out there . . . at least take it out on the other players first. I don't endorse dumping out the tribe's rice for strategic reasons but I do endorse J'Tia as a dynamic television personality. To this very day, Rory Freeman still regrets not burning the entire camp down.

The End Game

As exhausted as you must be by now, you've gotta stay sharp. A slight lapse here could be more costly than before.

Really look at who you're heading to the end with. Can you beat them? If you don't think you can beat someone, get them out of there. Period.

If you're really having a hard time getting someone out, don't play up their threat level. You can elevate their threat level in one-on-one conversations, but don't announce to the whole jury that Ben or Rachel making it to the end would mean they're winning. Because then when they do . . . they win. Perception is everything on *Survivor*, so don't treat the cockroach who keeps winning immunity or finding idols like they're amazing.

Win immunities and find idols. While you might act like you aren't that impressed if someone else does that, *you* want to be the person doing it.

Be honest with yourself about if the jury likes you. Tune in and you can tell. Are they laughing at your jokes or scowling at you? Do they seem pleased when you arrive at tribal with the immunity necklace or bummed out when you play your hidden immunity idol? Also pay attention to whose jokes they *do* laugh at. If someone is scoring laughs with that jury, add them to it, while you go laughing all the way to the bank.

> "So people reach out to me every once in a while when they're going on the show, and I try to tell everybody . . . 'Look, go and just have fun. You're not gonna win, so go and just have fun. Make moves, switch alliances, flip the game. Like, just go have fun.' That's what it's all about. Like, I think it's just good for TV."
>
> —Jeremy Collins, September 17, 2022

WHO SHOULD I PUT INTO FIRE?

Great job winning Simmotion! Now, you've (probably) got a fire-making challenge to contend with. The first thing to ask yourself is if you need to throw yourself into fire. I wouldn't, but you might have to if you answer yes to any of the following questions:

- Does it feel like you'll lose the jury vote if you don't do something extreme?
- Are you the only person good enough at fire to take out the one player destined to win the game?
- Did you spend most of the game voted out on the Edge of Extinction?

If you decide not to risk making the fire yourself, it's time to decide if you want to try to get the biggest threat out or drag them to the end to rob them of the opportunity of impressing the jury with their caveman magic fire abilities. It's really how you sell it. Dee seemed more dominant bringing Austin with her, but Xander seemed to lack awareness when taking Erika.

Once you've decided to send the biggest threat into fire, your last choice is picking against who. Here, you're just weighing who has a better shot at winning and who will be less mad at you for being in the challenge. Burning a jury vote might not be a fire-making challenge you can afford to lose.

HOW DO I WIN THE FIRE-MAKING CHALLENGE?

I know you already know how to make fire by now, so just try to stay calm, make sure you line up your base under the rope, and try to block the wind if you can. If your opponent already has a big flame going and you only have a little one, dump everything you've got in. The sticks, the husk, the kindling, your buff—you've got nothing to lose.

> ★ **BONUS POINTS** ★
>
> Be sure to smirk and say, "Is it hot in here or is it just me?" after you win. It signifies to the jury that you've stayed cool enough under pressure to drop a sick zinger after your big moment.

BEING A JUROR

Sorry you got voted out (or suck at making fire), but just because you're out of the game, it doesn't mean you're off the show.

Dress to impress. Who can forget Sol's vest? This is your chance to wow everyone. The editors can always edit out your subtle, brilliant gameplay, but they can't edit out what you wear on the jury. We thought we knew Andrew Savage after watching him for two seasons, but one well-timed jury beanie had us questioning everything.

Do something cool with your hair. Remember Lex's mohawk? Awe-some. Maybe it's finally time to try out that handlebar mustache?

Serve us looks. Go rewatch all the post-merge tribal councils in *Micronesia* on mute. It's no mystery why Eliza is the benchmark for best jury reactions. You want to be a reaction GIF on Twitter. Do something—stand up if it feels right.

Hold the finalists accountable. Have spicy questions ready, and don't let them off the hook with vague answers. We wanna see the finalists under the most pressure possible.

If you truly feel devastated, get a sick jury speech going. Sue Hawk, Kelly Goldsmith, and Reed Kelly were all met with scorn when they made their spicy speeches, but history looks back at Sue and both Kellys fondly. Take stock if you think any finalists might remove their teeth.

There is no right or wrong way to vote. If you want to vote for your friend, vote for your friend. If you want to vote against the person that pissed you off, that is your right. However, be prepared that the fans will judge your judgment. It's fair for you to vote however you feel, but it's also fair for them to feel however they like. There is no appeal in the *Survivor* jury vote process, but it will be indefinitely re-litigated online.

Examples of good jury questions:

- "Tell us why the people next to you don't deserve to win." Get them dunking on each other.
- "How many jury votes do you think you have locked up right now?" Put them on the spot and test their self-awareness.

Examples of bad jury questions:

- "What do you plan to do with the money if you win?" Boring, who cares?
- "Tell me about myself. How well did you really get to know me?" Maybe it's important to you, but we certainly don't care if you'll stay friends afterward or where you'll go on a little bro-date together.

Facing the Jury

Enjoy your Day ~~39~~ 26 breakfast and get ready for what may be the most important part of your game. Whether you're the front-runner or not, you can still blow it or catch up.

Be self-aware. This is the most important thing jurors look for. You could get jurors to overlook your mistakes, but it'll be much harder to get them to overlook you not realizing those were mistakes. If they saw you as a snake, they might accept the winning story of a snake who snaked the right people, but they'll never accept the winning story of an honest, loyal soldier who stood by their word. If they saw you as more of a follower, they might accept the winning story of someone who purposefully stayed back until it was time to strike, but they'll never accept the winning story of a bold leader who played from the front.

Conversely, highlight lack of self-awareness in your opponent. Recently in *45* and *48*, Dee and Kyle both buried Austin and Eva respectively by letting them declare something first and then body slamming them with an "um actually," revealing how unaware they were of what was really going on in the game.

Treat every question like a good question. Like in a job interview, no matter how stupid it is, you must find a way to answer it. If the juror clearly hates you and hits you with a loaded question, you can still answer in a way to try to win over a different juror on the fence.

Calculate which jurors you need to appeal to. Ideally, your game can appeal to everyone, but realistically, there'll be votes you know you'll get, votes you won't, and a few up in the air. Hit the up-in-the-air voters hard. Recognize when to cut bait on someone who has their mind made up and go for the swing voter. Figure out who's struggling with their mortgage and offer to pay it.

You're allowed to lie. Sometimes it seems like players think the deceptive part of the game is over and come into final tribal having drank truth serum. Sure, it's great to be honest about your gameplay, but if a salty juror wants an apology that you don't feel like making, grit your teeth and give them an apology you don't mean. Just don't tell the kind of lie that takes too much credit for something that isn't verifiably yours. Especially if someone on the jury feels like they deserve credit for that. They've already lost the game; all they have left is to cling to the little ways they've affected the season.

"And I feel that when you make people feel good, you can control them. It's kind of the opposite of the Russell thing, which is like, make people feel miserable; you control their feelings. I think he's half right. So with the ego thing, the idea is you figure out what a person believes about themselves and behave in a way around them that reinforces it so you're being to each person what they want you to be, and that extends into the jury if you can. . . . When you're pitching your case to the jury, you want to present yourself in a way that, again, does not threaten their self-identity. So I think you should choose a quality in your game that does not rub up against other people. So I don't think that you should say, 'I was the strongest player for this reason, I was the smartest player for this reason, I was the most strategic for this reason.' Because the chances are there's at least one person, probably several people on the jury, that feels, no, I'm the strongest person. No, I'm the smartest person. No, I'm the most strategic person."

—John Cochran, May 4, 2017

Talk up the jury. Package what you did and how you did it in a way that respects the competitors you beat out. The reason you had to cut them? Because they were playing such a good game and would win. Did Todd actually think that Jean-Robert was a huge strategic threat? Maybe not, but that doesn't matter. What matters is that Jean-Robert feels better being voted out by Todd for being too smart for his own good. Frame your story in a way that makes your win their win. Even though they got blindsided, they'll be able to sleep better knowing that the winner couldn't have won without them.

Keep calm if you're winning, fight like hell if you're losing. If things aren't going your way, you gotta jump in, interrupt, and contradict your opponent. But if things *are* going your way, be graceful—no one wants to see you kicking a goat while it's down.

The Reunion/After-Show

Okay, the season is over. Congratulations on this once-in-a-lifetime experience that maybe you'll be lucky enough to experience multiple times. Now you either have to wait eight months for the reading of the votes and a live reunion show or instantly have no time to process your feelings, get pizza shoved in your face, and have to answer more of Jeff's questions.

If they return to the live reunion show, have a little something prepared. Don't overexplain, own your mistakes, and maybe throw in a joke. This isn't an *On Fire* episode, this is live TV—you don't want Jeff to have to cut you off. And dress to impress. Who can forget Michele's iconic red dress or the following season's Michelle's iconic dragon dress? No matter how hard I try, I still can't shake the image of Tyson's tuxedo T-shirt or Brad's substitute gym teacher look.

However, if they stick to doing the after-show on the island, my only piece of advice is more of a plea. I am on my knees, begging you . . . do not eat the pizza. If you're a starving finalist and you cannot wait thirty more minutes to eat, fine. But if you've been on the jury, eating well every night, don't you dare stuff your face. We want to hear your answers, not hear you chew food.

If you're at all thinking about getting engaged to any of the contestants . . . take the leap and propose. If you're even slightly considering it, even a little on the fence, do it—no regrets.

After the Game

Regardless of how well you did, it's never easy to go from such an extreme high-stress situation back to regular life. A few pointers for settling back in:

Prioritize your physical health. I don't want to scare you, but plenty of players return with weird parasites and various other issues. You're not being over-cautious if you want any sort of symptom checked out.

Prioritize your mental health. You've been through a lot, so don't keep things bottled up. Lean on your support system and consider starting therapy if you haven't already. I was very bummed when I returned from *All-Stars* and probably the best thing I did was spend more time with my friends and family and less time reading about myself on the internet.

Seriously, do not go down the rabbit hole of Twitter/Reddit/whatever. The show is never going to get everything right and you'll also never be able to correct all the trolls and sincerely misguided fans posting inaccurate information. People will have their own opinions, which is their right, and they'll sometimes say rude and hurtful things, which I'm not excusing, but for your sake, you need to learn to somehow let that go. Easier said than done . . . even if you're Tony, returning home victorious, it's still too tempting to let ass-kisser Stephen Fishbach know that he needs to wipe the "s–t stains" off his glasses before rewatching the season that he's been so incorrectly commenting on.

Be a good sport. Whether you won or lost, made jury or were the first boot, if you can't laugh at yourself about what went wrong, you will never, ever be at peace with what happened. There are players I personally know in the community whose experiences on the show didn't go swimmingly. And yet, despite the disappointment, they were able to move forward, laugh about it all, and become staples of the fan community. There are others who are still sadly spiraling about what didn't go their way on this crazy, luck-based show.

Don't spoil the season. Keep it vague when fans and acquaintances ask how you did. Don't list the boot order of your seasons in an interview. I understand if you want to share how you did with your closest loved ones, but if you won, consider lying. How fun would it be if you told your spouse that you lost at fire so they watch the entire season waiting to see you get eliminated in the finale, and, boom, you win a million dollars? MVP of this is, of course, Chris Daugherty, who not only told his wife that he got voted out the night she came to the loved one's visit, but blamed her for it because she lost the loved one's challenge.

Have fun in the *Survivor* community! It's fun to play *Survivor*, but it's also fun to be a *Survivor* alumni. You're joining a (relatively) small group of people who understand what you've been through. Don't let it define your entire life, but come to the fan events—maybe even host a fan event in your town. I know there's been some unfortunate rabid fan reactions, like how the fan base scared Natalie White into obscurity, but, in my personal experience, the majority of the *Survivor* fans are kind, wonderful people.

If avoidable, try not to break up any existing *Survivor* marriages.

If you won a lot of money, prioritize paying off your debts, put money into a high-yield savings account, and be sure to set some aside for applicable taxes. Run this by Tasha Fox or any other actual accountant.

"When Trish and I were talking recently and she's getting ready to go out and talk publicly, motivationally, and she said, 'What do you think the hardest part of *Survivor* is?' And I told her the hardest part is, honestly, moving on. I think for anyone, winners, losers, first person out, Day 38 person. It really is processing the experience and moving on from it. It's harder than the rain. It's harder than the starvation, you know? And especially now, with social media."

—Kass McQuillen, October 4, 2018

GETTING TO GO ON *RHAP*

Okay, now let's get to the most important part of your experience. The day after your final episode airs, you get to . . . talk to me! You're more nervous than when you first got to talk to Jeff?! Well, you shouldn't be, but here's what I'd recommend for our chat:

Keep your answers tight. You'll have a lot of exit press to do that day so they'll only give us around fifteen minutes. Try not to ramble too much. You are always welcome back to do a longer interview later.

Mix up what you're saying in your exit press. The online fan base is dedicated enough to follow all the interviews, so don't worry about having to cover everything in every single one. Tell me a different story than you tell Gordon Holmes.

Don't tarnish other players with character attacks. It's not really fun. But if you truly feel the need to do so, at least get specific. Either state something clearly or keep it to yourself. No need to put weird cryptic messages out there.

SHOULD I SELL MERCH?

Sure. But I'd recommend waiting until your season ends.

SHOULD I GO ON CAMEO.COM?

Sure. And if no one is buying any Cameos . . . you maybe set your price too high.

RETURNEE SEASONS / OTHER SHOWS

If you're being invited back on a returnee season, you are way past needing any of my help. You're a master of this! But if I had to give you advice, I'd say never believe your hype too much. Always stay hustling and grinding like you did on your initial season. If you show up like your you-know-what don't stink, you're almost guaranteed to have a huge downfall. Make other players feel like they're working with you and not for you.

If you end up on shows other than *Survivor*, here are a few quick things to consider:

Big Brother: Stay asleep for the first month of the show. *Big Brother* is about playing the long game.

The Traitors: As Sandra figured out, the goal isn't to catch the traitors (because they'd just recruit new ones), but to cozy up to the traitors so they don't murder you, and then banish them all at the very end.*

The Challenge: Start a fight on your rookie season (bonus points if you get punched in the face) and ride out your alliances for ten years.

The Amazing Race: Definitely work on your cardio before you go.

Deal or No Deal Island: When facing the banker, you shouldn't care about putting big money in the pot—only focus on not getting eliminated. The final deal will always give you a 50 percent chance of being eliminated, so take any deal when your odds of sticking around are higher than fifty.

* Let's see how well this works out for me!

House of Villains: Producers seem to allow anything as long as it makes for a big television moment. So go ahead and cheat, as long as you keep it fun.

The Circle: Don't worry about catching the catfish. If someone is working with you, why does it matter if they are who they say they are?

The Mole: Go in as the Mole so you're in all the episodes.

The Genius: Learn to count cards.

Squid Game: The Challenge: This one might be too much luck to control. Be ruthless.

Beast Games: Same as *Squid Game*, but I think it helps if you're very Christian and bond with everyone over that.

Snake in the Grass: Don't worry, it's canceled.

SHOULD I START YET ANOTHER SURVIVOR PODCAST?

No.

World's Best Host
Russell Hantz
Dumbass Girl Alliances
Idol plays
For references, call Shambo

CHAPTER 7

Shred Your *Survivor* Résumé

That Jury's Still Out but You're Still In

"If a hyena came through camp and ate our mush, and then after he ate it, he turned around and licked his heinie, did he do it because that was animal instinct or to get the taste of mush out of his mouth?" This was the exact question posed by Big Tom from the jury at the end of *Survivor: Africa* to finalists Ethan Zohn and Kim Johnson. When Tom served on the jury five seasons later on *Survivor: All Stars*, his tone was a little different. "No hard feelings," he tells Boston Rob, extending his hand, before doing the classic hand-pull-away trick and dropping a hard, "Don't be stupid, stupid." In Africa, Tom ended up voting for Ethan, who was his friend and alliance member. Then in *All-Stars*, Tom ended up voting *against* Rob, who was also his friend and alliance member . . . but one who betrayed him. Neither time did any of the jury answers influence what Tom had set out to do. But it was pretty funny to see Kim Johnson, who never had a chance in hell of getting Tom's vote, attempt to sincerely answer how the hyena wouldn't be all that disgusted by eating the mush that she herself cooked all season.

The jury deciding who ultimately wins the game is what elevates *Survivor* from a great game to the greatest game on television. This isn't *The Amazing Race* or the aptly named *The Challenge*, where the winner of the season is decided by whoever wins a challenge. This isn't *Top Chef* or *Project Runway*, where you need to impress some chump judges to win. And this definitely isn't *American Idol* or *Last Comic Standing*, where America picks the winner by texting the name of their favorite contestant to the same toll-free number over and over again*—although Russell Hantz may have preferred that. The brokenhearted contestants who are eliminated hold the ultimate power, not just in deciding the winner, but in deciding what metrics to judge the winner by. What's important to one juror might not be as important to the person next to them. And while a jury of one season might value the social relationships built by a certain finalist, the jury of a different season might be more impressed by the strategic gameplay, or physical prowess, or just the cut of the jib of a different finalist. There is no one "correct" path to winning the game, which makes it endlessly interesting as an audience member (or podcast commentator) but understandably frustrating for a player. You're cold, you're hungry, and, on top of trying to suss out who is conspiring to get you voted out, you also have to worry about the dopes you *already did* vote out. It's a lot!

* Standard texting rates apply.

Human beings are complicated creatures, but we are creatures nonetheless. And creatures love certainty. On *Survivor*, players rarely experience certainty about when their next meal will be, if they'll be dry, how many trinkets their enemies have, and how many of their allies will even have a vote. So in an attempt to grasp any control of certainty in the game, the "*Survivor* Résumé" was invented. An annoying trend where players treat a game played half-naked on an island like it's a corporate ladder to climb. The idea is to "make a CV," populated with a collection of moves made throughout the season that, when printed out and faxed over to the jury, will certainly land them the job of Sole Survivor.

> "We're not seeing a lot of the characters like we used to where you got to really get to know the people in a different sense. Everyone's talking about strategy, and one thing I hate is there's always this résumé that all of a sudden these new players have to build. We hear more about, 'You got to do this because you got to build this résumé.' I don't know where that came from."
>
> **—Sandra Diaz-Twine, November 23, 2018**

Although it's hard to call it a "trend" when it's now been happening for nearly half the seasons of the show. It eventually created a feedback loop as the show cast more superfans, who approached the show with the nerd* energy and belief that if they turn in all their homework and study hard for the big test, then surely Teacher has to give them an A. When high-school student Will Wahl paraded around wondering if he should blindside Zeke just for the sake of building his résumé in front of the jury, it really made sense that a student working on his college applications would look at the game the same way. He may as well have thought, "Sure, I have good grades in the social game, but how do I show admissions my extracurricular strategy?" But

* As a nerd myself, I use the term lovingly.

sometimes you do everything you think you should and Teacher still doesn't give you an A. Sometimes professor Dr. Maria Shrime Gonzalez fails the young pupil Charlie, forcing him to retake the entire course.

The origin of all this résumé talk is interlinked with the origin of the "Big Movez" Era. Which makes sense, since if you were forced to have a résumé, you wouldn't fill it up with "medium-sized moves" to impress the jury. In season 27, the first *Blood vs. Water*, Hayden's attempt to sway Ciera to flip over to him from the majority alliance was based on convincing her that the jury wouldn't find her as impressive as the people she was aligned with and turning on them would be a pretty great move for her . . . yup, résumé. But the most important thing to note here is that Hayden was playing from the bottom. He *needed* Ciera, so whether or not his assessment of how she was perceived was correct, *any* flashy move by Ciera at that stage would help *him*. If nothing big happened and the status quo was maintained, he'd be out. Ciera herself was in the same situation on season 31, *Second Chance*, endlessly clamoring for others to make big moves. Résumé talk started as a misguided way to try to game the system and became a tool for a player in trouble to convince others to shake things up. So the real question here isn't whether Ciera made the right move flipping over to Hayden;* it's whether Ciera's flip would have been a meaningful tick on her theoretical final résumé. We'll never get to know for sure, but let's suppose the rock draw went the other way, with Tyson pulling the white rock (and Katie telling him that's *his* seat over there), and Ciera, Hayden, and Katie barreling their way to the final three. Would Ciera be able to convince the jury that what went down at the final six was *her* move, or could Hayden successfully argue that convincing Ciera to flip goes on *his* résumé?

The history of how moves are "counted" on a résumé is unclear at best. In season 33, *Millennials vs. Gen X*, Adam managed to get more credit for Ken turning on David than Ken himself—nothing in *Survivor* happens in a vacuum, and the jury's perception will trump whatever any finalist types up on their own résumé. You can claim in a job interview that your gap year traveling Europe made you knowledgeable and

* The correct answer is that she probably should've instead flipped a round earlier when they were targeting Caleb before a rock draw was forced.

worldly, but it's out of your hands if your prospective employer sees you as a bum who took a year off to party in Barcelona. Of course, this is all a moot point, since, in our hypothetical, Hayden and Ciera would only be battling for second place, after Katie Collins declares "it's a game, bitch" and sweeps the entire jury.

> "I agree with Sandra. I hate the word 'résumé.' I slightly throw up in my mouth when I use it myself. . . . I know I wouldn't want to vote for somebody who I think thinks about *Survivor* in the terms of résumé. I think what's more important is, like, ensuring that you play the game true to yourself and that you are like making active decisions that are in line with your story. I think it's less about a résumé and it's more about like your *Survivor* story."
>
> **—Sophie Clarke, November 25, 2018**

This "*Survivor* Résumé" may have started as a tool used by players on the bottom, but it also became a useful tactic for the jurors, themselves. I believe there is a harsh truth to the *Survivor* jury system: Jurors tend to vote for people they personally like. Maybe this is a hot take, but our favorite reality TV contestants aren't grizzled court justices—they're human beings who want their friends to succeed and their enemies to fail. However, human beings are also usually aware of how they'll be perceived on television.* After the first couple of seasons, most jurors have come in knowing they can't just go up in the finale and say, "I like you better, Sandra, I'm voting for you." Instead, they go up in front of the finalists and pretend they care the most about having survival skills . . . and then vote for Sandra anyway, regardless of what she or Scoutmaster Lill say. Even if Lill boiled the water you drank for the full thirty minutes! At the end of *Exile Island*, Shane berates Aras and Danielle about how undeserving they both are and how he can't bring himself to vote for either of them. So instead of choosing, he asks them

* Thankfully, not all of them, or we'd never get any delightful wackadoos.

to pick a number between one and a million. Aras chooses four and Danielle goes with ten.* Shane was one of only two votes for Danielle and, on his voting parchment, he scribbled some illegible six-digit number (the best I can make out is 489,489). However, later on, Shane admitted that the real number he was thinking of was, in fact . . . four! Four had always been his favorite number, which was clearly a piece of personal information Aras retained. Despite Aras nailing this one-in-a-million shot, he was never going to get Shane's vote because he had sworn to Shane on his yoga and went on to break his little yoga promise.

Honesty was big back in the early days of *Survivor*. Whichever finalist the juror liked better was the one they claimed played with more "honor" or "integrity." You weren't giving your friend a million dollars because they're your friend, but because you'd made a well-reasoned, objective decision about who played this deceptive game with more "integrity." Take Sarge in season 9, going up to face Chris and Twila. Now, I'm not disparaging Chris Daugherty's very deserved win, but Sarge obviously voted for Chris purely because Chris was his buddy and Twila backstabbed him. But Sarge couldn't bring himself to say on national television, "Hello, I am a sore loser, I'm voting for Chris." So instead he gave an indignant rant about how Twila swore on her son and how this was simply a horrible, uncrossable moral line.† But let's look at a hypothetical reverse situation where Twila swears on her son to the girls at the merge but ends up sticking with the boys and blindsides Ami. When Twila's sitting in the final two chairs, does Sarge go up there and tell her that she damned her son to hell for lying to the gals? Of course not. He tells her she's a hell of a woman, that he's proud to know her, and votes to give her a million bucks because it was only a problem when she lied to *him*.

* By *The Price is Right* rules, Danielle technically should've gone with five.

† He's been to Europe and people don't swear on their sons there!

As the game became more sophisticated, so did the players playing it. It became too embarrassing to say you cared about who lied less in a game predicated on lying, so this "résumé" business became a convenient cover to mask your own bruised ego. It's not that you like the person better; they're just objectively more qualified because they have XYZ on their résumé. It's not that you got passed over for a promotion because the boss decided to promote his own nephew; it's that his nephew had a terrific XYZ on his résumé.

> "Here's the thing about *Survivor*, Rob. If you're weak in the beginning, there's a chance that you're gonna be targeted. But once you get to the merge, you're golden. No one's gonna care for you and no one's gonna target you because everybody thinks they can beat you. And players like that are starting to win *Survivor* now because once they get to the finals, everybody's gonna want to vote for them because they don't really rub you the wrong way. . . . Because if you're on the jury and if you don't like somebody, you're not going to vote for them, hands down. Doesn't matter if they played the best game. . . . But I mean, it depends on the people that are on the jury. With my season, I voted for someone who played the best game, you know? And Susie, out of the three, played the best game."
>
> **—Ken Hoang, May 8, 2010**

The best part is, XYZ can be whatever you want it to be! When you happen to like Gabler on a personal level more than Cassidy, Gabler taking jury-threat Jesse out in fire is an incredible move that must be respected. But when you happen to like Tommy better than Dean, who cares that Dean took jury-threat Lauren out in fire? Maria can't say Charlie hurt her feelings and that's why she's going to vote Kenzie—instead, she has to make up a story about how she saw the fire in Kenzie's eyes when she defeated

Liz in a fire-making challenge that we now all know was an incredibly dragged-out, unremarkable showdown. If instead of season 9, *Vanuatu* was season 59,* Sarge would be up there raving about Chris's unbelievable play with his amulet-vote-steal-nullifier and telling Twila that her résumé really lacked in not being the one to take out jury-threats Eliza, Julie, and Ami in the mandatory final 4, 5, and 6 fire-making challenges. The show can continue to season 99 and I still wonder if anyone will have the courage to just say, "I'm voting this way because I like them better and I think it will be cool when my friend is a millionaire and buys me a nice dinner at Outback Steakhouse."

The artificial construct that anybody cares about your résumé is strongly reinforced by the producers of the show. I'm not saying they prod players to do certain things, but of course they love the idea that players are concerned that they might not have enough idol plays or blindsides for their résumé. Most production decisions, especially changes to game mechanics, are made to set the stage for the players to try wild stuff. The Shot in the Dark, one of the better New Era additions, allows every player to trade in a vote for a one-in-six shot at immunity, ensuring that *every* vote needs to be a blindside. Even the new final tribal jury questioning format in *Game Changers* was clearly put in place so that every finalist's game would be broken down into (not always sensical) chunks of outwit, outplay, and outlast to encourage every player to worry more about every aspect of their game. It's not clear if this has influenced any winner from season 34 on, but it's definitely given the jury more opportunity to pile on someone and explain that they won't vote for them because they just didn't win enough challenges or play enough advantages or—the aforementioned favorite new résumé-related rationalization—put themselves into fire-making.

The producers obviously want players to take big swings; it doesn't matter whether those end up being big hits or big mistakes, because they still might make big TV moments. Unfortunately, when editors play up the importance of big moves for the sake of the audience, this ironically often ends up leaving the audience frustrated. The more bombastic players like Boston Rob, Russell, and Aubry get a more favorable

* A boy can only dream that we'll leave Fiji one day.

edit and leave a large chunk of viewers confused when they are handily defeated by Amber, Natalie, and Michele, whose more subtle gameplay is more difficult to properly portray on screen. Prioritizing blindsiding the audience every episode can result in blindsiding them on the winner!

Some of the savviest *Survivor* players have ignored the flashy idea of the résumé, realizing the path to winning is often the boring one. Sophie Clarke deliberately and forcefully made the less exciting television move of sticking to the majority alliance, knowing full well that she would be able to beat Coach at final tribal. Her successful strategy was rewarded with being one of the show's most under-edited winners. Yet despite her tenth-place showing in *Winners at War*, her more overt gameplay led to an edit depicting her as the big, scary dragon Tony had to slay to win the game. Similarly, Michele's fighting-from-the-bottom third place in *Winners at War* garnered her more respect from the audience than her not-flashy social win in *Kaôh Rōng*. Ironically, both times, fans felt she deserved second place.

The takeover of "*Survivor* Résumé" thinking has meant a disconnect between what helps you win *Survivor* and what you think you're supposed to do on *Survivor*. The audience is complicit in this, as well. Those of us who watch, and especially those of us who commentate on the show, know that it's a much more exciting night when we get a big-time blindside instead of the safer, more subtle (and often smarter) move. So the producers want it, we want it, and we can't ignore the meta that the players themselves are now aware enough to know everyone around them wants it. They know what will get them airtime on the show, and it's not hiding under the radar to avoid making a big splash. As Zeke declared in *Game Changers*, he'd rather live with the regret of not making a move soon enough than the regret of making a move too late. Nobody wants to spend thirty-nine days* on *Survivor* to rarely be seen on television, even if they win. But if I may give a small piece of advice (which is more of a plea) to future contestants who plan to go out there and do as much as humanly possible . . . when you're filming your confessionals, even if the producers try to prompt it, do not use the word "résumé." Go ahead and say you're about to "blow things up" or "slay the dragon" or "tear the roof off this motherf—r" or whatever manner of speaking feels genuine to you. Just don't invoke the bland image of adjusting fonts and tinkering with margins in Microsoft Word.†

> "And what I think is unfortunate about the game is that not enough players get enough credit for what they decide not to do. Not enough players get enough credit for what they decide not to do in the name of strategy."
>
> **—Jamal Shipman, April 20, 2023**

The résumé ends up being a convenient misconception for the players, the producers, and the fans. It benefits nearly everyone except the ones who buy into this shared

* A boy can only dream that we'll get back to thirty-nine one day.

† Though I have no issue with the good people at Microsoft or their product, which I'm currently using.

delusion and don't realize that the emperor Richard Hatch actually has no clothes. Players end up making moves that are big but not good and whose motivations are confusing. I'm not saying only subtle social moves help you win *Survivor*, but I do think that you need to ask yourself if the big play you're about to pull off actually benefits your game or if it's just something you want to say you did. Even though Baby Andy didn't end up winning 47, his bombastic Operation: Italy was a thrill because it made perfect sense for him to take that risk at that stage of his game. When Tony and Jesse slice the throats of their number one allies Trish and Cody for a strategic purpose, we love it. Their hunger to win overpowers their genuine friendships and it is truly a beautiful, painful thing to watch. The show rarely gets any better than Tony looking Trish straight in her eyes and telling her yes, the money was worth him swearing on his dead father. We are like Romans in the Colosseum, cheering to see more blood spilled. But that magic dies when the gladiators aren't fighting for their survival but just to beef up their LinkedIn profiles. In season 46, half the cast blindsided their number ones because they thought that was what you have to do on *Survivor* now. It not only hurt their own games, with most of them getting voted out right after, but it proved to be a confounding chain of events to witness. "Betrayed my ally" isn't a good point on your résumé if you didn't need to betray your ally. Funny enough, Kenzie's win could be partially attributed to failing to vote out her number one, Tiffany. If she had succeeded in her plan, maybe Tiffany wouldn't have campaigned so hard for her on that jury.

So if the résumé doesn't matter, what does? Well, just like in real life, getting the job is about much more than one crisp piece of paper. Your cover letter, references, and the job interview itself matter a whole lot more. Your cover letter is your story—how you made it to the end, what your overall strategy was, maybe even some growth you had. The references are the people on the jury who will vouch for you or bury you. After losing the jury vote in back-to-back seasons 19 and 20, Russell declared there was a flaw in the game. And while jury management falls under Russell's responsibilities, it's no secret Laura Morett strong-armed the jury over her personal dislike for him. So I will partially agree with Russell here in the sense that, in a perfect world, the jury would be completely sequestered and not be able to influence each other. But we don't live in a perfect world. We live in a world where hot dogs come in packs of ten while hot dog buns come in packs of eight, and it's too impractical from a production standpoint to sequester every juror. Not to mention needlessly cruel to the early jurors who just had their dreams crushed and just want to commiserate with other losers while eating a bunch of hot dogs.

Which brings us to the final tribal council: the job interview itself. How you come across in a job interview matters much more than the bullet points on your résumé. Employers aren't hiring a list of facts about you; they are hiring a person they need to feel good about spending every single day with. And *Survivor* jurors are voting for which winner of their season will make them feel good about their experience as a whole. Since jurors are talking and comparing notes, the most important aspect of your job interview is to show self-awareness. The key is making the jury feel good about voting for you, which doesn't necessarily mean you have to kiss their asses (though that often helps) but does mean you have to validate their perception of you in the game . . . because it validates their perception of themselves. The clearest difference between résumé and cover letter is Dean presenting an idol he never had to use as just another thing he did, versus Maryanne presenting an idol she never had to use to change the perception of her to someone more in control than everyone thought.

Whatever point you want to make to the jury, be sure to make it with conviction. Take it from John Popper of Blues Traveler, whose biggest hit is a catchy tune with the lyrics being about how it doesn't matter what he says so long as he sings with inflection. Just like Bob Dylan, quoting Sam Cooke, once said that voices shouldn't be measured by how pretty they are, but only if they convince you that they are telling the truth. And who can forget when Baylor Wilson sang about stepping in gum, getting honey in her hair, having her Dairy Queen melt, movie theater floors, and various other sticky situations? It is, indeed, a sticky situation, as well as your responsibility, to manage the emotions of a pained jury.

The jurors are a bunch of hurt people, who just lost a game for a million dollars on a national stage. They're emotional and occasionally drunk* . . . which makes them even more emotional. They're clinging on to the last bit of power in the game they have left: their jury vote. And when you come at them with résumé talk, what they're hearing is someone dictating the terms on which they should base their decision. Jurors want their own autonomy, so figure out what's important to them and get their vote on their terms . . . not yours. And, all right, I'm big enough to admit that, when I was on the *Amazon* jury, I cast my vote for Jenna mostly because I liked her better than Matteo.

> "It was Day 39, we were waiting to go into tribal council, and me and Courtney were just laughing and joking, and Amanda was like, 'How can you guys be laughing right now? I'm trying to think. I'm trying to figure out what I'm going to say.' And I looked at her and I said, 'That's going to get you nowhere, Amanda. We are here on Day 39, and me and Courtney are celebrating. So you do you.' And I didn't want to go in and sound like a robot. I didn't want to go in and sound like I had this huge thing planned out. And I went in and I was like, 'I'm going to listen to what they say and then I'm going to answer.' And so, yeah, and it worked."
>
> **—Todd Herzog, February 18, 2021**

* "Blame it on the beer," as a different *Survivor*-contestant-turned-country-star Chase Rice once sang. Even though he and big NYC-bachelor Sash may've had more moves on their résumés, Fabio had more friends on the jury.

RHAP
RHAP

CHAPTER 8
The Rob That Sucks

How I Played *Survivor* for Two Seasons but Talked About It for Fifty

In the fall of 2001, with my late grandfather's camcorder, I filmed my *Survivor* audition tape. It consisted of my voiceover narration as I wrote a letter to Mark Burnett. I told them who I was, where I was from, and asked if there was any way for me to get "that Jerri chick's" phone number—I said I could understand Colby passing up a million dollars but he was an idiot for passing up Jerri. I never sent in the tape. What was the point? They were never going to pick me. And I was honestly terrified of the conditions of *Survivor: Africa*.

Instead, in the spring of 2002, I set my sights slightly lower and decided to apply for *Big Brother*. There were so many people applying for *Survivor*, how many could possibly want to be on *Big Brother*? Plus, if I got on *Big Brother*, I would get to leave work for three months, a way better deal than a quick thirty-nine-day sabbatical of *Survivor*. I made a different tape, in which I did a fictional post-win interview with an animated *Big Brother* host Julie Chen, voiced by my sister. I discussed the impeccable strategy which led to my *Big Brother 3* win and how all the women in the house wanted me (which my sister, as Julie Chen, claimed to not recall). I almost didn't send in that tape, either. Maybe I was scared, but more likely I was just being lazy. I had to go all the way to the post office?! Get a big envelope?! But on the way to the airport to go to Jamaica with my fraternity friends Floyd and Justin, I managed to find time in my busy schedule to drop that tape off at the mailbox outside the Wantagh Public Library. It was a memorable spring break—Floyd and I even competed in a *Survivor* competition at a bar. I made the merge but then it was rigged in favor of some bikini-clad girls.*

A few weeks later, this guy Teddy calls me up from *Big Brother* casting. I honestly thought I was being pranked. But it was real, and he wanted me to take the train to New York to meet with some casting executives. I took the day off work, beyond excited to meet anybody at all associated with making the shows I had only seen on TV. It was obvious it went well because my meeting went way longer than the others'. I talked about how I lived in my parents' basement so I'd probably get more privacy in a house full of cameras. I half-joked about how the women in the *Big Brother* house would *have* to date me since they'd have such limited options. They seemed to think I was funny and it was all very exciting, but the most I hoped for was that I'd get flown out to Los Angeles to be part of the fifty or so people in casting finals. I'd never been to California before. And suddenly, there I was. You hear about the beaches, the celebrities, but I'd say the ideal trip to Hollywood is being sequestered for seven days at the Universal Sheraton, meeting with executives and taking a battery of mental and physical tests. I finally got sent to CBS and met with twenty or so suits, including Les Moonves, the head of the network at the time. The meeting went great, and I flew home that night already prepping mentally to go on *Big Brother*. A few weeks later, I got a call

* Little did I know this would be my second-best showing of my three *Survivor* outings.

from casting director Robyn Kass that it wasn't going to happen. I was devastated. I remember getting sad drunk and my dad yelling at me. When I finally stopped feeling sorry for myself, I committed to improving myself by next summer so I'd get cast on *Big Brother 4* instead. I started by quitting smoking—I'm not sure why I thought being a smoker is what prevented me from getting cast, but it made sense at the time.

That September, *Survivor: Thailand* had just premiered when I got a phone call from someone in Lynne Spillman's office. "Hey, would you wanna be on *Survivor*?" I was asked casually as my heart dropped through the soles of my shoes. It seemed what had happened was that my *Big Brother 3* slot went to this guy Josh Feinberg, another dorky white guy, also from Long Island. Josh was a big character on the show and *Survivor* was actively looking for a Josh Feinberg–type to round out their latest cast.* And who better to fill that archetype than the other guy they were considering? So I was back on a plane to Los Angeles, back to the same battery of tests and interviews. I met with a lot of the same CBS execs from a few months prior, so honestly, I wasn't even treating this as a way to get on *Survivor*. I was only looking at this process as a way to get in good for *Big Brother 4*. Finally, I had the big meeting with Jeff Probst, Mark Burnett, and my old pal Les Moonves. Right before, Lynne pulled me aside and told me not to mention *Big Brother*, because Mark *hates Big Brother*. But I should definitely mention that I wrote my college paper on how *Who Wants to Be a Millionaire* and *Survivor* changed television. Not a problem. I did my superfan spiel and stuck with my shtick† about struggling to get dates. They asked me which *Survivor* women I'd love to get with and I made a joke about going out with *The Australian Outback*'s Alicia Calaway and how she'd kick my ass. As fate would have it, I'd end up on a tribe with her a year and a half later . . . and she would kick my ass. After this meeting, I went back to the waiting room and some casting handlers came to tell me I was going to be on the sixth season of *Survivor*. Again, I thought I was being pranked. More specifically, I asked if I was being "X'ed," which was what they said on Jamie Kennedy's

* I'd say I did a bit better on *Survivor* than Josh did on *Big Brother*. I definitely cried a lot less.

† Not really a shtick.

hidden camera prank show (not to be confused with that era's Ashton Kutcher's hidden camera prank show *Punk'd*). It became clear I was being neither X'ed nor punk'd when they took me to Cedars-Sinai, the hospital my wife would eventually work at as a nurse, and gave me so many inoculations that I could barely see straight. I got sent home the next morning, knowing that in four weeks, I would leave for *Survivor*.

I cannot overstate how big a deal this was. In 2002, less than one hundred people had ever played *Survivor* . . . and *I* would be one of them?! I (very much incorrectly) assumed I would be one of the last people to get to play. The show was still a phenomenon but slipping a little in the ratings. I mean, how long could it realistically last?

I only had a month to prepare. They gave me a shopping list and I had to get doubles of everything. Back then, online shopping wasn't quite what it is now. Where the hell could I get two pairs of Speedos out on Long Island? And did I have to wear a Speedo on the show?! I had never worked out in my life, didn't have a gym membership, and could barely swim. I owned a couple of dumbbells and I tried to run the track a couple times in the chilly October days. I knew getting in shape was out of the question, so I decided to put on weight instead. I took weight-gainer, frequented McDonald's, and put ice cream in all of my shakes. I went into *Survivor* the heaviest I'd been in my life. At least I knew I wasn't going to die of starvation. I'd still worry about dying, though. Many a night, I'd wake up in a panic—what the hell was I thinking going out there? It was going to be a disaster. My parents were also extremely concerned and confused about the whole thing. They hadn't taken any of this seriously until I came home and showed them my inoculations. Now my weird obsession was becoming real and they could not imagine it was going to go well for me.

This was before the show was even on DVD, so you couldn't easily go back and watch previous seasons. Podcasts weren't a thing yet, so I devoured whatever blogs and message boards I could find about the show. David Bloomberg wrote "Why _____ Lost" articles, a resource breaking down why each person got voted out. I read a book by Peter Lance called *The Stingray* about Richard Hatch's Machiavellian strategy, and a *Survivor* field manual written by Mark Burnett (which didn't end up being particularly helpful). I had no master plan going into the game. I just knew I wasn't ever going to try to be a leader and I wanted to remain flexible. At the insurance office where I worked, we used some European software; after getting approval from my boss to go on the show, I made up a cover story that I was being sent to that software's company headquarters in Prague for a while to . . . I guess get better trained? Instead, I flew to Miami, where I was temporarily quarantined at a hotel. I had just ordered a room service burger as my potential last meal when two producers came in with a camera. Was I ready to know where I was going? they asked. I had already read on the *SurvivorSucks* forums that the next season was rumored to be set in the Amazon, but I still played along with being surprised. The other thing they couldn't wait to tell me was that, well, the Speedo they made me get? That was because the Amazon has a small fish that likes to swim up your urethra. So I'd better always wear my Speedo in the water if I didn't want to have to get my penis amputated—not exactly an item on my *Survivor* bucket list.

> "It's such a concentrated experience that nobody else can understand. And then, it's like another concentrated experience inside of that that, like, you know, you have your own season. Like, the people who haven't played *Survivor* don't get it, and then people who've never played your season don't get it."
>
> **—Jenna Morasca, January 24, 2023**

From Miami we flew to São Paulo and, from there, to Manaus. Then, there was a series of ground and boat transportation leading us deep into the Amazon rainforest. The final step was a wet landing, as they say. We got off the boat straight into the water, and were instructed to shuffle our feet so we didn't accidentally step on a stingray. The sun was setting when it sunk in how much trouble I was in. We ate at a mess hall, where Mark and Jeff addressed us with a rousing pre-game speech. "If you didn't want to go on an adventure," Mark Burnett taunted us, "you should've gone on *Big Brother*!" *Oh God, he hates me*, I thought. And if I wasn't terrified enough, they had nature guides take us out on canoes into the water to show us how real it was.* They shined their flashlights around, illuminating red circles surrounding us, which they informed us were the eyes of crocodilian caimans. "They really hate it when we do this!" they told us before banging a bunch of pots that they'd clearly brought on the boats for this exact purpose. If they hate it, maybe let's stop doing it?! Between the crocodiles and stingrays and piranhas and that urethra fish, it seemed that simply being in the Amazonian water could kill you. So, with the exception of a brief moment in a challenge later on, I had zero intention of getting near the water my entire time there.

After a few days of press stuff and nature training, we got woken up at six a.m. to finally get to do the thing. It was so surreal watching Jeff do multiple takes of the "thirty-nine days, sixteen people, one survivor" intro. When we were split into tribes, we finally learned that the twist theme of the season would be men versus women. My gut reaction was a little disappointment. We hadn't been allowed to speak to any of the other cast members, but there were a lot of preseason social games going on purely based on eye contact and facial expressions. I felt like I had great facial-expression-related relationships with more of the women than the men. I also wasn't too opposed to getting to know Heidi specifically. Pretty quickly I realized how much I benefited from being on a tribe of all men. Going in, I was concerned about being a physical liability to my tribe, both in the challenges and building the shelter. But suddenly, being on a tribe with seven other men, it was like, great, we'll have enough guys who can fish and build stuff. And since we'll already have plenty of muscle for the challenges, maybe someone good at the puzzles would suddenly be more useful. It also helped me a lot that two of our buffest guys, Dan and Ryan, totally choked in our first challenge on the balance beam.

The first night was the scariest. I wasn't nervous about the strategic game; I was nervous about the elements. I was scared I would fail instantly, completely fall flat on my face. I'd never even been camping before! Not only was I worried about having a (no offense) Brandon Donlon experience out there, I genuinely thought I might die. Sleeping on the floor of the Amazon jungle in just your normal clothes is a harrowing

* Which, believe me, was *not* necessary. I was not pulling an Emily Flippen and pushing back on how real this was.

experience. I really wanted to prove to the tribe that I was a hard worker. Who cares how or where to build the shelter, but if anyone needed something done, I would give it my all to get it done. I might've overdone it and given myself some heat exhaustion. Great, now I'd be the sick guy at the start of the season who gets voted out for being sick. Fortunately, it passed, and I soon realized I was probably not going to die out there. And, spoiler alert for those who haven't seen my season . . . I did not, in fact, die. I found myself fifth in an alliance of five guys. Not the worst spot to be early on, to be safe for a few votes at minimum. But still I struggled to bond with the men. These were not my kind of guys—none of them really watched TV or went to the movies. I've never been much of a macho guy, but I thought I could, at the very least, bond with the men about professional sports. But no—while I was into normal sports like professional baseball and football,* these fellas were into the likes of FIFA, cycling, and crew. So talking about chicks was the only way to get a good response out of them.

I found my place on the tribe as the fun guy. *Survivor* could get very boring—lots of downtime, waiting around with nothing to do. So I became the guy entertaining everyone with jokes, stories, ideas for games. Back then, we were each allowed to bring a personal item with us. I figured I didn't need a picture of my parents, so I chose to bring something fun instead, something we could play with or create activities out of. Originally, I wanted to bring my desk bell. I had grown up watching game shows and decided to buy a desk bell to use for our *Family Feud* board game. I ended up bringing it to college with me and used it to punctuate whenever somebody made a particularly great joke. When someone said something really funny or very true, I'd hit the bell like a symbol crash. The bell even featured in the *Survivor* audition tape I never sent in. Production, however, correctly figured me constantly ringing a bell would mess with their audio. I also considered an Etch A Sketch, but ultimately landed on the Magic 8 Ball. Asking the Magic 8 Ball questions ate up some time and bought me some goodwill, as well as some camera time. I do admit, I could be a bit of a ham on the show.

* Love my notoriously lovable and not-so-lovable losers, the Mets and the Jets.

Would I have organically said I "missed my calling as a lumberjack" when I was poorly chopping wood if there wasn't a camera on me? Probably not. But I wasn't there to *not* be on a TV show. Plus, the producers were really encouraging me. It became a feedback loop where I would say something funny in my interview and they would laugh and I would try to chase the next laugh at any cost. If you watch my confessionals, you'll notice I'm talking rather slowly. That's because when I started a sentence, I didn't quite know how that sentence would end. I was just searching for the most outlandish thing to say on the fly. It didn't necessarily make sense to call the women's tribe the camp of the vagina monologues but the producers seemed into it so I kept going. I was also TV-savvy enough to know what sorts of confessionals they would need. So when I said that I might vote with Ryan, I might vote with Roger, it wasn't because I hadn't already made up my mind; I just knew that would most likely be the last confessional they'd air before tribal. I was such a screen hog, I even used giant block letters when writing my votes because I hoped if my handwriting was super large and clear, they'd use my vote as the final vote each episode.

Things took a turn for the better at the swap. Not only did I get swapped with Alex, my closest ally from my initial Tambaqui tribe, I finally got to be around some of the younger women, Jenna and Shawna, both of whom I instantly got along with. More importantly, I got linked up with Deena. On the *Big Brother* season I didn't get cast on, there was this cunning player Danielle Reyes (of later *Traitors* fame) who strategically ran the house with her secret alliance with this younger guy Jason. I actively wanted a Danielle to my Jason—an older woman who no one would suspect I was working with. Deena was perfect. She was a highly logical player and we were going to play a game no one would see coming. Socially, I had finally found my group, and, strategically, I had found my secret partner. Now I was really cooking. Things only got better and better from there, with the highlight of the season being when I won the final seven immunity. Overall, I did better than I thought I would at the challenges. I didn't embarrass myself, probably because I didn't have to swim. But the final seven challenge wasn't some fluky dexterity thing—it was answering questions about who knew the tribe best, something I took real pride in. Everyone was so happy for me when I won, and I was looking around at the six other players, thinking, *Wow, everybody believes I'm their ally. Tomorrow I'll betray and crush the dreams of three of them, but for now, I'm on top of the world.* When Jeff put that necklace around my neck, I said it was the best day of my life. And it really was—until my kids ruined it.

My sons recently asked me unprompted if I had ever won individual immunity. Oh boy, pull a chair, kids. I fired up Paramount Plus. Here we go, season 6, episode 11! But as soon as the challenge started, my kids were like, "Hold on, Dad, this is questions. This isn't *Survivor*, this is *Big Brother*!" Well, sorry, it was a mental challenge! Jeff asked who there used sex as a weapon and my sons were freaking out: "Oh my God, why are they saying this?!" "I don't know! Those were the questions they asked!" Jeff followed up with asking who there we had a crush on and the kids lost it, like, "Dad, why are they being like this?!" By the time Jeff asked who there we'd want to see pose nude in a magazine, my wife had come downstairs and she was furious I was showing this to them. Their jaws were dropped and they didn't even know what they were watching. I wasn't running through an obstacle course or solving a puzzle; Jeff wasn't yelling, "Rob's really doing it!" As far as my kids were concerned, this wasn't even *Survivor*.

There's probably a lesson here about keeping expectations low. Going out there, all I cared about was getting invited to *Survivor* parties after the show was over. I mean, I was one of the ninety-six people total who had played—they *had* to invite me places. I wasn't aiming to become an icon of the show; my only goal was to *meet* the icons of the show. Each additional day I had out there felt more and more like playing with house money. And speaking of money, I never for a single second dreamed of actually winning the million dollars. It wasn't until deep into the season that Heidi told me there was prize money beyond first and second place. I can't remember the specifics, but it was like third place got $85k, fourth $75k, and so on. I couldn't believe it—I didn't even have five thousand dollars to my name, so any of these amounts might as well have been a million dollars.*

I can honestly say I did not take any part of the experience for granted. Day 38, my final day in the game, I still remember taking time to admire how beautiful the sunset was before heading to my doom at tribal council. After Jenna voted me out at the final three, I said in my confessional that I wasn't going to stop smiling until my torch was out, and you know what? I'm still smiling. I wasn't putting on a brave face, either. Everything truly went a million times better than I ever could have anticipated. Short of winning the show, I felt like I experienced every single aspect I could of *Survivor*, my favorite TV show.

Final tribal council was on a Thursday, I flew back on Friday, my parents picked me up at the airport Saturday, I watched football Sunday, and I was back to work 8:30 a.m. Monday morning. My cover story of going to Prague was not holding up. I looked awful, I had lost thirty pounds, and I physically was not able to stay awake past six o'clock at night. A *Survivor* season was currently filming and the world's biggest *Survivor* fan, who made everyone in the office do a *Survivor* pool, just coincidentally went missing and lost a bunch of weight? People didn't know, but they knew. It was super exciting leading up to the show airing. They did a strange cross promotion (that they never repeated) where, if you went to a Saturn dealership and test drove a car (like the Saturn Ion that Matteo ended up winning), they would give you a DVD with preseason interviews with the cast. I can't tell you how many Saturns I test drove to get my hands on multiple copies to give to friends. Sorry to all the salesmen whose time I wasted—the next car I purchased was a Mini Cooper.

* Heidi also wanted her, Jenna, Alex, and myself, regardless of who won the million, to all go into business together and buy a Sonic. Which I definitely did not want to do. I had to rat out her plan to producers, as conspiring to share the prize money broke the rules. In hindsight, I could've been a hamburger franchise mogul by now. Maybe you were right, Heidi. Sorry.

My life did not immediately change when the show started airing. I did not become an instant celebrity—more of a niche one. But from my experience, at least, being a niche celebrity is the perfect amount of fame. It's the best of both worlds: I can go to a *Survivor* event and be famous, and I can still go to Kroger's and be a nobody. Like changing from Superman to Clark Kent without the trouble of putting the glasses back on. Except for a few times at CVS and one time in traffic, I didn't really get recognized when my season was airing. I also don't have a very specific look, like a Rupert. If a person stops me, it's likely that they're confusing me for a friend of a friend they met once. This was also before social media, there was no Cameo.com, so I wasn't exactly reachable by people that watched the show. During my run, I read anything and everything about me that was posted online. I know a lot of castaways receive an unnecessary amount of hate from the audience and I'm sorry to report that I experienced absolutely none of this. I'd go on *SurvivorSucks* and find that all the strategy people loved me, all the character people loved me, everyone loved me. Since the internet was invented in 1983, for all I know, I may be the only person who ever had a good time reading about themselves online.

My parents started throwing weekly watch parties, inviting lots of people over. Even though they were originally against the idea of me going on the show, now they loved it. When I was growing up, they always saw me as a goof. My mom worked at the same insurance office as me, so that's where she began to see that the son she raised wasn't a complete idiot. For my father, though, I think seeing me on *Survivor* might have been the first time he was actually proud of me. He didn't like that I was studying communications; he wanted me to go to school for business, do something respectful. But once his son was on *Survivor*, he couldn't wait to tell everyone. I was obviously the star of these watch parties—I mean, it's not like my family was rooting for Dave Johnson. Some players get a bad edit, but I loved my edit. I went into this grateful to just be on one episode, but I got to dominate the screen time of all thirteen. Did I say some stuff that makes me cringe a little now? Sure, but I don't have any deep remorse.

Every other week there's a new Reddit thread from someone discovering *The Amazon* and being shocked at the "misogyny." I do understand the world is a lot different now, but back in 2003, the men, myself included, weren't presented in a damning way, but rather comedically. It was like, hey, these guys are idiots, here's how these idiots talk. I do regret calling Roger a bigot. I didn't then or now agree with his views on gay people, but I do wish I had chosen different words. Roger had a tough life. He served in Vietnam, he had lost a daughter. On reflection, he was more of a Rudy than a right-wing talk radio guy. I'm sure he was excited to watch himself on television with his family and I could've condemned his opinions without hitting him with a sledgehammer. I also feel bad about how I shut down Dan Lue's concerns at our second tribal council. From my perspective, Dan wasn't on the outs with the tribe because he was Asian; it was because he aligned himself with Ryan. I still think Dan got voted out because he was frankly bad at playing *Survivor*. But now that I'm twice that age, having seen more of the world, it's obvious his feelings on the matter were more valid than mine. If he felt there was some innate bias against him as being the only non-white member of the tribe, it's something worth seriously considering. And despite how frustrated Roger may have been with Dan's work ethic, he definitely should not have said he was going to give him a kung fu chop. C'mon, Roger, I was trying to help you—work with me a little!

> "It's ten years and I've always wanted to say, you know, the last show when I got tossed, it was brutal. And I hardly ever go on the internet, but anyway, I did. And there was an article, some guy was saying about how he watched that show, and he said, 'Never had that happen before or subsequent to where they treated, you know, right from the get-go.' You knew I was gone. And absolutely add insult to injury was when you guys took my clean underwear."
>
> **—Roger Sexton, February 7, 2013**

Someone who seemed to particularly enjoy me on the show (though maybe not everything I said about my female castmates) was my sister's friend Nicole. She had missed my family's first watch party but showed up the second week. After each episode, the younger people would all go to Mulcahy's for drinks. Nicole went and we really hit it off. Rinse and repeat a few weeks and, suddenly, I had my first ever (and hopefully last ever) serious girlfriend. I never got mobbed by rabid fans at Mulcahy's, but I did have my first kiss with my number one fan Nicole there. I was trying to slow play it, though. I was kinda being the reverse version of *48*'s David Kinne. Rather than trying to win a million dollars on *Survivor* to keep my girlfriend from dumping me, I wanted to make sure Nicole wasn't dating me just because I might become a millionaire soon. I was very guarded and didn't even bring her to the finale. We had only been dating a month or two, and this *Survivor* business was *my* thing. Even though I didn't bring her, I did give Nicole a shout-out by announcing on live TV that I did finally get a girlfriend, though after seeing how I played, she didn't believe a word I said.

Finale night was huge. My family and I took a limo into Manhattan. There, by the Ed Sullivan Theater, I was recognized left and right by fans of the show. I only got third, but Jeff called me the smartest player to never win the game. And I did get to achieve my dream of meeting so many *Survivor* alumni. It was incredible. Now, this is the part of the story where I should start returning to planet Earth, but only a month later, I was invited back to New York City along with the rest of my season's final six for the CBS upfronts. That's where networks parade the stars of all their shows out in front of the shareholders and advertisers. We're hanging out backstage at Carnegie Hall, waiting for our turn to go onstage, when I notice Richard Hatch is there. And Rudy. And Ethan. And Jerri. I asked what they were doing there and Richard seemed surprised I hadn't heard about . . . the *All-Stars*. So we go out onstage to tip our cap to the crowd, Destiny's Child (minus Beyoncé) is there performing "Survivor," and all I'm thinking is, *Wow . . . they're going to bring people who played* Survivor *back to* Survivor? I had assumed this was a one-and-done-type deal, but I'd done pretty well . . . could *I* be asked back? At the after-party, I found myself at a table with Mark Burnett and Phil Rosenthal, the creator of *Everybody Loves Raymond*. Phil was incredibly nice and a big fan of the show, and he asked Mark in front of me if I was going to be on *All-Stars*. "Is the pope Polish?" Mark quipped back rhetorically in his patented British accent. I'll save you a Google search—at the time, the pope *was* Polish. So only a few weeks after my season ended, I was already preparing to go back on the show.

This time, I got a personal trainer and began to (somewhat) seriously start working out. From my perspective, I was one balance challenge away from winning a million dollars. I quit my job at the insurance company, which really hurt my boss's feelings. Les Feingold was a family friend who graciously gave me that opportunity, took me under his wing, and gave me early exposure of how to run a company—even though the insurance business is a lot different from the monkey business I now operate. Les had also been incredibly flexible with me taking time off to pursue my reality dreams. But to be perfectly honest, once I had returned from *Survivor*, I ceased to be a functional employee anyway. Seven out of the eight hours of the day, I was either surfing the web for *Survivor* stuff or chitchatting on the phone with Jenna Morasca. I hate to say it, but if you're an employer, there's really no benefit to letting your employee go off and get a big head on some television show. Joke's on me, though. My friend Justin also worked there and stuck around in the insurance industry, ending up way more successful than me. He just sold his own brokerage company for a lot more money than I would've gotten if I had won *The Amazon*, *All-Stars*, and, why not, *Winners at War* combined.

That summer, *All-Stars* was looming large. I wasn't necessarily pre-gaming or building alliances, but I was attending a lot of charity events that other players would be at, trying to get in good with everyone. I probably saw Boston Rob five or six times that summer. He hosted a Labor Day party and a lot of people who ended up on the cast were there. I felt like I was rubbing elbows with all the right folk and was set up great. Was I feeling myself? Yeah, of course. My expectations going into *All-Stars* were much higher than *The Amazon*. My story was that Jeff called me the smartest person to never win; I'm about to change that. Or, if I didn't win, I'd still make it real far and be real famous. To me, I was from season 6—basically the New Era. While these old-schoolers were going to just stick with their starting alliance, I was going to run circles around them with my fluid gameplay. I was feeling confident to an embarrassing degree. I went on a trip to California with Jenna and Heidi and we ended up meeting up with Colby and Jenna Lewis. I was talking with Jenna Lewis at some bar and she asked me what I thought her chances were of being put on *All-Stars*. I told her that I honestly didn't think it was looking too good. She called me an a-hole and told me she *was* going to be on. Not only did she outlast me by a lot, but now she's coming back for *50*. Proves what I knew. A harbinger of my many poor season 8 reads to come.

> "I rewatched *All-Stars* recently because my daughters wanted to see how physically difficult it was because I was trying to explain, like, without water for four days . . . they had to send the medic to take our blood pressure, make sure no one was gonna die and have a huge lawsuit. But it was just brutal. So we watched like four or five episodes around it so I could show them when Ethan sits down and was like, 'She's like the godfather of this team.' And then I stopped it. I was like, you can't see Mommy get bad. Like, it gets bad from here on out."
>
> **—Jenna Lewis, September 27, 2015**

Before the game started, I was sequestered with what turned out to be my entire tribe at what turned out to be Michael Bolton's dad's house. I didn't know they were going to be my tribe yet—three tribes of six weren't a thing before *All-Stars*. I just saw Boston Rob come in, followed by Amber, Big Tom, Alicia, and Sue. I thought, *Awesome, these are all people I'm on great terms with already. This is going to be a cake walk!* What

I underestimated was the impact of my season being so fresh in everyone's minds. Jeff's "smartest player to never win" comment made me the hot new thing. And no one likes the hot new thing. It didn't help that when they were doing preseason interviews, Boston Rob overheard some journalist introducing her segment with, "We're here on location with legendary players like Rob Cesternino and Richard Hatch." She might as well have said, "We're here on location, painting big, juicy targets on the backs of Rob Cesternino and Richard Hatch." She didn't even throw me a bone and list me *after* the most iconic winner the show had then seen.

I never really found my footing in the tribe. The role I served on *The Amazon* as the funny guy was not working with this crew—this tribe didn't have room for my antics. The more I tried to become better liked, the more it had the opposite effect. But I still felt like I had a good connection with Boston Rob and was in a four-person alliance with him, Amber, and Big Tom. When Rob and Amber started being an item, I thought that was great—now they were a real target. Turns out, Amber liked Alicia a lot more than me and convinced Boston Rob to bump me in the four for Alicia. Every *Survivor* player likes to view their season through a lens of their own importance, so I'll just go out on a limb and claim that was Amber's winning move. I didn't feel good about going to tribal on Day 12. The thing about having all the votes go my way during *The Amazon* was that I wasn't quite equipped to recognize when they weren't. It just felt a bit odd how little scrambling there was. Jeff read Alicia's vote against me and my vote against Alicia. But once that second "Rob C." vote came out, I was in shock. The rug got pulled out from under me and I was completely pissed. When Jeff read the third vote, I clearly mouthed the f-word, which they somehow forgot to blur. Against my will, I became the hundredth vote-out in *Survivor* history.

When I got back to Ponderosa, I was so salty and depressed. I couldn't process that it was all so suddenly over. It killed me because it wasn't supposed to be like that. But what could I have done? I guess I should've not sat out of the immunity challenge and won it on the puzzle? Even if I'd had hours' warning that I was getting voted out, I don't know if I could've gotten the votes against Rob or Amber. Maybe all I could've tried was to be more of a Phillip to Rob and go further up his ass. I wasn't faithfully playing the part of the loyal court jester. Even then, it seemed Rob correctly pegged me as someone that was going to be trouble down the line. Unlike some of these idiots on the season, I definitely would've gone rogue and flipped on Rob and Amber in the merge. So, as much as it sucks, it was a good call on Rob's part and I do take solace now knowing what he would go on to do. At least I didn't get taken out by some chump.

> **"You're not still mad about that, are you, by the way? . . . Just so that we can clear the air here, like, the reason why we did get rid of you was because you were a huge threat. I mean, like the way I wanna play the game, I always wanna play with people who, you know, I have the ability to control and, clearly, you know, I wasn't gonna be able to control you. So, we had to get rid of you. It was out of respect, buddy."**
>
> **—Boston Rob Mariano, October 24, 2012**

It's hard to capture how hard and how fast everything came crashing down. It was barely over a year from when I got the call asking me if I'd consider going on *Survivor* to that precise moment. I had just turned twenty-five, and the last fourteen months of my life had been taken up with getting cast on my favorite show, becoming a star of my favorite show, instantly being invited back to my favorite show, and then blowing it all on my favorite show, specifically blindsided out by my favorite player on my favorite show. It's an understatement to say I was devastated. It felt like all the goodwill I had built up in *The Amazon* was ripped away from me. When I said that, shy of winning, I felt that I had experienced everything I could on *Survivor* my first season . . . turns out I didn't consider the experience of having everything go horribly wrong. But that's *Survivor*, baby. There was a lot of self-pity, a lot of struggling to understand what my life would be now. What's sort of nice and beautiful is that I can look back at this time knowing where I'd go and what I'd become. I can't say *why* this happened, but *because* this happened, my life ended up taking a pretty cool trajectory. But that's results-oriented thinking. At the time, this sucked so hard.

To twenty-five-year-old me, this was basically as bad of a thing as could happen. I might've been more okay if I got to stay at Ponderosa, hang out with more of the pre-jurors, possibly see Jeff here and there, and still feel like I was in *Survivor* world. But after the Richard Hatch/Sue Hawk incident, they decided to send the first few pre-jurors on their trip earlier. I wouldn't say I was the number one victim of that incident, but it certainly didn't help my situation. Jenna went home to be with her mother and Richard had insane demands to get put up in his own private whatever, so it was just Tina, Rudy, and myself sent to Patagonia. While the younger group of Ethan, Colby, and Jerri were partying it up in Mexico, I was freezing my ass off with the older crowd at the southern tip of Argentina. Don't get me wrong, I have nothing but love for Tina and Rudy, but it was a long three weeks. Tina was dealing with her own stuff, having been voted out first, and had no interest in trying to make me feel any better. She was trying to enjoy the experience—go fly fishing, go horseback riding up a mountain. I was just wallowing, getting drunk and trying to find cigarettes, not in the right headspace to appreciate anything. I was missing my mother's fiftieth birthday, I was missing Nicole. It's one thing to miss this kind of stuff while playing *Survivor*. It's another to miss them while stuck in purgatory, playing Cranium with Rudy and Tina.

When I got back, I didn't even have to tell my parents how it went. My mom went out for the loved one's visit to the Amazon so she got the hint when she wasn't booked on a flight to Panama. My grandma also instantly pointed out I hadn't lost weight. She was originally excited that I was on *Survivor*, calling herself "the famous grandma," but after seeing *Pearl Islands*, was rather disappointed that I never mentioned her on the show. At least Jonny Fairplay talked about *his* grandma. The one great thing I had going for me was Nicole. I would've been in much worse shape if I didn't happen to also be totally in love, in the honeymoon stage of a blossoming relationship. The sting of what I had gone through was also starting to wear off a little with the incoming press for the season. We were going to premiere after the Super Bowl, our pre-game interviews were airing, and I was being talked about all over the media. Even though I knew it wasn't going to go well, it was nice that people were so excited for me.

My wound reopened when the season started to air. Feel free to play me the world's smallest violin, but it sucks going from someone who broke records with the amount of confessionals on air to someone who was barely on the show. And when I *was* on the show, I felt miscategorized. Say what you will about me, but I was not lazy around camp. I guess the editors needed a simple reason to justify my boot. Within two years, I had experienced both a strong edit and a flop one; had experienced both running the show and being run off the show. With the highs and lows, I can now relate to pretty much every contestant that's ever been on. I didn't tell my family, but it was pretty obvious which night I was going to be voted out since I didn't attend their watch party. I had to do my exit press the next day so CBS put me up in the city, and to make up for not taking her to my last finale, I brought Nicole with me. The only benefit of getting voted out was that I at least got my own little media week. It was cool going on Howard Stern, David Letterman, and Regis and Kelly, even if Regis really butchered my last name.

Episode 4, appropriately titled "Wipe Out!," came and went, and I was no longer on the show. *Survivor* is like a supernova in terms of how much it changes your life and then suddenly burns away. One day, you're a star. The next day, you're nothing. My dad really thought I didn't get a fair shake—he might've been the first critic of the "dangerous fun" that comes along with small tribes. People seemed bummed to see me go but eventually my brief stint on the show was lost to time. I didn't get a single question at the *All-Stars* reunion, and when the cast reunited the next morning on the CBS *Early Show*, Jeff rubbed salt in the wound, saying that he didn't ask me any questions because I made zero impact on the season. He wasn't wrong, but he didn't *have* to say it! I didn't care about losing the money, but I really cared about losing all the hypothetical opportunities I had in my head. What was I supposed to do now? Did I go crawling back to my insurance job? Could there still be any opportunities for washed-up reality stars?

Well, that was the question producer Scott Zakarin had. He'd co-founded a company called Creative Light Entertainment and wanted to find something to be done with former reality contestants who were just callously discarded by the industry. Former

Big-Brother-contestant-turned-agent Josh Souza reached out to me and I got offered $1,000 a month to blog for them on the Fishbowl website and pitch them ideas. I was more than happy to do this; I couldn't believe someone from Hollywood wanted to work with me, and I couldn't believe it when they eventually asked me to move to Hollywood to work full-time. Nicole felt that I was prioritizing my career over her, but even though I'm not some sort of God of Rizz, I was able to convince her into a long-distance relationship until she graduated from nursing school and could join me in Los Angeles. I ended up doing various projects with The Fishbowl, including a television series called *Kill Reality*, which was like *Project Greenlight*, but instead of serious filmmakers, it was a bunch of reality nuts living in one house, making a schlocky slasher film. We had cast members from *The Bachelor, The Real World, The Challenge*, and, of course, *Survivor*, with the likes of Jonny Fairplay, Ethan Zohn, and Jenna Lewis (hot off her run on *All-Stars*, an appearance in Eminem's "Without Me" music video, and a different hit viral video). Unfortunately, the funding fell through on the movie itself, *The Scorned,* so they tried to fund it out of the show's budget, expecting to recoup some money on DVD sales; instead, it was a flop, and the company ultimately went out of business. We started a new media company with all the same people from The Fishbowl, producing YouTube videos, but that lost all of its funding after the 2008 financial crash. Again, I wasn't the number one victim of what happened in 2008, but I certainly didn't benefit. It's completely bonkers that I ever, for a single second, was even slightly concerned that Nicole might've only been interested in me for my hypothetical million dollars. She was really put to the test when I had no money for many, many years.

At this point in my life, I decided to go all-in on trying to break into comedy. After a brief unsuccessful attempt at stand-up, I became more focused on the writing side. I was taking classes, writing spec scripts,* and doing the typical LA aspiring television writer thing. I liked writing jokes, but unfortunately, I lacked the daily writing discipline required to succeed. This was pre-Cochran, so I didn't know that all I had to do was say I wanted to write for television during the live reunion show and get

* A television spec script is basically a fancy way of saying "fan fiction." I wrote a *30 Rock* spec.

instantly put on some Will Arnett show. Desperate to get any attention on my writing, I started a website, appropriately named RobHasAWebsite.com. My priority became getting any eyeballs (or earballs) on the site, so I began to podcast. I've always been a fan of talk radio—I loved Howard Stern and had SiriusXM in my car. I became an early adopter of podcasts, listening to stuff like *The Bill Simmons Podcast* or some show where they talked about the TV show *Lost*. The podcast I started doing was mostly just me chatting with Nicole about this or that. She seemed to run into a lot of celebrities so she'd talk about stepping on 50 Cent's shoe or almost running over Weird Al with her car. We probably only had twenty or so of my friends listening, but I treated it like a great experience to learn various technical things which could be applicable to all the media jobs I was applying for.

> "Never watched the show again. A lot of fans ask me like, 'Hey, you know, do you keep up with the show?' And I'm like, 'No, I really don't.' And I think at the ten-year reunion, I remember somebody came up to me and was like, 'Oh, I loved you from *All-Stars* and *Thailand*.' And I was like, 'Oh, thank you very much, who are you?' And they were like, 'Oh my God, I won, you know, *Survivor* season blah, blah, blah.' And I was like, 'I'm sorry, it's nothing personal.' They were so offended. I was like, 'You know, it's not, it's nothing personal. I just, I don't watch the show. PTSD.'"
>
> **—Shii Ann Huang, September 19, 2019**

I had stopped watching the show. I was experiencing some *Survivor* fatigue, and now that it wasn't my job, I symbolically wanted to move past it. I dipped my toe back in to see some returning faces on *Micronesia* and couldn't resist watching the Russell-mania of *Samoa*, but what I really got caught up in was all the excitement brewing for the upcoming *Heroes vs. Villains* season. This couple, Jo Ann and Stacy, invited me to talk about it on their podcast called *Survivor Fans*, which, as far as I'm aware, was the first ever *Survivor* podcast. They had started with *Palau* and are still going strong. I called into their show, rambled for a while about the season 20 cast, and definitely caught the bug. It reminded me of one of the more successful projects out of The Fishbowl—when they had Jenna Lewis and me host a weekly radio show recapping what happened that week on *Survivor*. It was incredible. We would talk about *Survivor* . . . and people would actually listen! This was clearly the prototype for *Rob Has a Podcast*. I even incorporated my desk bell into it.

After the first episode of *Heroes vs. Villains* premiered, so did the inaugural episode of *Rob Has a Podcast*. Every week, I would talk about what just happened on *Survivor* with Nicole, the First Lady of Podcasting. For the third show, we had Jonny Fairplay on as our first guest. It was absurdly easy to get huge guests—many castaways hadn't been asked to do interviews in a while, so they were more than happy to chat. That first season, we had Todd, Yau-Man, Penner, Hatch, Eliza, and Stephen Fishbach, of course. Jenna and Ethan were still dating so they came on as a duo, as did Kathy Vavrick-O'Brien and Natalie White (who were not dating at that particular time or ever). Lex specifically requested to come on the April 2 show, which turned out to "coincidentally" align with the episode his betrayer Boston Rob got voted out. While I lacked the motivation as a screenwriter to make my own self-imposed writing deadlines, it turns out I get real motivated by not letting other people down. If there was any audience at all waiting to listen to me talk about *Survivor*, I felt way too guilty not putting the episode promptly out there.

I had the pleasure of interviewing Sandra after her win, and during the following season, *Nicaragua*, I somehow got added to the list of people doing exit press. It's still weird to me that they let us do exit press, like I'm an actual journalist. The podcast became in a lot of ways the record of *Survivor* news, but I still had plenty of imposter syndrome. I was just talking to these people in my bedroom. Then for *Nicaragua*, I was one of a few former contestants CBS asked to write for their website. Someone on the message boards was very excited that Boston Rob was going to be blogging about the latest season. Luckily another helpful fan stepped in to correct them: It wasn't that Rob, it was "the Rob that sucks." Instantly I co-opted this moniker in an ironic, self-deprecating way (deep down, I may have agreed with it a little).

At the beginning of *RHAP,* I put out lots of shows that weren't about *Survivor*, not wanting to get pigeonholed as just a "*Survivor* guy." I was still pretty snakebitten from my last outing and figured it would be embarrassing to be the guy that couldn't let go of the fact that he was on some TV show a hundred years ago. This was the earlier days of Twitter. I was very active on social media, so if anyone was talking about anything like Rebecca Black releasing *Friday*, I would do a show about it. It got to the point where I would end up doing fewer and fewer shows with Nicole. She's a big personality and she loved podcasting (mostly because she loved having a little corner of the world where people knew who she was), but she was a full-time nurse and didn't have the unlimited hours I did. So if this was going to be successful, I couldn't wait on Nicole to finish saving actual lives before I could hop on the mic to discuss Charlie Sheen going crazy. I was getting more steam with the podcast, but I still couldn't envision doing it full-time. I knew a guy who got so much attention for making a (pretty mediocre) web series, so I was still treating the podcast as a way to bring attention to my (pretty mediocre) writing. Just like I went through *Survivor* casting hoping it would help me with *Big Brother* casting, I was hoping *RHAP* would create an opportunity for me, not realizing that, just like a decade ago, *Survivor was* the opportunity. I was applying to so many jobs at the time and, if any of those had panned out, I would not be where I am today.

In 2011, I attended this three-day self-improvement seminar thing. It came highly recommended from Parvati and her friend/*Survivor* casting associate/*Amazing Race* contestant Erika Lynn Shay. I've always loved self-help-type stuff, so even if this particular one did seem a little pyramid-schemey, I shelled out five hundred bucks and took my chances. Their big philosophy was not to blame anyone for your problems—that everything in your life was your own fault. These tenets came with an assignment: Call your parents and tell them you love them. Let go of any baggage you may have and accept they did the best they could. As a kid, I never felt that my dad had a high opinion of me. We got closer as I got older and my experience on *Survivor* had helped with that. But still, when we spoke, it usually ended up being more surface-level conversations about sports.

I wrote up a whole outline of everything I wanted to say to my dad and called him that very Tuesday. He was a little resistant at first to having such an unprompted vulnerable conversation, but I pressed on and told him all the things I'd always wanted to say. In return, he opened up to me about how his father never showed him much affection and how he never learned how to do that. He went on to tell me how much he loved me and how proud he was of me. The conversation went better than I could've ever expected. That Friday, I got a phone call from my mother. Turns out, that amazing conversation I had with him would be the last I'd ever have with him. Out of nowhere, my dad started to experience chest pains. They called an ambulance, went to the hospital, and they lost him. This was the biggest coincidence that had ever happened to me. We were always concerned about his weight, but we had no reason to believe he was going to pass anytime soon. I had all this time in my life to have this conversation, and I thankfully got to have it, not knowing it would be my last chance to. I was at my mother's house afterward looking through photographs, and it really hit me that I needed to figure out what I was doing with my life. My father was a police officer, working hard for many years to provide for his family. But here I was in my thirties, and what the hell was I doing? Still cobbling things together and treating my obsession like a side gig. If I was going to stick with this little podcasting thing, I needed to pour all my efforts into it. No more effin' around.

I bought a bunch of podcast equipment and set a goal that I needed to make $75,000 a year from *RHAP*. I added Amazon affiliate links to the site so the listeners could support the show by doing their usual online shopping. But my big hustle in the early days was selling *Big Brother* live feeds. Back then, you got ten bucks in commission for every person you convinced to pay CBS for the feeds. I created content that went along with watching the live feeds, like recaps, and bingo cards, and even put together a team to obsessively cover them. This is how I met Taran Armstrong, who has since been a staple of *RHAP Big Brother* coverage. Some people have jobs and they don't have all day to watch the live feeds, so Taran's job was to watch the live feeds for them. That July, we made $3,700 peddling the live feeds—still well shy of my $75k goal, but getting there. We got lucky that *Big Brother 14* was a particularly exciting season, just

as we got lucky that we were heading into *Survivor: Philippines*. It was fortuitous that the dark era of *Survivor* coincided with us figuring out the growing pains of making a podcast. We had so much fun doing live recaps immediately after the *Big Brother* episodes that I thought to do the same for *Survivor*. And who better to join us than Stephen Fishbach, who was already blogging about *Survivor* for *People* magazine and had been a regular guest on *RHAP*. Stephen loved the idea and we dubbed ourselves the Know-It-Alls, a tongue-in-cheek name about how we know everything about *Survivor* (except how to win).

During our *Philippines* coverage, we had Jeff on the show for the first time, as well as Boston Rob. Two major coups. The latter had just joined Twitter and I tweeted at him that the real Boston Rob would never join Twitter—so to prove me wrong, he came on the podcast. But just as *RHAP* started to go well, personal stuff got hard. In October, Nicole had a miscarriage. After I did Penner's *Philippines* exit interview in November, he and his wife, Stacy, invited Nicole and me over for dinner. I was sharing what we were going through and told Penner that, even though I really wanted children, it was scary not having a stable job. His advice was that babies make bread—you have a kid, you figure it out. The next morning, I was in the bathroom, kinda hungover, and Nicole burst in, shoving a positive pregnancy test in my face. As Penner accurately predicted, I got another job, but his crystal ball forgot to mention that I would get laid off shortly after that. So I ended up with a two-month-old and no real job, and I had so many *RHAP* commitments, I was basically unemployable. Who wants a guy who needs to take off work early on Wednesdays and then can't work Thursdays so he can talk about his favorite reality show? Nicole was especially supportive during this time. She's the kind of person who is not great when it comes to the small stuff. If I happen to eat the last apple in the refrigerator, she will cuss me out. Yet she's amazing with the big stuff. If I happen to be unemployed and pursuing my pipe dream while we're struggling to pay for a newborn, she's unwavering in her support. She didn't doubt me, even when I was doubting myself.

In 2014, it all changed when I launched the Patreon.* I felt very sheepish asking listeners for money, but I didn't know if I could continue to make the show. Hundreds of people signed up right away—people that loved the show and didn't want it to go away. I can't begin to tell you how grateful I am to all these people. We started a Facebook group for the patrons. Finally, the people who loved *RHAP* could connect with one another. It was a magical time of white-hot energy and support for one another. Online discourse gets a bad rap, especially when it comes to anonymous people on Twitter yelling at each other, but there was something about the early days of Facebook that led to a wonderful, kind community. Around this time is when I started podcasting with Tyson, fresh off his *Blood vs. Water* win. We began discussing offbeat topical news stories on *News AF*, along with star of *The Hills* Spencer Pratt (who quickly burned out on our nonsense). Over the years, I've gotten to build incredible relationships with former-players-turned-podcasters, such as *Cagayan*'s purple-pants badass Brice Izyah and *Africa*'s popcorn-eating badass T-Bird Cooper. This is also when

* If you aren't familiar, it's basically a safe-for-work version of *OnlyFans*.

my frequent collaboration with Mike Bloom began, who for God-knows-whatever reason had mysteriously reached out to me under the guise of Mr. X.

As we did more and more shows, I was building on inside jokes within our small community. *Survivor: San Juan del Sur* is when we introduced the soundboard, a classic talk-radio staple. Any funny or weird thing that got said on the show got put on the soundboard and replayed and memed into infinity. I will still casually drop a "love you, Bay," here and there. In his book *Tribes*, Seth Godin describes what has become my basic business philosophy. Godin argues that you can have an extremely successful career if you can just find a thousand true fans. Like running a successful alliance on *Survivor*, Seth wrote that successful leaders focus more on tightening the tribe, rather than growing it. So that's why I've always tried to cater to the most hardcore fans. Will *most* people want to listen to a four-hour-plus podcast about *Australian Survivor*? Probably not. But if there are *any* fans passionate enough to want to, then I will be there for them. What started at maybe a hundred people listening to me ramble has grown to around fifty thousand people listening per episode. That's fifty times more than what Seth said I even needed!

> "I have been an *RHAP* patron for years, as many people know. . . . There's an archive out there, a very deep archive. People can snoop if they want. I have talked with Rob—how many hours have we talked? This is before I even probably heard an email from *Survivor* . . . It's a very, very full circle."
>
> **—Andy Rueda, May 27, 2025**

I knew *RHAP* had really arrived in 2015 at the uncreatively named Podcast Awards in Las Vegas, where we won the top prize: the People's Choice Award. Maybe you're not impressed, maybe you're rolling your eyes at some podcast award but, for your information, we beat . . . *Serial*! In my acceptance speech, I joked about how *RHAP* beating *Serial* was such a huge mystery that it should be explored in the second season of *Serial*. This was a big deal for me because the People's Choice was a pure fan vote, so it was a measure of how strong your fan base was. I knew I didn't have the best podcast of 2014. I didn't have the funniest or the most interesting one. But I clearly had the most dedicated listeners. So unlike Stephen Fishbach's "Fishy," which is a broken system rewarding losers for losing, this award proved I had built the best community.

My kids don't appreciate what I've accomplished because their only points of reference for what I do are people like Mr. Beast, who are a thousand times bigger than me. To them, I'm an unsuccessful loser compared to some random YouTuber making all the *Minecraft* videos they watch. And sure, what I do *is* mostly silly. One of the most popular segments on the podcast was when Josh Wigler and I did a weekly *Survivor* song parody contest, called the Wand-Off.* I can still make myself laugh remembering Corey B's tribute to *David vs. Goliath*'s medically evacuated Pat Cusack with "Pat's Tweaked Back's Alright" (to the tune of "Backstreet's back, alright!"). But what isn't silly about it is building an ecosystem for people to connect about what they care about—a place for passionate fans, amazing podcasters,† and even fellow players. In 2020, *Marquesas*'s Sean Rector reached out to me, wanting to have a roundtable with other black contestants, sharing their experiences being on the show—oftentimes, as their tribe's sole person of color. This snowballed into him creating the Black Survivor Alliance Group, which met with CBS executives and Jeff Probst and led to CBS implementing a diversity initiative for all their reality shows. Now I'm not going to sit here and declare myself the great white savior of *Survivor*. I'm just proud that the unserious platform I've built allowed for necessary serious conversations.

A few times, I've flirted with a return to *Survivor*. Nicole and I were amongst the many who got a preliminary call for *Blood vs. Water*. Even though the timing wasn't right (Nicole was pregnant with Dominic), we did enjoy the swirling rumors that maybe we'd be on the cast, and we definitely fanned those flames, teasing a "big

* Named after the first boot of *Palau*, Wanda Shirk, who, despite her limited screen time, sang her way into all of our hearts.

† I work with too many incredible podcasters to name in this book, all of whom I love like my children—and, just like my children, who my favorite is shifts from day to day, depending on who made me the least mad most recently.

announcement." It got to the point where Aras was G-chatting me threats that, if I didn't tell him I was going to be on the season, he would make sure I was the first one voted out. Then they reached out to me about possibly being on *Game Changers*. They'd already got half of the Know-It-Alls for *Cambodia* and now they wanted the better half. But my son Anthony was just two months old, so, again, not a great time to leave home. I got another call for season 40 when the rumored theme at the time was something like *Winners vs. Best to Never Win*, but once they landed on only bringing back winners, I was naturally cut. My phone then stayed rather quiet until August 2024, when I received a call about season 50. They were making a lot of calls, but I was truly honored to be considered for such a milestone season of *Survivor*.

> "I'd just like to say, now that I understand what it takes to make a podcast, I have even more respect for what you've been doing for the last many years. . . . You have a point of view. I now understand why you do it the way you do it, 'cause I've now been trying to learn how to do a podcast and realized you have to have a point of view on that podcast. You have one on yours."
>
> **—Jeff Probst, February 25, 2024**

I did my testing and my background check, and talked to the psychologist. I didn't feel that, of all the 700+ people who'd been on the show, I was one of the twenty or so hottest they'd want back, but as the months went by and I still wasn't cut, I started believing it was actually possible. Similarly to after I had been cast on *The Amazon*, I'd wake up in a panic—what the hell was I doing?! Me, back on *Survivor*? I've spent years building up this reputation and it felt like walking back into the casino and risking it all. Nevertheless, I got a flint and started practicing making a fire. I'm no Gabler, but I got to the point I could get it done. I had one Zoom call with the producers and I felt like I blew it. Or at the very least, I was a little tight. I never really got a chance to get rolling, and before I knew it, it was over and Jeff was thanking me for my time. Like my run on *All-Stars*, I didn't connect well with the group I was with, it was over rather quickly, and I had a lot of disappointment about how it all went down. I wondered if they thought that I wasn't *that* excited to go back. Which I was, but also maybe a little . . . apprehensive about it all. My understandable apprehension must've bled through. They're looking for "f—yeah," not "sure, I would, but . . ." After this call, I really dug deep and realized that, just like when *Survivor* was my entire life at twenty-one and I didn't have any expectations, I had to accept that, at forty-six, *Survivor* was still one of the most important things in my entire life, but I had to let go of some expectations. I needed to let go of any fear of embarrassing myself on television (again) and try to come around to the idea that, no matter what happens, good or bad, first boot or Sole Survivor, it was worth playing for.

A couple of months later, I was in the car with my family when I got a call from an old friend. My kids were so excited to hear a legend on the line, but he asked me to take him off speakerphone. It was Boston Rob, recently off a fun run on *The Traitors*, the hot new show on the block which pulled reality stars from all the shows into one singular multiverse of messy cutthroat competition. It was a real full circle moment. The guy who crushed my dreams twenty years earlier was presenting me with a new amazing opportunity. He told me that the *Traitors* producers had asked him for my number to invite me onto their fourth season. I was incredibly flattered, but I told him I was still in the mix for something else, cough cough wink wink. "What's better," he asked me, "a bird in the hand or one in the bush?" Good question. My call with the producers of *The Traitors* went very well and I was able to say all the things I didn't get to say on my *Survivor* call. As insane as it may sound now, there was a moment in time where it seemed possible that both *Survivor* and *The Traitors* were interested. I took a long weekend to really, truly consider which show I'd pick, if it was up to me. My head and heart were in disagreement. My head said doing *The Traitors* made a lot of sense. I get to present myself to a whole new audience and diversify my portfolio a bit. And it comes with way less of a downside. If I was the first murdered or banished on *The Traitors*, it would be a lot less humiliating than if I was the first boot of *50*. Sure, I'd have fun with it, be tongue-in-cheek and self-deprecating about it . . . but it would follow me forever. Plus, not being able to podcast about season 50 would be a big loss for me. For fifteen years I'd covered every season; how could I miss *this* one?

But when I was truly honest with myself, my heart said I had to pick *Survivor*. I can get deeply emotional now just thinking of what it would mean for me to spiritually be back on *Survivor*. I love *The Traitors*, but no part of me is going to want to cry on my first day at the castle.* *The Traitors* is an incredible opportunity but it's not going "home." *Survivor* is my home. Back when I was sitting in Ponderosa, pouty and pathetic, I never thought there was any realistic possibility to have a third chance to play *Survivor*. Either *Amazon* was a fluke or *All-Stars* was a fluke, and I wanted to prove the latter. I wanted to prove all the haters on *SurvivorSucks* wrong. I was ready to march back into that casino and bet it all on red (or black or blue or whatever color buff I'd get). I was ready to be rebirthed in that New Era mud and show everyone that I'm actually really good at this. That I'm not all talk, that I can walk the walk. That I could be the old-school player that is able to bridge the gap with the new-school players. That I could play a strategically disciplined game while remaining flexible and keep up with all the crazy twists and turns. I never let myself dream that I would win *Survivor 50*, but just that I could show up and place on *50* . . . could show people and myself how much I've grown from the twenty-four-year-old idiot into the person I'm really proud to be. Even the possibility of being selected for *50* touches me on such a deep level. But ultimately, going back on *50* would not be my destiny. On an otherwise uneventful weekday, they called me to let me know that I was no longer in contention.

Look, I'm a lifer for *Survivor*. I found this show when I was living in a flop house in Oswego during Summer 2K and that show took a shot on me and gave me everything in my life. My wife, my children, a wonderful career I could've never dreamed of, are all because of *Survivor*. *Survivor* will always be a part of my story, but going back on *Survivor* may not be. Buried deep down, I was still somewhat carrying what happened on *All-Stars* with me. I was looking to *Survivor* as my redemption. But maybe it's not a redemption story I need; just a new chapter. And *Traitors* could be that chapter. But whether that

* I hope I don't have to eat these words. Much more looking forward to eating that breakfast buffet.

goes great or ends up being a total disaster, it'll never be *Survivor*. As cheesy as it sounds, *Survivor* represents my life. And once that fire's gone, so am I. But my fire for *Survivor* has never gone out . . . even when my torch got snuffed for the second time. Would *50* be my last chance to return to the show? My burnt-up Magic 8 ball says "signs point to yes" but who knows? Maybe they'll need some old schoolers to round out the cast of a *Third Time's the Charm* themed season. And I'd still be younger than Rudy the first time he played if they called me for *Survivor 100*. Don't lose my number, Jeff.

It stung not making the cast, but I loved being in the casting mix. Yes, it would've been great to have Jeff announce my name on *The Early Show*, but, not gonna lie, I also just loved reading the rumors about me maybe heading to Fiji. I even enjoyed fanning the flames a bit, dropping little "clues" on the podcast about working on my grip strength. Beyond anything I've done or will do on television, what's made my journey special is having this relationship with the audience that I don't think a lot of other reality stars could ever experience. Yes, I started a podcast network, but it's really a relationship business. A podcast is a strangely intimate medium. I'm literally inside people's ears day in, day out, while they're at the gym, at the store, traveling all over the world. Nobody really listens to a podcast while they're experiencing their great highs in life. Podcasts are there to help people in the not-so-fun times. To distract them from their mundane commute or while they're doing the dishes. Sometimes I'm there for people going through serious medical treatments. I've heard from many people that in times of extreme isolation, especially during Covid lockdown, *RHAP* was one of the few ways they truly felt connected. I don't know if the shows are anything special, but I do know that I've been firmly consistent in putting them out. I've been remarkably reliable in this reality world, which is built of the flakiest of flakes. When Jeff himself was introducing season 48 at a live event in New York, he threw me a rogue compliment. He compared what he was trying to do on *Survivor* to what I had done on *RHAP*. That I started with this small box, but within this box, after years of doing the same thing, I've found universes. And it's true. Making the podcast is the greatest joy of my professional life and I truly believe that it's what I was put on this planet to do—to take this passion and knowledge of these shows we love and build a hub. A town square for the fans, for the players, for the alumni—even some production people are listening. I have quite literally found my tribe. And the tribe and I speak every day.

> "I don't want to talk about this. You know what I wanna talk about, Rob? You're a jerk. . . . Here's my impression of you: You'd have somebody on the thing, and you'd be like, 'So, what do you think of Mike White?' And they'd be like, 'Oh, you know, I like him. You know, he's good.' Or whatever . . . 'Yeah, yeah, yeah. Okay. Are you a fan of his films? Are you a fan of Mike White? Are you a fan of his movies?' And he'd be like, 'Well, people like, oh, I like *School of Rock*.' 'Oh, yeah? Have you ever seen *The Emoji Movie*? I got a DVD for *The Emoji Movie* I can give you.' How would you like it, Rob, if you, like, heard me on something and I'm like, 'Are you a fan of Rob Cesternino? Are you a fan of Rob? Are you, are you a fan of his?' Like, 'Oh, yeah, he's good.' 'Well, have you heard his Leesa mattress commercials with his wife? I can burn you a DVD of that!' . . . 'Have you seen *The Emoji Movie*?' Oh, my God. And this is the guy I was like, oh yeah, I hope, like, I'll have my game like Rob Cesternino because he was such a good judge of people. I was like, oh, my God, this guy can't give me freaking two positive words!"
>
> **—Mike White, December 20, 2018**

Do people get mad at me? Of course. Believe it or not, people on reality TV tend to have sensitive egos. I'm talking for so many hours a week, I'm going to eventually share an opinion that rubs someone the wrong way—or worse, someone else on my network shares a hot take that, for some reason, I have to take the blame for. J'Tia wore a green "I Heart Nerds" shirt on *Cagayan* and was rather upset with me because I dared question if she truly did or did not, in fact, heart nerds. Mike White famously tore me a new one during his *David vs. Goliath* exit interview because I did not fairly assess his game in my coverage (and I admit I was in the wrong). And I once had an awkward supermarket run-in with *Philippines'* Carter Williams. Don't even get me started on the various troubles I've created for myself with *Big Brother* contestants, where I tend to be a bit faster and looser with my coverage.

But more often than not, I'd say I'm generally appreciated in the *Survivor* world. I'm particularly moved by what the great Shane Powers once said about me. We were doing a live show during *Winners at War* in celebration of *RHAP*'s ten-year anniversary. Stephen and I were onstage at a now-closed bar in Mid-City, Los Angeles, recapping the episode, but there were some interruptions coming from the alumni in attendance. After we politely asked them to keep it down several times, Shane stormed the stage, grabbed a mic, and cussed everyone out. But after he was done swearing he continued on, "Thirteen years ago . . . Rob asked me to do his internet radio thing. This was before podcasts, it was before anything. He had a string with two Styrofoam cups on either side. I called in, I s—t on him for an hour. And it's twelve years later. And what he has built is an absolute example of one plus one plus one plus one equals *this*. And in the twelve years that he's been doing this . . . he has created a community of people that have a like-minded interest. And in the meantime, you've helped each other with your families, you've been there for each other when you were sick; what has happened here is super, super important. I don't come to these things ever and I came here tonight because we all need to recognize, not only what Rob has built for his family and him, but what he has built for all of you guys and us." Shane has since referred to me as the propaganda arm of *Survivor*, but he can't take away how nice he made me feel that night.

Final Words

Next Time on *Survivor*

When *Survivor* came on, I felt that a veil was lifted from society. It cynically opened my eyes—this is how the world really works, this is how people truly operate. Everyone is just constantly lying, trying to pull one over on each other. Hungover, my buddies and I would go to Dunkin' Donuts, get giant iced coffees, and engage in subterfuge. We'd tell the morning crew that we were there last night and the late shift was talking all sorts of smack about them. Then we'd go back that evening and tell that crew how much crap the morning crew was talking about *them*. There was no end goal to this, and, eventually, the two shifts compared notes and we were no longer welcome at the Oswego Dunkin'.

It's ironic that a show rooted in the appeal of watching people plot against each other ended up creating such a beautiful community. For millions and millions of people, *Survivor* is part of their week; friendships are based on it, romances have bloomed from it, and we find ourselves to be fans of something bigger than us, connected to this worldwide network of lunatics. As watered down as it can feel sometimes, we still catch a glimpse here and there of what originally made us fall in love with this insane show where people eat rats on an island.

What would we do if *Survivor* ever ends? Over twenty-five years later, it's tough to fathom. Will the old episodes hold us over in our hearts? Will we still discuss Cochran's flip, debate if Aubry should've won, and forever wonder who smuggled in that beef jerky? What will become of the alliances we made along the way? What will we do on Wednesday nights? And what will become of me? I hope it's a question we never have to answer.

For many years, I felt like *Survivor* was always two seasons away from ending. At points, it seemed that it couldn't go past Jeff Probst. But we also couldn't imagine *The Price is Right* without Bob Barker. Now, *Survivor* is such a fixture, with a lucrative, repeatable setup in Fiji, that it seems likely that just like *Jeopardy!* or *Wheel of Fortune*, it'll (outwit, outplay, and) outlast us all. Who knows what the era after *50* will bring us. Will it be a continuation of the New Era? Or another reinvention of the show, just like after season 40? Will this hypothetical New New Era bring even more twists and turns, or will we see a return to more classic social strategy? Who will be the new fan favorites? And are we bound to see some Mariano kids running around Fiji?

I don't have the answers for anything. My track record of making predictions on my show is tenuous at best. Happy to show how wrong I often am by locking in, in print: Tiffany as my season 50 winner pick, beating out Kamilla and zero-vote Jonathan in the final three. Chrissy is the first boot, Jenna Lewis loses fire, and Savannah gets screwed over after her closest ally Colby loses his vote playing some dangerous dice game.

The truth is, my podcasts are fine, but I didn't do anything earth-shattering. *RHAP* became a thing because so many people care about the institution that is *Survivor*. It's a worldwide phenomenon that only seems to be growing in recent years. When we were all in lockdown, so many new fans discovered *Survivor* on Netflix. I never heard of a single new *Big Brother* fan that came out of the pandemic. And as more and more A.I. slop is shoveled at our faces, maybe there'll be a larger clamoring for reality. Everyone always debates which seasons to introduce their friends to *Survivor* with, but if you really want to recruit your loved one into our little cult, tell them there's someone on the show that reminds you of them. People are incredibly self-absorbed, so, similarly to when you're playing *Survivor*, if you make it about them, you'll have them hook, line, and sinker. And hopefully, they remind you of someone on *David vs. Goliath* and not *One World*.

"Hell no! *Survivor* ain't fun," the incredible Keith Nale once said in the middle of a torrential downpour. "Going on a cruise is fun, you know? Going fishing's fun. Going to play golf's fun." I'll agree with Keith that playing *Survivor* can be hard, but I wouldn't go as far as saying golf is fun. I've also never been on a cruise, but I've been on a few boats and I got seasick. What's actually the most fun is watching a great goddamn episode of *Survivor*. Going back to my Dunkin' days, there's still nothing better than watching a juicy blindside unfold. Nothing beats a compelling, self-interested player betraying the person they love. Nothing's more satisfying than seeing it play out slowly, like a Shakesperean drama, with a surprise ending that feels inevitable in retrospect.

Survivor is like pizza: It's better when you enjoy it with friends. And while we may have our own preference of favorite toppings, even bad pizza is pretty good. Yes, even Fijian pizza, which many a contestant has called out as the worst pizza in the world. So grab a slice and enjoy the show.

> "'Cause I'm mad about this, Rob. I'm not happy about this, I'm gonna tell you right now. All you new schoolers or whatever, what are we calling it? The New Era? The pizza sucks. Stop acting like it's good. Because if we keep acting like the pizza's good, that damn Jeff is gonna keep serving it! It's awful. And you all know it. It's cardboard. And they throw some cheese and they slap a little bit of sauce and some red s–t, probably ketchup, and they serve it to you like it's pizza. It's horrible."
>
> **—Bret LaBelle, April 9, 2025**

ACKNOWLEDGMENTS

To Nicole, Dominic, and Anthony, thank you for all your patience as I attempted to split my time between being a husband, a dad, and the leader of the *Survivor* community. I'm sure I didn't always get it right but I am eternally grateful that you haven't decided to vote me out. I love you more than I could ever put into words on a page or in a podcast.

Like many of *Survivor*'s great moves, I could not have accomplished bringing this book to you without many allies along the way. Most notably was my #1 write-or-die, Alex Kavutskiy. Alex, you were a dream collaborator to work on this book with. You're an incredibly gifted talent and your friendship has been the greatest part of this project.

To Sean deLone, thank you for taking a chance on a *Survivor* book from a man who only knows how to talk. Thank you for all the creative freedom you gave us to describe why we love *Survivor*. To Sam Bond, your beautiful artwork has elevated this book so greatly. It's been an honor to see your work bring these words to life. And always, thank you, Michael Glazer, for all your sage counsel. You've helped me with *RHAP* in countless ways over the years and your friendship has known no bounds.

To my fellow Know-It-All, Stephen Fishbach, thank you for writing the beautiful foreword to this book. No matter what *Survivor* has thrown at us, it's been the journey of a lifetime to cover it with you.

To my mom and dad, thank you for letting me follow my *Survivor* dream—even if you were very rightfully concerned! And to my brother, Danny, and my sister, Lisa, thank you for all your love and support across everything that I do.

Thanks to Jennie Butler, Naomi Calhoun, Ryan Elder, Shannon Guss, Sam More, and Akiva Wienerkur for all your insightful feedback that truly helped us write this book.

Thanks to the community of *RHAP* podcasters, staff, patrons, and listeners. I thought it was my dream to go on *Survivor*, but I learned that my true dream was getting to spend all of my days talking about it with you.

Finally, to Jeff Probst and the entire team responsible for making *Survivor*, I have so much respect and admiration for what you've built over a quarter century. We may have strong feelings about the decisions that you've made, and we thank you for having the grace to let us discuss those differences at great length. While we may not see eye-to-eye all the time, I know that those decisions are never made because of a lack of caring for the franchise you've built. We should be so lucky that the people responsible for ALL of our institutions cared about them as much as you. Everything I have in some way comes back to you believing in me and keeping *Survivor* alive. Thank you for the adventure of a lifetime.

ABOUT THE AUTHORS

Rob Cesternino, the two-time *Survivor* player referred to by Jeff Probst as "the smartest player never to win *Survivor*," is the creator and host of *Rob Has a Podcast*. Since 2010, Rob has covered reality TV shows such as *Survivor, Big Brother, The Amazing Race,* and more. The show has won five People's Choice Podcast Awards. Rob is a proud husband, father of two, and friend to thousands in the *RHAP* community.

Alex Kavutskiy is a mostly unemployed filmmaker and television writer but full-time *Survivor* superfan. He resides in Los Angeles, California, with his girlfriend, Jennie, and their two cats, who viciously hate each other.

Sam Bond is a certified medical illustrator, game developer, avid doodler, and *Survivor* superfan based out of Chicago, Illinois. Her work can be found on Instagram @reality.paintz.